New Regional Authorities

The idea that regional organizations rightly occupy a central place in human rights, global governance, and international intervention has come to be taken for granted in international politics. Yet, the idea of regions as authorities is not a natural feature of the international system. Instead, it was strategically constructed by the leaders in the Global South as a way of maintaining their voice in global decision-making and managing (though not preventing) outside interference. Katherine M. Beall explores changes in the norms and practice of international interference in the late 1970s and early 1980s, a time when Latin American and African leaders began to empower their regional organizations to enforce human rights. This change represented a form of quiet resistance to the imposition of human rights enforcement and a transformation in the ongoing struggle for self-determination. This book will appeal to scholars of international relations, international history, and human rights.

KATHERINE M. BEALL is a Lecturer at the University of Massachusetts, Amherst. She received her PhD in Political Science from the University of California, Berkeley, and has previously worked at the UN International Criminal Tribunal for the former Yugoslavia and the US Embassy in Croatia.

Her research has received awards from multiple American Political Science Association sections.

New Regional Authorities

Self-Determination and the Global South

KATHERINE M. BEALL
University of Massachusetts, Amherst

Shaftesbury Road, Cambridge CB2 8EA, United Kingdom

One Liberty Plaza, 20th Floor, New York, NY 10006, USA

477 Williamstown Road, Port Melbourne, VIC 3207, Australia

314–321, 3rd Floor, Plot 3, Splendor Forum, Jasola District Centre,
New Delhi – 110025, India

103 Penang Road, #05-06/07, Visioncrest Commercial, Singapore 238467

Cambridge University Press is part of Cambridge University Press & Assessment,
a department of the University of Cambridge.

We share the University's mission to contribute to society through the pursuit of
education, learning, and research at the highest international levels of excellence.

www.cambridge.org
Information on this title: www.cambridge.org/9781009645560

DOI: 10.1017/9781009645591

© Katherine M. Beall 2026

This publication is in copyright. Subject to statutory exception and to the provisions
of relevant collective licensing agreements, no reproduction of any part may take
place without the written permission of Cambridge University Press & Assessment.

When citing this work, please include a reference to the DOI 10.1017/9781009645591

First published 2026

Cover image: Watercolor Layered Blue Dots / saemilee / DigitalVision Vectors / Getty Images

A catalogue record for this publication is available from the British Library

Library of Congress Cataloging-in-Publication Data
Names: Beall, Katherine M. author
Title: New regional authorities : self-determination and the Global South /
Katherine M. Beall.
Description: Cambridge, United Kingdom ; New York, NY : Cambridge University Press,
2026. | Includes bibliographical references and index.
Identifiers: LCCN 2025028860 (print) | LCCN 2025028861 (ebook) | ISBN 9781009645560
hardback | ISBN 9781009645614 paperback | ISBN 9781009645591 epub
Subjects: LCSH: Regionalism–Developing countries | International agencies–Developing
countries | Self-determination, National–Developing countries | Human rights–Developing
countries
Classification: LCC JF60 .B428 2026 (print) | LCC JF60 (ebook)
LC record available at https://lccn.loc.gov/2025028860
LC ebook record available at https://lccn.loc.gov/2025028861

ISBN 978-1-009-64556-0 Hardback
ISBN 978-1-009-64561-4 Paperback

Cambridge University Press & Assessment has no responsibility for the persistence
or accuracy of URLs for external or third-party internet websites referred to in this
publication and does not guarantee that any content on such websites is, or will
remain, accurate or appropriate.

For EU product safety concerns, contact us at Calle de José Abascal, 56, 1°, 28003 Madrid,
Spain, or email eugpsr@cambridge.org

Contents

Acknowledgements		*page* vi
1.	Changing Approaches to Interference in the Global South	1
2.	Self-Determination through Regional Authority	33
3.	The Imposition of Human Rights Enforcement	62
4.	Latin America and the Emergence of Regional Authority over Human Rights	88
5.	From Non-Interference to African Enforcement	118
6.	Short-Circuiting Regional Institutions in the Middle East	146
7.	Regional Authority and Self-Determination in International Politics	170
References		185
Index		224

Acknowledgements

There are many people who helped make this book possible, to whom I am extremely grateful. I have been lucky to receive feedback from and have helpful conversations with countless people over the years that I was working on this project, and I thank all of them for their generosity and constructive engagement.

I want to give special thanks to the members of my dissertation committee at Berkeley, who cared enough to give me critical feedback, and from whom I received the perfect mix of guidance and space that helped me to sharpen and improve my project while figuring out for myself exactly what it would be. Susan Hyde, who chaired my dissertation committee, read countless drafts and memos and was so supportive as I developed my project. Michaela Mattes was always generous with her time and feedback, and she helped me to internalize the kind of critical voice that is essential for doing research. Vinnie Aggarwal is one of the main reasons I developed an interest in international political economy, an interest that turned out to be central to this project. Early on, Vinnie gave me tough feedback on my writing for which I will always be thankful, because it pushed me to develop my writing skills and to be more thoughtful about my writing. Aila Matanock, in addition to giving me invaluable feedback on my research, helped me learn from an early stage what research is. I was lucky to get to work with her on research in my first years of graduate school.

I thank the people that attended my book workshop: Charli Carpenter, Erik Voeten, Soo Yeon Kim, Gino Pauselli, Sabrina Arias, and Zoe Ge. I am incredibly grateful to them for reading my manuscript so carefully and engaging with it so constructively. Their thoughtful feedback greatly improved the project, and I feel lucky to have been able to talk through my project with such a supportive and encouraging group.

Acknowledgments

The IR Theory community has also been a source of support and community as I have worked on writing this book. In particular, I am grateful to have been awarded the Nuno P. Monteiro dissertation award, which gave me encouragement that what I was doing was worthwhile, and for being given the opportunity to participate in and get feedback from the IR Theory Virtual Workshop. I would like to offer special thanks to the organizers of the workshop, Stacie Goddard, Jennifer Mitzen, and Sebastian Rosato, as well as to Orfeo Fioretos and Martha Finnemore, who generously gave their time to join the workshop to discuss my project.

I also owe many thanks to Helen Milner, who gave me the opportunity to be a postdoctoral fellow at the Niehaus Center for Globalization and Governance. It was during the year that I spent at the Niehaus Center that I was able to revise my dissertation into a book. I was lucky enough to have a cohort of postdocs and visiting fellows – MD Mangini, Matt Malis, Rachel Schoner, Calvin Thrall, Noah Zucker, Haillie Lee, Alastair Smith, and Erik Voeten – who kindly listened and offered their thoughts and feedback over and over again. The Niehaus Center also provided me with generous funding that allowed me to host a book workshop. And, of course, thanks to Jen Bolton for going above and beyond in making the workshop happen.

Finally, I want to thank my family for being excited with me at every step.

1 Changing Approaches to Interference in the Global South

The late 1970s and early 1980s were a time of major change in the practice of international interference. Prior to this time, leaders throughout the Global South had opposed any interference in their domestic affairs – even public comments from other governments – as an unacceptable violation of their sovereignty.[1] However, in these years, leaders in Latin America and Africa began to empower their regional organizations, the Organization of American States (OAS) and the Organization of African Unity (OAU), to enforce human rights in ways that involved interference and to speak of this regional enforcement as legitimate. Since then, regional organizations have become central to human rights enforcement, international intervention, and global governance.

What explains this change, and why did it not happen in other regions, namely the Middle East and Southeast Asia? I argue that the decision to accept international interference was part of a strategy by leaders in Latin America and Africa to establish their regional organizations as authorities over human rights, accepting interference within their regional organizations and asserting the authority of regional enforcement vis-à-vis other enforcers. They adopted this strategy in response to new forms of pressure that challenged their states' self-determination. These pressures did not arise in the Middle East or Southeast Asia, and as a result, leaders in those regions continued to reject all interference.

---

[1] I use the term "Global South" to refer to a group of states that share important features, including historically high levels of economic dependence and material weakness, a disadvantaged position in the global economy, late industrialization, low state capacity, and significant experiences with colonialism and imperialism. These states have identified and organized themselves as "Southern" states, including in groupings like the G77 and Non-Aligned Movement, as well as more broadly under the banner of "South–South Cooperation." In spite of significant heterogeneity, these states pursued many of the same goals and self-consciously grouped themselves together.

For leaders in Latin America and Africa, insisting on non-interference and asserting regional authority over human rights were two different strategies for accomplishing the same goal of limiting the external imposition of rules and safeguarding self-determination. One strategy created a hard shell around the state, while the other created mechanisms for filtering and managing outside involvement and amplifying the region's influence over interference. Once the first strategy no longer worked, they switched to the second.

The decision to accept regional human rights enforcement was a significant change in state practice toward sovereignty and the norm of non-interference, as well as an important moment in the emergence of regional organizations as central to legitimate intervention. In Latin America, the "doctrine of non-intervention" had developed in response to European intervention in the nineteenth and early twentieth centuries and was adapted to the threat posed by the United States and "Yankee imperialism." In Africa, the emphasis placed on non-interference and territorial integrity in the post-independence years led to accusations that the region was a "club of dictators." In Southeast Asia, non-interference became a cornerstone of the "ASEAN way," the set of norms and practices governing state behavior within the Association of Southeast Asian Nations (ASEAN). In the Middle East, states demanded respect for non-interference by external powers, while a regional order governed by strict respect for one another's sovereignty *within* the region was consolidated between 1967 and 1973.

Because of historically high levels of material weakness and economic dependence, leaders throughout the Global South have benefitted from norms and rules that prioritize legal equality over material power in inter-state relations.[2] Following formal decolonization, many saw their newly won sovereignty as undermined by great power meddling, political pressure, and foreign control of their economy. In response, these leaders argued for and institutionalized increasingly strict and expansive rules about sovereignty and non-interference. In other words, decolonization transformed rather than ending the struggle for self-determination.

Across these regions, state and non-state actors also placed great value on sovereignty as the realization of the collective right to self-

---

[2] Clapham 1996; Jackson 1990; Jackson and Rosberg 1982; Krasner 1985, 1999.

determination, while non-interference was understood as a corollary to this right and a means for realizing it against imperialism and neo-colonialism. Regional organizations respected non-interference, and they were also important tools for institutionalizing this norm and policing violations. Even where human rights institutions were set up within regional organizations, they were given no authority to interfere in member states' domestic affairs, and member states mostly ignored them.

However, in the 1970s, the paths of these regions diverged. In Latin America and Africa, leaders began to give up their strict opposition to interference, developing or dramatically expanding institutions for the enforcement of human rights within their regional organizations. At the same time, they called for others to defer to regional efforts to enforce human rights. In Latin America, leaders began to ratify the long-dormant American Convention on Human Rights *en masse*, consent to visits from the Inter-American Commission on Human Rights, and collectively challenge governments' human rights violations during meetings of the Organization of American States. They gave new authority to the Inter-American Commission, increased its budget, and allowed it to carry out its tasks. They also accepted the authority of the Inter-American Court on Human Rights. These institutions had been ignored or actively undermined since they were created, when leaders suddenly began to accept their authority and facilitate and augment their work. The Inter-American human rights system has since been regarded as one of the most effective in the world.[3]

In Africa, leaders passed a resolution calling for the creation of a regional human rights charter and a commission to enforce the charter in 1979, and they adopted the African Charter on Human and Peoples' Rights in 1981. The charter established the African Commission on Human and Peoples' Rights, an independent commission of human rights experts empowered to "resort to any appropriate method of investigation" to address human rights violations, including receiving and acting on accusations made by individuals and NGOs.[4] The charter came into effect in 1986. Since that time, regional and sub-regional human rights institutions have proliferated. A human rights court was set up in 1998, and in 2000, the OAU was transformed into

---

[3] European Parliament 2009: 5; Forsythe 1991; Goldman 2009: 857.
[4] Organization of African Unity 1981: Articles 45(2), 46, and 60.

the African Union and given unprecedented authority to intervene militarily in member states in response to war crimes, genocide, and crimes against humanity.⁵ The African human rights system is generally considered to be less effective than Latin America's, with the latter benefitting from greater democratization in the 1980s. Nevertheless, African human rights institutions were designed with real power and autonomy, and their creation represented a real and significant shift away from the norm of non-interference.

By contrast, leaders in the Middle East and Southeast Asia continued to reject any interference and refrained from creating institutions that permitted even minimal interference long after these changes took place in Latin America and Africa. What regional human rights institutions have been created came about much later, have weaker powers, and are subject to greater state control.

In the Middle East, the members of the League of Arab States set up a human rights commission in 1968. However, the commission was made up of government representatives rather than independent experts, and its powers were distinctly respectful of sovereignty. Its mandate included facilitating dialogue, raising awareness, and coordinating member states' external human rights advocacy. In practice, it focused almost exclusively on advocating for the rights of Palestinians.⁶ A string of proposals for expanding the organization's human rights mandate and institutions in the 1970s and 1980s went nowhere, and it was only in 2004 that a human rights charter, establishing a new human rights commission, finally received enough ratifications to come into existence. Even then, the new commission remains limited in important ways. It cannot receive information about human rights violations from individuals within member states, considered a crucial piece of a human rights enforcement system. A human rights court, created in 2014, can only receive complaints from states and state-approved NGOs.⁷ Saudi Arabia is the only state to have ratified the court's statute.

Southeast Asian leaders made their first steps toward creating human rights institutions within ASEAN in 2009, establishing the ASEAN Intergovernmental Commission on Human Rights. Like the

---

⁵ African Union 2000: Article 4(h).
⁶ An-Na'im 2001: 712–14; van Hüllen 2015.
⁷ League of Arab States 2004: Article 48, 2014: Article 19.

Arab League's commission, the ASEAN commission has no formal authority to investigate or challenge member states or to even consider their domestic human rights records. It is also, as its name suggests, a commission composed of government representatives rather than independent human rights experts.[8] The ASEAN Human Rights Declaration, adopted in 2012, is a statement of voluntary standards, not a set of legally binding obligations.

The consequences of this regional divergence have persisted and now extend beyond human rights. Regional and subregional organizations in Latin America and Africa have developed a wide range of institutions for democracy promotion and election monitoring, counterterrorism, civil conflict resolution, and anti-corruption. They have authority to monitor, criticize, sanction, and suspend member states. By contrast, while regional organizations in Southeast Asia and the Middle East have expanded into new issue areas, cooperation in sensitive political issues has remained much more limited and less institutionalized. Institutions that have been set up tend to be respectful of sovereignty, operating to a much greater degree under the control of the governments whose policies and behaviors they're meant to challenge.

What explains the sudden shift in approach to interference in Latin America and Africa, and why did leaders gravitate toward institutionalizing human rights within their own regional organizations? Why did this change occur only in some regions, while others held firm on the norm of non-interference for much longer and to a much greater degree? Each of these regions had developed similar practices and beliefs with respect to non-interference, and each derived significant strategic benefits from this norm. All valued sovereignty as the realization of the right to self-determination and saw non-interference as a means to realize this right in the face of pressures from more powerful states. Yet, out of these four regions, it was only in Latin America and Africa where the 1970s marked the beginning of a major transformation in how leaders approached state sovereignty, a transformation which spread to many other sensitive areas of these states' domestic politics.

In this book, I argue that this divergence was the result of diverging strategies for using institutions to resist the imposition of enforcement in the face of different pressures experienced by these regions.

---

[8] Association of Southeast Asian Nations 2009.

It represented a transformation of the political struggle for self-determination. As articulated by Edem Kodjo, Secretary General of the OAU and one of the architects of the African human rights system, its creation was motivated by "the twin objectives of liberation vis-à-vis the rest of the world and the internal democratization of African societies."[9] This project, and the goal of self-determination, united democratic leaders, human rights advocates, and dictators whose governments were engaged in serious violations of human rights.

In the mid-1970s, Western governments began to enforce human rights by incorporating human rights considerations into their economic relations with developing states. Western governments leveraged developing states' weakness and their economic dependence on the West to push acceptance of and compliance with human rights standards. Human rights had occasionally entered into their decision-making about trade and development assistance before this, but it was only in the 1970s that these policies became common and widespread.

These policies were seen throughout the Global South as neocolonial and imperialistic; they clashed with widely held views about the principle of self-determination. However, simply objecting to the policies, including with appeals to sovereignty and the norm of non-interference, was ineffective. The citizens of Western states and prominent civil society groups had started to accept and even demand interference in response to serious human rights violations, while leaders like US President Jimmy Carter had themselves started to think of interfering in support of human rights as both legitimate and permissible under international law.

In Latin America and Africa, these interventionist policies became the new status quo, substantially altering leaders' decision-making over whether to accept interference. Interventionist enforcement was going to happen one way or another, and the question now was *who* would interfere and *how*. It was at this point that leaders in these two regions began to establish their regional organizations as authorities over human rights. This change happened unevenly by region because the pressures were uneven. Western governments targeted Africa and Latin America, where doing so was relatively cheap and easy and did not jeopardize other important foreign policy goals, while largely

---

[9] Kodjo 1990: 273–74.

subsuming human rights to other political and economic goals in the Middle East and Southeast Asia.

This strategy combined and appealed to widely held beliefs about the legitimacy of international institutions and local self-rule, and it leveraged concerns in the West about legitimate relations with weaker, post-colonial states. Because of this, where regional institutions met certain expectations about what enforcement ought to look like, Western leaders were willing to accept the authority of regional organizations and defer to their enforcement. The most important expectation was that regional institutions must be empowered to interfere in their members' domestic affairs.

I focus here on attempts to establish regional authority over human rights, but I argue that this strategy has been used much more widely. Developing and advocating for the idea of regions as authorities has been an important way for different political actors in the Global South, both within and outside of government, to increase capacity and space for self-rule. It has helped them resist the many pressures they face from more powerful actors, manage outside involvement in their region, and increase their own influence over global decision-making.

Establishing regional authority over human rights was an important example of this strategy. It was also an important moment of transformation away from this strategy being used to support state sovereignty and toward accepting interference as long as it was supported by or carried out through regional organizations. In fact, this reshaping of international authority has been especially pronounced in the area of human rights. Regional organizations are central to the international enforcement regime, with the relatively weak global regime standing in contrast to regional systems, whose human rights courts "have no global parallel."[10] The most substantial form of enforcement – judicialization – exists exclusively within regional organizations.[11] Prominent advocates of human rights like the European Parliament and the International Commission of Jurists have characterized regional organizations as "fundamental" to the global human rights regime,[12] "constitut[ing] the main pillars of the international system for the promotion and protection of human rights."[13]

---

[10] Voeten 2017: 119.
[11] Heyns and Killander 2013: 3; Pevehouse 2016: 487; Voeten 2017: 119.
[12] Sahraoui 2004: 339.   [13] European Parliament 2009: 5.

This is despite the fact that, in many ways, human rights are poorly suited to a regional approach and clash with the idea of regional authority, as universality represents a core, defining feature of human rights. A UN study group, convened in 1968 to discuss the idea of regional human rights commissions, voiced concern that human rights were a "universal problem,"[14] and "United Nations activities alone could ensure a uniform application of accepted norms."[15] In a volume released in 1982, Karel Vasak, a major figure in human rights known for developing the idea of "three generations" of rights, observed that, in the 1960s, regional approaches to human rights had been regarded with suspicion, seeming to represent a "breakaway movement" that challenged universality.[16]

Regional authority is not a natural or obvious feature of the international system, and the many downsides, weaknesses, and failures of regional organizations in the Global South are well-documented. Regions are home to significant rivalries and conflict; engage in biased decision-making; contain substantial linguistic, cultural, and political heterogeneity; and lack resources and political will for effectively dealing with regional issues.[17] Instead, regional authority has been strategically constructed by actors that benefit from their regional organizations having a stronger voice and greater representation in global politics as it affects their region.

The argument presented here speaks to larger questions about the current world order and, in particular, how regional organizations came to be taken for granted as legitimate and effective sites for policy-making and global governance. It helps explain how appeals to the norm of regional solutions to regional problems, which recognizes a right for regions to address matters internal to themselves and promotes the idea that they are uniquely well-suited to do so, came to take on an almost ritualistic quality in global governance.

Appeals to this norm are part of the rhetoric of great powers, who use it to frame and justify their foreign policies. US representatives have extolled the importance of "African-led security efforts" in combatting terrorism, noting that "African leadership for African problems can lead to solutions."[18] Xi Jinping has promoted the idea of "Asia for

---

[14] UN Commission on Human Rights 1968a: Para. 26.
[15] UN Commission on Human Rights 1968a: Para. 29.   [16] Vasak 1982: 451.
[17] Diehl 2007; Hettne and Söderbaum 2006.   [18] Thomas-Greenfield 2023.

Asians" as the Chinese government works to limit US influence in the region.[19] United Nations Security Council resolutions and debates routinely acknowledge the important role of "relevant" regional organizations. The UN Secretary General holds annual coordinating meetings with representatives of regional organizations, and in a 2022 address, Secretary General António Guterres characterized cooperation between regional organizations and the UN as "essential."[20]

This idea of regional authority has reconfigured the logic of collective legitimation, with regional organizations becoming an important source of legitimation for global action.[21] In establishing regional organizations as both legitimate authorities and legitimizers of global action, leaders using this strategy have increased space for self-determined action in the context of a constraining and hierarchical international system.

1.1 Overview of the Argument: Self-Determination Through Regional Authority

In this book, I argue that leaders in Africa and Latin America created, accepted, and expanded regional human rights enforcement institutions as part of a strategy to establish their regional organizations as authorities over human rights. By creating alternative enforcement institutions and arguing that others ought to respect and defer to these institutions, they were quietly pushing back against the imposition of human rights enforcement by Western governments. Leaders in these two regions became willing to relax their absolute rejection of international interference in pursuit of the larger, overarching goal of self-determination. Leaders in the Middle East and Southeast Asia, by contrast, retained their strict stance toward non-interference for much longer and to a much greater degree because they did not encounter these same forms of imposed enforcement.

In developing this argument, I conceptualize self-determination to include self-determination over international rules. It is this conception of self-determination that I draw from to talk about the imposition of human rights enforcement. This form of imposition is distinct from "cultural imperialism," or the imposition of Western values onto non-

---

[19] Jakobson 2016.   [20] Guterres 2022.
[21] Barnett 1995a: 428; Claude 1966; Hettne and Söderbaum 2006.

Western peoples and societies, a common criticism of human rights. Imposition as I discuss it in this book is not about the content of rules or even the existence of a historical relationship of colonial or imperial domination, though these dynamics may also be present.[22] Instead, it is about how states, and the people within them, are bound by rules and how those rules are enforced. In fact, many leaders and activists in Global South viewed guarding individuals' human rights from abuse by their state as important, and they were actively involved in promoting human rights in some contexts, including in institutions they shared with former colonizers. They did so at the same time as they rejected the exploitation of economic dependence as a means of enforcement.

I build on theorizing on self-determination from the fields of psychology, philosophy, and feminist and indigenous theory, which share a perspective on self-determination as consistent with and potentially realized through cooperation, interdependence, and the surrendering or pooling of sovereign decision-making authority.[23] This understanding forms an important part of how state and non-state actors throughout the Global South have long advocated for self-determination as a necessary basis for legitimate relations between states and the legitimate exercise of power in the international system.

What would it mean for international rules to be self-determined? How is self-determination realized in a system of sovereign states? The international side of self-determination has often been treated, both in scholarship and in practice, as synonymous with, or most fully realized through, sovereign independence and strict non-interference – in other words, with the complete exclusion of outside actors and rules.[24] As I discuss in Chapter 2, expanding and policing rules of non-interference, including within regional organizations, was one important strategy for realizing self-determination. It accomplished this goal by restricting forms of interference or pressure that would undermine self-determined action.

---

[22] I am grateful to Desmond Jagmohan for pointing out this distinction to me.
[23] deCharms 1968; Deci and Ryan 2000: 233; Dworkin 1988; Friedman 2003; Kingsbury 2000; Lightfoot 2021; Mackenzie and Stoljar 2000; Mahmood 2011; Ryan and Deci 2006; Shrinkhal 2021; Xanthaki 2007.
[24] Cameron et al. 2006; Cassese 1995: 5–12, 205–73; Fabry 2010: 9–14; Goddard 2012, 2015; Goodman and Jinks 2013; Moore 2014: 133; Schmitter and Karl 1991: 81–82; Simon 2017; Walzer 1983: 62.

1.1 Overview of the Argument

However, for anti- and post-colonial leaders, activists, and scholars, self-determination was not achieved by sovereign statehood alone nor, conversely, did its full realization require the total exclusion of external rules or authority.[25] Significant forms of cooperation, delegation, and outside interference could be consistent with, and even expressions of, self-determination. For example, some anti-colonial leaders in French colonies in Africa and the Caribbean advocated for self-determination in the form of equal integration in a reconstituted, democratic French federation. Anti- and post-colonial leaders also commonly sought self-determination through the pooling of sovereignty into regional federations.[26]

Rather than strict sovereignty, independence, or autarky, self-determination was about the nature of international cooperation and interdependence. Realizing the principle of self-determination in the international system meant ensuring that international institutions and inter-state relations met certain standards for the legitimate exercise of power. Specifically, it required states, and by extension the people within them, to be able to *domestically affirm* international rules, meaning the decision to accept rules and their enforcement would be the product of domestic decision-making processes, and to *meaningfully participate* in the enforcement of rules, or to take part in and influence the design and enforcement of rules to which they were subject.[27] In other words, international interference, monitoring, and policymaking can be consistent with self-determination if they are domestically affirmed by the people of a state and if those people retain, through their government, the ability to equitably participate in the implementation, elaboration, and enforcement of international rules. This, of course, necessitated the democratic representativeness of governments, who provide a crucial link between people within states and the international system. As I discuss in the following pages and in Chapter 2, many leaders and activists championed democracy within states alongside reforms to democratize the international system.

The goal, then, was not to be free from any international authority or to eliminate interdependence. Instead, recognizing the reality of

---

[25] Anghie 2005; Bedjaoui 1979; Cassese 1995: 55–57; Chimni 2007; Gathii 2020; Getachew 2019; Grovogui 1996, 2002; Jagmohan 2020; Wilder 2015.
[26] Getachew 2019; Simon 2017; Wilder 2015.
[27] For discussions on affirmation and participation, see Stilz (2015) and Markell (2008).

their dependence and the necessity of cooperation, the goal was to reshape inter-state relations and to change the nature of their interdependence. Guyanese historian and prominent anti-imperial activist Walter Rodney offered a typical articulation of this perspective in his influential 1972 book, *How Europe Underdeveloped Africa*, contrasting imperialistic economic dependence on Western metropoles with "mutual interdependence" that preserved the "capacity to exercise choice."[28]

International institutions were one of the main tools used by leaders and activists in the Global South to ensure that international relations met these standards. Institutions were an important part of translating abstract ideas about self-determination, authority, hierarchy, and dependence into real decision-making rules and standards for behaviors. Putting these ideas into practice involved creating or reforming international organizations, designing treaties, and elaborating on existing legal principles with the goal of placing decision-making on an equal playing field and eliminating the many forms of international domination that persisted after independence.[29]

It was this understanding of self-determination, and new challenges to it that arose in the 1970s, that motivated leaders in Latin America and Africa to regionalize human rights enforcement. At this time, governments of Western states faced pressure from their citizens and from global civil society, who had become suddenly, intensely interested in human rights violations around the world and demanded that their governments take action to defend human rights and to stop supporting violent, abusive leaders. Western governments responded by tying access to economic cooperation to developing states' domestic human rights records and increasingly weighing their relations with developing states against international and domestic demands – and their own growing desire – to privilege human rights in their foreign policies. The United States under the presidency of Jimmy Carter was perhaps the most prominent and consequential government that adopted these policies, but during this time, they were also adopted by a number of European governments, notably the United Kingdom, the Netherlands, and the Nordic countries, and they were introduced into the external policy of the European Economic Community in the second half of the 1970s.[30]

---

[28] Rodney 1972: 31. [29] Anghie 2015; Getachew 2019; Salomon 2013.
[30] Eckel and Moyn 2013; Keck and Sikkink 1998; Lorenzini et al. 2022; Moyn 2010; Sikkink 1993, 2004.

1.1 Overview of the Argument

Initially, this enforcement took the form of *ad hoc*, targeted responses to the most extreme cases of human rights violations, like those in Chile under Augusto Pinochet and Uganda under Idi Amin. However, Western governments soon expanded and institutionalized these enforcement policies by introducing human rights into their relations with a wider set of developing states, rather than just those governments responsible for gross violations of human rights. They also shifted from applying sanctions in response to only the most serious violations to adopting a system of pressure and inducements aimed at increasing the overall observance of human rights around the world. Much of the Global South could now expect that human rights would factor into their economic relations with the West, through both formal policies and informal, behind-the-scenes decision-making.

These enforcement measures created new policies to which states were now subject, but to which they did not consent, and which were designed and implemented in contexts where they were unable to exercise influence. This was, in fact, largely the point of human rights conditionality.[31] Latin American and African leaders that encountered these policies objected to them, including by appealing to the norm of non-interference. However, their objections were made ineffective by the new beliefs that had taken hold about the legitimacy of interfering to protect human rights.

This changed the decision-making calculus of leaders encountering this new pressure. It was no longer a question of whether human rights would be enforced in ways that involved interference, but who would enforce them and how. Under these new circumstances, leaders preferred to have human rights enforced in institutions where decision-making rules gave them a say in human rights priorities and enforcement and where they would not be held up for one-sided judgement.[32]

It was in response to this pressure that leaders moved to establish regional authority over human rights. Doing so involved two non-sequential steps. First, leaders accepted regional authority, meaning that they created, accepted, and expanded regional human rights institutions and cooperated within their regional organizations to act on human rights violations. Second, they asserted to actors outside of the

---

[31] Hafner-Burton 2010.
[32] Regional and domestic civil society actors would also benefit from effective institutions that were more responsive to regional actors.

region – including Western states, international NGOs, and bureaucrats of global international organizations – that regional organizations should be regarded as authorities over human rights within their regions, and they should be given a voice over human rights enforcement being carried out within their geographic domain.[33] This required developing the idea that regional organizations were an appropriate place for human rights to be enforced, something that was not taken for granted at this time. In many cases, they argued that regional organizations were the *more* appropriate authority for addressing human rights violations and that actors outside of the region should defer to them.

These two steps were linked. The goal was to persuade Western governments, and the citizens and civil society actors demanding these governments respond to human rights violations, that they should accept regional organizations as authorities over human rights. To accomplish this, regional institutions had to be designed in ways that would meet these different actors' expectations of what constituted acceptable enforcement, and leaders had to actually accept and cooperate with them. This meant, most importantly, that regional institutions needed to be empowered to interfere in states' domestic affairs, including by investigating domestic human rights violations, commenting on domestic practices and policies, and recommending or ordering changes.

Leaders within targeted regions that genuinely supported human rights and dictators that were abusing human rights had similar beliefs and overlapping motivations that led them to adopt this strategy. This included the desire to push back against the imposition of enforcement and to ensure equal influence and voice over enforcement to which they were subject. Even those leaders that genuinely supported human rights nevertheless had principled objections to the use of economic enforcement, and they became important agents in advocating for regional institutions with real power and independence. For authoritarians and leaders abusing human rights, self-determination was a matter of both principle and strategy, as these pressures threatened their regimes and were regarded as illegitimate domination and imperialist interference. Their indignation pushed them toward

---

[33] On authority, see Barnett and Finnemore (2004), Blau (1963), Lake (2009), and Tallberg and Zurn (2019).

1.1 Overview of the Argument

regional enforcement and made them open to accepting more challenging authority than they otherwise would have if their goal was regime survival alone.

This strategy was effective because it appealed to the beliefs of Western governments and their domestic publics about the normative value of self-rule and the legitimacy of acting within international institutions. This thinking was articulated in a 1978 internal policy document prepared by Jimmy Carter's Director of Policy Planning, Anthony Lake. Under a section titled "The Perception of Arrogance," Lake suggested that "We should now be consulting with others – at the UN, in the OAS, and with other regional leaders (e.g., in black Africa) – about *their* suggestions for effective human rights strategies in their areas, in the context of their own cultural, economic, and political situations."[34] Where leaders in Africa and Latin America were willing to enforce human rights, and where regional enforcement met Western leaders' expectations of what constituted legitimate and effective enforcement, Western leaders were willing to accept the authority of regions.

As I discuss in Chapter 4, the first steps toward establishing regional authority over human rights were taken by Augusto Pinochet's government in Chile in 1975, which became the first and most intense subject of these new enforcement policies. The Chilean government argued that actors from outside of the region should accept the OAS as the appropriate authority to deal with human rights within Latin America. They did so, however, as a regime survival strategy, accepting regional enforcement in ways that attempted to manipulate and undermine the regional system, paper over their abuses, and placate critics. The Chilean government's attempts to manipulate the regional system to deflect pressure were transparent and failed, but their actions carved out a new path for responding to this newly emerging human rights pressure.

This strategy was quickly transformed from mere manipulation of regional institutions into more genuine acceptance of regional authority once the rest of Latin America became involved in 1976, and again after Jimmy Carter's administration widened the US's economic enforcement policies to cover the entire region in 1977. Latin

---

[34] *Foreign Relations of the United States* 2013: Document 105 (hereafter "*FRUS*"). Emphasis in original.

American leaders that supported human rights enforcement believed in the regional system. They also objected to both US-dominated enforcement and the use of economic conditions as counter to the principle of self-determination. In response to the US government's policies, leaders throughout the region, including authoritarian governments, began to accept genuinely challenging authority within the OAS and to assert regional authority over human rights. Once African governments began to confront these pressures several years later following international attention on Idi Amin's government in Uganda, they adopted this same strategy, creating a regional human rights system from scratch.

Regional variation in whether this change occurred is explained by whether or not regions were targeted by economic enforcement policies. Past research has established that human rights are often subsumed to other strategic concerns in Western foreign policy.[35] Though Western governments were responding to pressure from domestic constituents and international civil society, they retained considerable discretion over their global human rights policies, and they tended to apply human rights pressure where it was relatively cheap, meaning there were few tradeoffs or chances of it damaging other important priorities, and easy, where pre-existing relationships and institutions were available into which human rights could be introduced and where greater leverage meant that the likelihood of success was high.

However, rather than making decisions on a state-by-state basis, Western governments devised their human rights policies with entire regions in mind. This resulted in what the US State Department Director of Policy Planning referred to in 1978 as "regional discrimination."[36] The United States and Western Europe had similar constraints in designing their foreign policies, including massive increases in oil prices, Cold War politics, and a global recession; similar opportunities, in terms of the regions in which they had substantial leverage;[37] and similar foreign policy goals, including establishing peace in the Middle East, maintaining access to oil, and expanding into new export markets. They independently developed patterns of enforcement that emphasized human rights in Latin

---

[35] Dietrich and Murdie 2017; Dunning 2004; Grigoryan 2020; Jamal 2012; Levitsky and Way 2006: 383, 386; Nielsen 2013.
[36] *FRUS* 2013: Document 105. [37] On leverage, see Levitsky and Way 2006.

1.1 Overview of the Argument

America and Africa, while consistently overlooking or down-playing violations in the Middle East and Southeast Asia. Where Western countries *did* apply pressure on human rights in the latter two regions, it tended to be much more limited and symbolic.

This regional discrimination meant that Latin America and Africa faced new and unprecedented pressure on an issue that had previously been treated as purely a matter of domestic politics. In response, Latin American and African leaders adopted the strategy of establishing regional authority over human rights. By contrast, in the Middle East and Southeast Asia, human rights remained subsumed to other economic and security concerns in the foreign policies of important donors and trade partners in the West, and leaders in these regions continued to treat human rights as a domestic matter not subject to interference.

The argument presented in this book is an elite story, with leaders throughout the Global South motivated by, wielding, and acting on the basis of shared understandings of the principle of self-determination. It was leaders that made decisions about how to engage with the norm of non-interference and pushed to establish regional authority over human rights. Many benefitted from an understanding of self-determination that increased their own space for autonomous decision-making and delegitimized international pressure that challenged them personally.

However, this was not just an authoritarian strategy of regime survival. In important ways and at crucial moments, it was led by democratic leaders and human rights advocates, who saw the realization of self-determination, democracy, and human rights *within* states as linked to and of equal importance as their realization in the international system. These democratic leaders and human rights advocates played an important role in pushing for regional institutions to be designed with real power. Additionally, as I elaborate on in later chapters, this understanding of self-determination drew from shared beliefs about self-rule that were also held by non-state actors within these regions. Leaders throughout the Global South were shaped by these ideas and drew from them in their utilization of regional organizations.

This shared ideational basis motivated widely held understandings of what it meant for self-determination to be realized for sovereign states and how this principle was undermined by a hierarchical international system. A distinct set of domestic and transnational civil society actors operated alongside more well-known transnational human rights advocacy networks and, in many cases, provided different understandings of and explanations for some of the same human rights abuses. This included arguing that human rights violations were rooted in usurpation of democratic rule by imperialist governments and global capitalists. The case of Augusto Pinochet's Chile, which was largely responsible for igniting the international human rights movement of the 1970s, was one example of this.[38]

1.2 Other Explanations for Changing Approaches to Interference

The expansion of human rights institutions and changing attitudes toward sovereignty and international interference have received significant scholarly attention, and existing scholarship has offered many possible answers to the question of why leaders in the Global South softened their stance on the norm of non-interference and empowered their regional organizations with greater authority over sensitive political issues like human rights. These existing explanations offer important insight into aspects of these changes. However, they also overlook or fail to account for many patterns and dynamics that accompanied these normative shifts and institutional developments. I briefly discuss six existing explanations: norm diffusion, democratization, the rise of transnational advocacy, forum shopping for weaker mechanisms, establishing regional autonomy, and a prior preference for regional enforcement. For each, I discuss how the argument presented in this book accounts for behaviors that these explanations don't anticipate.

The first three explanations – norm diffusion, democratization, and the rise of transnational advocacy – overlap significantly. They explain the shift away from non-interference by looking to changes in global norms and practice, domestic politics, and the interaction between these domestic and international factors. First, looking at global changes, leaders altered their stance on the relative importance of sovereignty and human rights in response to changing global norms. Some became persuaded of the importance of human rights, while others were pressured to accept them.[39] Some leaders responded to

[38] Chomsky and Herman 1979; Kelly 2013a, 2013b, 2018; Tulli 2021.
[39] Hafner-Burton 2005; Keck and Sikkink 1998; Lutz and Sikkink 2001; Risse-Kappen et al. 1999.

1.2 Other Explanations for Changing Approaches

new material incentives to positively engage with human rights, such as the availability of foreign aid for states that ratified human rights treaties or demonstrated their compliance with human rights norms.[40] In some cases, leaders engaged with international institutions tactically, as a way of fending off international pressure. However, having done so, human rights created new resources for both domestic and international actors to push for societal transformation.[41] The transnational human rights advocacy network, which first emerged in the 1970s, was an important source of this pressure, connecting domestic and international civil society and channeling pressure on human rights-abusing governments.[42]

Changes in the global environment interacted with and often reinforced changes in states' domestic politics, with the most important domestic change being democratization. Leaders of democratizing states had new material incentives to adopt and positively engage with regional human rights institutions and new beliefs that this was the right thing for them to do. Political liberalization within states removed reasons to resist international human rights enforcement and created new incentives to use international institutions to "lock in" political reforms. The political costs of accepting international human rights enforcement, including the loss of national decision-making autonomy, thus came to be outweighed by the benefits of accepting this authority, benefits which also included development assistance, trade, foreign direct investment, and tourism.[43] These domestic changes also created new desires to be (and be seen as) good citizens of the liberal community of states.[44] Democratization sometimes occurred in the context of pre-existing regional norms of pan-regionalism that were conducive to rethinking sovereignty.[45]

---

[40] Blanton and Blanton 2007; Farber 2002; Garriga 2016; Hafner-Burton et al. 2015; Hyde 2011; Isham et al. 1997; Jensen 2003; Landman 2005.
[41] Risse-Kappen et al. 1999, 2013; Simmons 2009.
[42] Moravcsik 2000; Risse-Kappen et al. 1999, 2013; Simmons 2009.
[43] Blanton and Blanton 2007; Coe 2019; Cole 2009; Farber 2002; Garriga 2016; Hafner-Burton et al. 2015; Hyde 2011; Isham et al. 1997; Jensen 2003; Landman 2005; Moravcsik 2000; Pevehouse 2002, 2005; Poast and Urpelainen 2013; Pritchett and Kaufmann 1998.
[44] Finnemore and Sikkink 1998; Hyde 2011; Keck and Sikkink 1998; Lutz and Sikkink 2000.
[45] Aggarwal 1985; Coe 2019.

These explanations account for many of the dynamics that were important in bringing about and consolidating changes discussed in this book. Norm diffusion shifted the global normative environment within which leaders responded to pressure on their human rights records and changed the calculations of leaders who encountered this pressure. The emerging transnational human rights advocacy network was an important part of this normative change and was responsible for much of the pressure on individual governments, though it was also the case that Western governments retained substantial discretion over where and how to pursue human rights enforcement.

It was certainly the case that democratization incentivized leaders of newly democratic states to ratify regional human rights treaties, and differences in democratization within regions help to explain the different outcomes in Africa and Latin America. In Latin America, substantial democratization in the 1980s consolidated the move toward regional enforcement and created conditions in which the regional system could flourish. By contrast, in Africa, democratization took place a decade after states created regional human rights institutions and was much less extensive than in Latin America. As a consequence, it wasn't until after the end of the Cold War that the regional human rights system really began to function, and once it did, it remained less effective and more constrained by member states.

However, these explanations also fail to account for important dynamics surrounding the creation, acceptance, and expansion of human rights institutions. Most notably, they fail to explain the systematic lack of alignment between actors' attitudes toward human rights and their attitudes toward human rights *enforcement*. Leaders that supported human rights often opposed and harshly criticized forms of enforcement that they regarded as counter to the principle of self-determination. They even cooperated with authoritarian leaders to push back against the imposition of human rights enforcement from outside of the region.

At the same time, these same leaders welcomed and supported extra-regional enforcement that conformed to the principle of self-determination and, in many cases, tried to reform global enforcement and create new global institutions that were more consistent with self-determination. This was the case with the creation of a UN High Commissioner for Human Rights and the addition of human rights institutions to parliamentary bodies shared by states of the Global

South and Europe. These explanations also do not explain why, as states democratized and their human rights records improved, they tended to gravitate toward regional institutions over UN institutions, even where enforcement was similarly challenging.

These explanations also do not account for the fact that, prior to the 1970s, leaders of democracies and those that supported human rights had frequently prioritized the norm of non-interference over human rights enforcement. In both Latin America and Africa, important changes in regional attitudes toward human rights and non-interference occurred at times when levels of democracy were low and oppression was widespread. Furthermore, periods of liberalization in both the Middle East and Southeast Asia did not bring about changes in attitudes toward non-interference with respect to human rights.

Finally, and more fundamentally, these explanations fail to fully grapple with the symbolic, historic, and strategic significance of sovereignty in the Global South, where non-interference was widely viewed as a corollary to and means of realizing the right to self-determination. The campaign for the New International Economic Order (NIEO), which was launched in 1974, was aimed in part at limiting economic interference and enhancing economic self-determination in developing states. It was widely supported by states across regime type, representing a distinct, alternative conception of global justice.

Rather than being persuaded of sovereignty's moral flaws, actors across these regions emphasized the normative value of sovereignty and grappled with its tension with individual rights. The idea was shared widely, by both state and non-state actors, that self-determination as realized through sovereign independence and non-interference was itself an important human right. Many civil society actors placed blame for human rights violations, in part, on the exploitation and domination of countries by global capitalism and powerful Western states, an understanding of human rights violations that is far less compatible with Western states acting as agents of enforcement or with a system of human rights enforcement that involves leveraging the economic dependence of the developing world to impose changes in policy or behavior.[46]

Another explanation for these changes is that leaders were attempting to hide behind weaker regional human rights institutions,

---

[46] Kelly 2013a, 2013b, 2018; Tulli 2021; Uribe 1975.

engaging in a type of forum shopping.[47] However, as I show in subsequent chapters, regional institutions had their shortcomings, but they also represented a real, significant break from the norm of non-interference. Rather than toothless institutions created by governments to hide or obscure domestic oppression, these institutions represented a difficult compromise between actors that genuinely wanted better enforcement of human rights and those that stood to be immediately and directly challenged by human rights. This compromise occurred in the shadow of Western enforcement pressure. Many leaders were reluctant to accept these institutions, and once regional institutions were in place, democracies and human rights advocates remained important proponents of them.

Finally, it may have been the case that leaders were attempting to establish regional *autonomy* or had a general, prior preference for regional enforcement. In other words, leaders were attempting to *exclude* extra-regional interference and to *replace* outside enforcement with regional enforcement. They were driven by their belief in the legitimacy of regional organizations, their perception of extra-regional enforcement as domination, and their desire to localize human rights norms to be more consistent with regional human rights norms.[48]

Though there was a systematic preference for regional enforcement of human rights, it was not the fact that these authorities were regional *per se* or that they enforced regional versions of norms that drove this preference. In fact, leaders that supported human rights were frequently open to and enthusiastic about cooperating with extra-regional enforcement where they saw it as consistent with the principle of self-determination, even in cases where it involved cooperation with former colonizing powers. It is also the case that regional institutions and enforcement often did not clearly reflect regional norms, and the very idea that there are internally consistent regional conceptions of human rights is itself contested. The African human rights charter includes content that is said to be more specific to African norms – including individual duties and collective rights – but also includes all the individual rights that are often said to be "Western." In Latin America, regional conceptions of human rights were already very similar to understandings of human rights outside of the region, and

---

[47] Abbott and Snidal 2000; Helfer 1999; Moravcsik 2000.
[48] Acharya 2004, 2009, 2011; Duursma 2020.

Latin America had played an important role in the construction of human rights norms and institutions in the UN.

Instead, as I argue and attempt to demonstrate in this book, the preference for regional enforcement was due to the fact that regional organizations allow their member states greater opportunities for participation and are more accountable to them. Leaders that supported human rights attempted to reform outside enforcement to make it more equitable and consistent with self-determination rather than eliminate it altogether. Even if leaders had wanted to exclude outside actors, in regions that were vulnerable to interference, this simply may not have been a realistic option. Where there was norm localization, as with the inclusion of the right to development in the African Charter, this may have been a consequence of the ability to meaningfully participate rather than the primary goal.

1.3 Empirical Approach

Both my argument and empirical analysis use a historical institutionalist approach. Historical institutionalism emphasizes the ways that the development and transformation of institutions are the product of power struggles that unfold over time. The design of institutions is, in part, a contest over who can exercise power and how. This approach also gives special attention to the timing and sequencing of events, including how the decision-making calculus of political actors and the constraints under which they operate change over time.[49] Actors made decisions in time, responding to the environment with which they were confronted. This included novel and unprecedented developments like the breakthrough of human rights in the 1970s. They made fateful decisions, including decisions over how to design regional institutions and how and whether to engage with them, and they encountered and responded to unintended consequences of these decisions. In developing my argument, I theorize contingency, critical junctures, and unintended consequences as playing an important role in explaining the creation and development of regional enforcement mechanisms.

In adopting a historical approach, I also attempt to tell a story that reflects the world as it was when these changes took place, rather than

---

[49] Fioretos 2011; Mahoney and Thelen 2015; Moe 2005; Pierson 2004; Rixen et al. 2016.

seeing regional institutions from the perspective of a "post-sovereign" world. From the latter perspective, many of the institutions that were created and ways of engaging with those institutions that emerged appear unexceptional and even inadequate. Putting these changes in their historical context highlights how dramatic they were, representing significant and unprecedented shifts in how state actors engaged with international interference.

My main empirical evidence consists of three in-depth case studies, examining the Organization of American States, the Organization of African Unity (now the African Union, or AU), and the League of Arab States (or Arab League). I have chosen these organizations because it was in these "macro" regional organizations that states first moved to engage with human rights. These organizations are critical for understanding the decision of states to empower regional organizations with authority to enforce human rights.

In each of these three regions, a strong norm of non-interference had long guided inter-state relations, and in each, leaders used their regional organizations to institutionalize and enforce this norm. In the first two cases, the OAS and OAU/AU, the dependent variable, the compromising of the norm of non-interference, was realized. In the third, the Arab League, it was not. These three regions are also similar and different across important potential explanatory variables, which allows me to consider competing explanations. These include their past engagement with human rights, the degree to which human rights norms cohere with regional norms, levels of regional democratization, and history of a pan-regional identity.

I selected the Arab League for an in-depth case study rather than the Association of Southeast Asian Nations, another important regional organization which also maintained its strict stance toward non-interference. I do so because, within the Arab League, there were early moves to institutionalize human rights in the late 1960s and early 1970s which were curtailed after the changes in Western human rights enforcement in the 1970s. This early institutionalization provides leverage for assessing how the onset of policies challenging states' self-determination over human rights affected the decision-making of leaders in the region.

Examining the Arab League also helps to address two possible alternative explanations. The first is that variation across regions was simply the result of pre-existing attitudes toward human rights. For both the Arab League and the Organization of African Unity, global human rights norms clashed in significant ways with regional norms, yet in Africa, states managed to overcome this lack of coherence to create regional institutions with many features of a "Western" human rights regime. The second alternative explanation is that variation between regions in whether they compromised on the norm of non-interference is explained by the existence of a pan-regional identity, which ultimately made regions more receptive to softening sovereignty norms.[50] In fact, pre-existing pan-Arab, pan-African, and pan-American identities had historically been an important part of politics in each of these regions. Yet, Middle Eastern leaders resisted interventionist human rights enforcement of any sort long after Africa and Latin America had begun developing their own regional institutions.

Though I do not devote a chapter in this book to tracing the development of human rights institutions in Southeast Asia, dynamics in this region also align with the expectations of my argument. I show in Chapter 3 that, as with the Middle East, Western governments refrained from pressuring Southeast Asian leaders on human rights because doing so would conflict with other, more important foreign policy goals. At this time and in subsequent decades, leaders continued to adhere to the norm of non-interference, a cornerstone of the "ASEAN way." It was only in the late 2000s that leaders in ASEAN began to develop their own regional human rights institutions, which consist of non-binding and inter-governmental mechanisms aimed at promoting human rights and encouraging cooperation rather than permitting interference.

1.4 Regions and Agency in a Hierarchical World

This book speaks to central questions about world order – why the current world order looks the way that it does, how states engage with this order, and how it is reified or transformed by their engagement. I point to the central role of the Global South in creating an international order in which regions and regional organizations are regarded as having special knowledge, legitimacy, and effectiveness in dealing with issues within their own geographic domain. I treat as my object of study something which has become largely taken for granted:

---

[50] Coe 2019.

the unique effectiveness and legitimacy of regional organizations. This idea is most evident in the norm of regional solutions to regional problems, a constitutive norm of the international order which articulates a right for regions to special voice over issues affecting them. I explore how establishing regional organizations as authorities has been a way to expand opportunities for voice, participation, and agency by the Global South in the context of a constraining and hierarchical international system.

This active shaping of the international order to privilege regions has been a recurring theme since the end of World War II. As this book makes clear in the case of human rights, regions are not inherently legitimate or effective sites for policymaking. An international order in which regional organizations are regarded as having special status, authority, knowledge, and legitimacy is, in large part, a product of strategic efforts by actors that benefit from their own regional organizations having greater voice and representation.

During the drafting of the UN Charter, it was the independent states of Latin America and the Middle East that pushed for greater recognition of the authority of regional organizations, along with the idea that these organizations should be autonomous from rather than subordinate to the UN. They did so against the ambivalence of the great powers and small European states, who worried that regional organizations would undermine the UN's authority and reproduce the same alliance politics that had led to two world wars.[51] Over the next two decades, a "wave" of regionalism, driven largely by decolonized states forming new organizations, dramatically expanded the number of regional organizations. This expansion was accompanied by questions on the part of the great powers, policymakers, and scholars as to the desirability of regionalism and the appropriate relationship between regional organizations and the United Nations.[52]

A second wave of regionalism after the end of the Cold War was characterized by substantial expansion of the authority and scope of many existing organizations, alongside renewed debates over the role, autonomy, and authority of these new, more assertive regional organizations and the implications of this for the authority of the United

---

[51] Barnett 1995a; Claude 1956; MacDonald 1965: 4–11, 19; Yalem 1962: 461.
[52] For scholarship addressing this question, see Akehurst 1967; Bebr 1955; Eide 1966; Gross 1965: 537; Halderman 1963; MacDonald 1965: 4–11, 19; Mower, Jr. 1969; Padelford 1954; Wilcox 1965; Yalem 1962: 461.

1.4 Regions and Agency in a Hierarchical World

Nations and post-Cold War global governance.[53] In both waves, actors from the Global South played important roles in advocating for the authority of regional organizations and their autonomy from the UN.

A large body of scholarship has problematized the naturalness of regions, asking how regions are formed and how they become meaningful such that they take on the quality of "regionness."[54] By contrast, there has been less work that questions the naturalness of regions as legitimate sites for policymaking, asks how the authority of regions and a norm of regional solutions to regional problems came to be consolidated, or attempts to understand why and under what circumstances actors from outside of a region, including powerful states, would accept and defer to regional authority.

In addition to speaking to questions about world order, this book also engages with scholarship on international institutions and delegation, bringing it into conversation with scholarship and active debates on international hierarchies. Recent scholarship in IR conceptualizes hierarchies as persistent, non-voluntary structures of domination and subordination that are formed through things like material inequality, asymmetric interdependence, unequal integration into the international system, and inter-subjective beliefs about status.[55] This body of work argues that, from the perspective of subordinate states, "most hierarchies are neither rational nor legitimate; they are just there, seemingly unmovable."[56]

This scholarship challenges earlier work on international hierarchy that conceptualized hierarchies as voluntary, mutually beneficial contracts entered into volitionally and accepted by subordinate states as legitimate.[57] In his influential book, *Hierarchies in International Relations*, David Lake applies this thinking to US hierarchy in the Caribbean. Lake argues that the United States provides domestic order

---

[53] Acharya 1994, 2004, 2007, 2009; Acharya and Johnston 2007; Börzel and Risse 2016; Buzan and Waever 2003; Fawcett 2004; Fawcett and Hurrell 1995; Fawcett and Seranno 2005; Hettne 2000; Hettne and Söderbaum 2006; Hettne *et al* 1999; Katzenstein 2005; Milner and Mansfield 1997; Söderbaum 2016; Söderbaum and Shaw 2003.
[54] Adler et al. 2006; Barnett 1995a; Dirlik 1992; Hemmer and Katzenstein 2002; Hettne 2005; Hettne and Söderbaum 2000; Hurrell 1995; Waever 1993.
[55] Bially Mattern and Zarakol 2016; Getachew 2019; MacKay 2019; Mukherjee 2022; Spanu 2020; Zarakol 2017.
[56] Pouliot 2017: 119.   [57] Ikenberry 1998; Kang 2005; Lake 2009.

to Caribbean leaders and protection against domestic threats to their rule, and in exchange, Caribbean leaders accept the US government's right to issue orders and punish non-compliance. In contrast to this, I suggest in this book that the US is itself often the primary threat to Caribbean leaders and domestic order. US hierarchy often operates like a protection racket in which the "choice" faced by Caribbean governments is to either accede to US demands for compliance, which come with economic and security support, or to face pressure, subversion, or even open intervention by a state with which they are utterly outmatched.[58]

This points to both the possibilities for and limits on agency and autonomous decision-making by weaker or dependent states in a hierarchical world, limits which scholarship on international cooperation and delegation have tended to overlook. The decisions of governments of weak or dependent states to cooperate, delegate, or accept international interference are deeply affected by the hierarchical international environment, the need to avoid antagonizing more powerful actors, and the inefficacy of overt resistance. I explore how hierarchy structures the decision-making of subordinate states, including decisions to participate in international institutions and accept and comply with demands from these institutions or from more powerful states. In doing so, I challenge scholarship on international cooperation and delegation that treats decisions to cooperate or delegate – to align policies with other states, ratify treaties, and join or participate in international organizations – as contractual, voluntary decisions made rationally in pursuit of benefits, or as the product of beliefs regarding the legitimacy and appropriateness of certain institutional forms or cooperative goals.[59] Like hierarchies, international institutions are often simply there, appearing to weaker states as inescapable features of the international system.

---

[58] Lake (2024) addresses this criticism, reconceptualizing the relationship as an equilibrium in which neither the subordinate nor the dominant state have an incentive to alter their relationship. However, in doing so, he excises from the relationship any sense of authority in terms of rightful or legitimate rule.

[59] Abbott and Snidal 2000; Börzel and van Hüllen 2015; Hafner-Burton et al. 2015; Hawkins et al. 2006; Ikenberry 1998; Keohane 1984; Meyer and Rowen 1977; Moravcsik 2000; Stone 2008; Tallberg et al. 2020; Thompson 2006. Other scholarship is more ambivalent about the benefits of international institutions for its weakest members (Gruber 2000; Kim 2010; Moe 2005).

1.4 Regions and Agency in a Hierarchical World

Having identified these limits on agency and autonomous decision-making, I also highlight the importance of agential, self-determined action as a distinct foreign policy goal and the different ways that actors in the Global South use international institutions to navigate this hierarchical international system to allow for self-determined action and decision-making. Some strategies have been overt and confrontational, aimed at immediate and radical reform.[60] Others have been quietly subversive. These approaches include foot-dragging, mimicking compliant behavior, or telling more powerful states what they want to hear.[61] One such approach involves delegating authority to a regional organization, with leaders empowering their own regional organization as a way to increase their voice over both regional and global decision-making. Where leaders expect that overt resistance or contestation will be costly and ineffective, they may pursue these more quiet or accommodationist approaches because they do not look on the surface like contestation or resistance.[62]

Regional organizations are an important tool for transforming hierarchy.[63] One reason that leaders in the Global South have created regional organizations and expanded their scope and authority is to reshape their international environment to be less hierarchical and to allow more space for self-determined decision-making. Oftentimes, this is not about increasing a region's isolation, independence, or autonomy. Within a hierarchical international system in which they occupy subordinate positions, increasing the authority and status of regional organizations and arguing for the legitimacy of regional self-rule is a way for weaker states to transform hierarchies to increase their voice and to expand opportunities for participating in global decision-making.

Finally, this book contributes to debates and scholarship on international norms and human rights. I provide a different understanding of why states would support human rights, or other international norms, while objecting to their enforcement. Rather than this simply being a case of what Stephen Krasner refers to as "organized hypocrisy," supporting a norm only when it is instrumentally beneficial or aligns with other strategic goals, I argue that leaders may

---

[60] Anghie 2019; Gathii 2020; Getachew 2019; Salomon 2013.
[61] Bayart 2000; Hyde 2011; Kat 2021; Scott 1985, 1990; Tieku 2013.
[62] Friedman and Long 2015; Scott 1985.
[63] Beall 2022; Friedman and Long 2015; Long 2017; Long and Friedman 2020; Tickner 2014.

genuinely care about human rights but view certain forms of enforcement as inappropriate. As I show, leaders in the Global South viewed the use of economic pressure to enforce human rights as a violation of the right to self-determination, as well as contrary to norms of sovereign equality, partnership, and universal representation.[64]

A large body of scholarship on the history of human rights has identified the 1970s as the time when the modern human rights regime took shape. It was at this time that human rights, as they are now understood and enforced at the international level, were consolidated.[65] I identify an important and under-explored part of this change: the transformation of human rights into a regional issue, with regional organizations becoming one of the main pieces of international human rights enforcement. Though some regional human rights institutions had existed prior to the 1970s, regional enforcement changed dramatically in the 1970s. Additionally, it was only in the 1970s that the idea took hold that regional organizations should be at the center of the global human rights regime. I show that these transformations were a strategic response to another change that occurred at this time – the sudden incorporation of human rights into the foreign policies of Western states.[66]

The rest of this book proceeds as follows. Chapter 2 lays out my argument in two parts. I first explore the concept of self-determination as it was understood by state and non-state actors in the Global South to govern legitimate relations between states and the legitimate exercise of power in the international system. I elaborate on two conditions that distinguish between international authority that is consistent with or even an expression of self-determination and illegitimate domination: domestic affirmation and meaningful participation. These conditions

---

[64] On legal equality see Finnemore (2003). On universal representation, see Finnemore and Jurkovich (2014). On partnership, see Oyewumi (1991) and Autesserre (2016).

[65] Borstelmann 2013; Brier 2015; Burke 2015; de Waal 2003; Eckel 2019; Eckel and Moyn 2013; Kelly 2013a, 2013b; Lorenzini et al. 2022; Mohandesi 2017; Morgan 2011; Moyn 2010. There is some debate over this claim about the 1970s, but this relates to questions regarding how to understand the changes that took place in the 1970s (Anghie 2013), the degree to which there is continuity between the 1970s and earlier periods (Hoffmann 2016: 280–281), whether or not later periods were more significant (Hoffmann 2016), and the precise starting point of these shifts (Jensen 2016).

[66] Burke 2011; Eckel 2019: 190–242; Lorenzini et al. 2022; Sikkink 2004.

capture how the relationship between self-determination and international rules was understood by a diverse set of actors that were motivated by similar concerns over global inequality and the exploitation of the weakness and economic dependence of post-colonial states. I discuss the important role of international institutions in realizing this principle and limiting practices that conflict with it.

Second, I detail how expanding the scope and authority of regional organizations can be a way to create these conditions. Regional organizations and regional governance provide opportunities for states to participate more effectively in international decision-making, to limit the use of power to impose rules, and to manage the involvement of outside actors in the region. Their formal design, including decision-making rules, consultation mechanisms, and membership composition, and their informal norms, like consensus decision-making, institutionalize broader participation in decision-making and restrict the imposition of rules. I expand on my argument that, in the case of human rights, persuading others to accept and defer to regional authority necessitated giving regional institutions authority to interfere in members' domestic affairs.

In Chapters 3 through 6, I turn to providing empirical evidence for my argument. Chapter 3 explores the changes in the global human rights regime that took place in the 1970s. At this time, Western governments began to impose human rights enforcement by incorporating human rights considerations in their trade and aid relationships with developing states. They did so first in an ad hoc, targeted manner and then as a widespread and institutionalized system of carrots and sticks. Due to the presence or absence of countervailing economic and national security interests, these policies affected Latin America and Africa, while the Middle East and Southeast Asia were spared these same pressures. Transnational human rights advocacy networks emerged at this time, demanding and legitimizing action by Western governments to enforce human rights throughout the world and delegitimizing appeals to the norm of non-interference by leaders in the Global South.

The changes detailed in Chapter 3 demanded a new response by leaders in Latin America and Africa. Chapters 4 and 5 examine how the strategy of establishing regional authority over human rights emerged in these two regions in response to economic pressure, evolving into an approach employed by democracies and a range of actors that supported human rights enforcement, as well as by authoritarian states that were challenged by human rights enforcement. In Chapter 6, I look at the Middle East, a region in which these changes did not occur. As I discuss, the breakthrough of human rights in the 1970s coincided with the Middle East's increased geopolitical importance in Western foreign policy and the explosion of oil wealth in the region, effectively short-circuiting advances toward developing human rights institutions that had taken place up to this point.

In Chapter 7, I conclude by discussing the implications of this argument for other areas of international relations scholarship and for contemporary international politics. I discuss the ongoing importance of regional authority and self-determination in the international politics of the Global South. I also consider how theorizing from the perspective of the Global South can lead to more complete understandings of contemporary political phenomena, providing better explanations for things like dissatisfaction with liberal norms and institutions, openness to cooperation with illiberal powers by states that respect liberal norms, and present-day dynamics of regionalism, including the creation of "new" regions and the growth of "authoritarian" regional organizations. I consider the implications and long-term effects of human rights – a discourse intended to empower people and provide them with the agency to realize their own freedom – being implemented in ways that undermine self-rule and limit political agency.

2 | *Self-Determination through Regional Authority*

Why did leaders in Latin America and Africa create and accept regional human rights institutions that could interfere in their domestic affairs, while leaders in the Middle East and Southeast Asia did not? Why have regional organizations assumed such a central role in the enforcement of human rights? In this chapter, I argue that both of these developments – the decision to empower regional organizations with interventionist authority and the central role that regional organizations have come to occupy in enforcing human rights – were the product of efforts to establish regional organizations as authorities over human rights. To accomplish this, these leaders became willing, for the first time, to accept interference in their states' domestic affairs. These changes varied by region because the imposition of enforcement varied by region.

The norm of non-interference had long protected these states and their leaders, however imperfectly, from intervention, pressure, and meddling by powerful states. However, as Western governments began to disregard this norm and enforce human rights in Latin America and Africa, the decision confronting leaders changed from whether to accept interference to *who* would interfere and *how*. In response, leaders in these two regions began to accept the authority of their regional organizations to enforce human rights by interfering in their domestic affairs. This was not merely an authoritarian survival strategy. Democratic leaders that supported human rights and authoritarian leaders that were violating human rights worked together to create regional enforcement institutions in response to what they regarded as a one-sided imposition, and they created institutions with real teeth.

As I discuss in this chapter, sovereignty and non-interference were not ends in themselves. Arguing for strict observance of these rules was a strategy for using international institutions to limit forms of pressure and interference that leaders saw as undermining their states' self-determination. However, once these rules no longer constrained

33

powerful states, leaders confronting interference needed a new strategy. Whereas before they had argued that interference was illegal and illegitimate, they began to argue that legitimate interference should be carried out by regional organizations.

I develop my argument in two parts. I first expand on the concept of self-determination to incorporate self-determination over international rules, and I explain what it is such that it could be realized by delegating to a regional organization. As I discuss, self-determination was seen by many post-colonial leaders, thinkers, and activists as only partially realized by independence, and they viewed their states as subject to continued forms of international domination that persisted after independence and undermined their self-determination.[1] I then lay out what it would mean for international rules and their enforcement to be self-determined versus being imposed. I argue that what mattered was meaningful choice in becoming and remaining subject to rules and effective voice over their enforcement.

Second, I develop my argument that leaders expanded the authority of their regional organizations in response to the imposition of human rights enforcement. I define authority as legitimate power, where legitimacy is a socially constructed understanding of rightful behavior rather than an objective quality. An actor or institution is an authority when it is accepted as having the right to issue rules and to enforce those rules by demanding compliance and punishing non-compliance. For those that are directly subject to authority, they accept that they have a duty to comply with these rules and orders. For others, recognizing authority means accepting that an actor or institution has a right to have its voice, opinions, and judgments listened and deferred to.[2]

In establishing a regional organization as an authority, members of the regional organization accept the authority of the organization over themselves by creating and ratifying treaties, setting up or expanding the mandate of enforcement bodies, and cooperating within the regional organization to enforce rules. The goal of doing so is to persuade others outside of the region to accept and defer to the regional organization's judgments and its right to handle issues within its purview. This translates into a two-part strategy in which member

---

[1] Anghie 2005; Getachew 2019; Grovogui 1996, 2002.
[2] Barnett and Finnemore 2004; Blau 1963; Lake 2009; Milner 1991.

states build and cooperate with regional institutions and assert to others the authority of regional organizations over rules and their enforcement.

In the process of establishing regional authority over human rights, leaders in Latin America and Africa became willing to accept interference in their domestic affairs. The reason for this was that, to persuade Western governments, international organizations, and international and regional NGOs to accept the authority of regional organizations over human rights, regional institutions had to meet certain expectations of what constituted appropriate and effective enforcement. Central among these was the expectation that human rights enforcement should involve international interference.

Regional institutions created new opportunities for leaders to appeal to norms of local self-rule and to leverage concerns about illegitimate domination in order to argue that regions have a right to participate in and take the lead on enforcement within their own region – said another way, that actors outside of the region should accept and encourage regional solutions to regional problems. Because of this, Western governments, as well as international NGOs and bureaucrats of global organizations, were responsive to and even supportive of appeals to accept regional enforcement, provided that it met certain standards.

This strategy was carried out within a single issue area and was often focused on establishing the authority of an individual regional organization. However, it also required making arguments about the authority of regional organizations more generally, and it drew from previous argumentation about the authority of regional organizations. Because of this, the larger, cumulative effect was to build on and further naturalize a more generalized idea of regional organizations as authorities.

2.1 Self-Determination and International Rules

What is self-determination such that delegating to a regional organization could help to realize it? In order to understand the strategy pursued by leaders in the Global South, it is first necessary to understand the problem that these leaders saw themselves as attempting to solve, the outcome that they sought to achieve, and the importance of international institutions for achieving it.

Self-determination is a standard for the legitimate exercise of power, both between and within states.[3] According to this standard, people have a right to constitute the political authority under which they live and to participate in the wielding of this authority, including exercising accountability over it or casting it off.[4] The 1960 UN General Assembly Declaration on the Granting of Independence to Colonial Countries and Peoples defines it as the right of peoples to "freely determine their political status and freely pursue their economic, social and cultural development" and to be free from "alien subjugation, domination and exploitation."[5]

Self-determination is a contested term, and it has often been understood as synonymous with or most fully realized by sovereign statehood.[6] In this view, self-determination in the Global South was realized by decolonization, which, by extending sovereignty to colonized peoples, brought an end to foreign rule and brought formerly colonized territories and peoples into the international system on the basis of sovereign equality.[7] However, another perspective, one commonly held in post-colonial societies, was that formal independence failed to fully realize self-determination.[8] Instead, post-colonial activists and leaders pointed to "new imperialisms" that emerged in the wake of independence.[9] Ghanaian independence leader Kwame Nkrumah vocally and persistently denounced the undermining of sovereign authority and decision-making as neo-colonialism.[10] Prominent international jurists denounced as a betrayal the failure of decolonization to fully undo colonial control.[11] New criticisms emerged about the undermining of states' economic self-determination, the absence of which Senegalese legal scholar UO Umozurike argued left behind a "hollow sovereignty."[12] Latin American scholars and leaders similarly

---

[3] Cassese 1995: 5; Franck 1992; Scott 2012.
[4] Cassese 1995; Dahl 1989: 91; Getachew 2019; Grovogui 1996; Jackson 1990: 74–78.
[5] UN General Assembly 1960: Preamble, Article 1.
[6] Cameron et al. 2006; Cassese 1995: 5–12, 205–73; Fabry 2010: 9–14; Goddard 2012, 2015; Goodman and Jinks 2013; Moore 2014: 133; Schmitter and Karl 1991: 81–82; Simon 2017; Walzer 1983: 62.
[7] See Jennifer Pitts's (2018: 10–15) discussion of this narrative, including as it appears in the English school of international relations scholarship.
[8] Anghie 2005; Getachew 2019; Krasner 1985: 4; Wilder 2015.
[9] UN General Assembly 1968: Para. 80. See also Lerner 1980: 70–71; Jaguaribe 1979; Prashad 2007: 34.
[10] Nkrumah 1965.   [11] Anghie 2015; Gathii 2020.   [12] Umozurike 1970: 80.

2.1 Self-Determination and International Rules

noted the undermining of autonomy, or the capacity for self-determined action, by economic dependence.[13]

In this perspective, rather than the international system having expanded to incorporate the non-Western world on the basis of sovereign equality, colonized peoples were already unequally integrated into the international system. Decolonization had merely extended formal sovereignty while preserving forms of domination, inequality, and dependence that undermined the meaningful exercise of sovereignty. International rules and institutions denied decolonized states equal voice and influence; international legal standards and unequal treaties that had enabled colonialism continued to be recognized and applied; and the global economic system continued to relegate the Global South to the role of producers of raw materials for and economically dependent on the developed world.[14] Understood in this way, the international system continued to limit self-rule after states became formally independent, with these states entering the system of sovereign states already bound by rules to which they did not consent.[15]

Property rights and foreign ownership rules were frequently singled out as examples of these continued limits to self-rule. Under colonialism, control of much of colonized territories' natural resources had been sold by colonial powers to foreign companies. Upon independence, Western governments expected post-colonial states to honor these contracts and to adhere to the broader international regime regulating property rights and compensation for expropriation. Many post-colonial leaders rejected this expectation, pointing to their lack of involvement in creating these rules and their "permanent sovereignty over natural resources," and nationalized or aggressively taxed their natural resources and foreign-controlled industries. These actions were met harshly by Western powers who, in some cases, provided material support to overthrow governments and, in other cases, conducted their own military interventions. Western-dominated

---

[13] Jaguaribe 1979; Lerner 1980; Russell and Tokatlian 2003; Sunkel 1969; Tickner 2014.

[14] Anghie 2005; Corrales and Feinberg 1999; Finnemore 2003: 30–31; Getachew 2019; Grovogui 1996; Jaguaribe 1979; Lerner 1980: 71; Pitts 2018; Sunkel 1969: 25, 32; Tickner 2014: 77–78; Thornton 2018; Wilder 2015.
On similarities between these claims in post-colonial Latin America and later decolonized regions, see Anghie (2005: 209).

[15] Anghie 2005.

financial institutions often made access to resources contingent on respect for property rights and privatizing state-owned industries.[16]

In this perspective, formerly colonized states did not enter the international system as independent, autonomous actors that then made volitional decisions to cooperate, accept international rules, and pursue integration. Instead, at independence, they were already deeply and unequally integrated into the international system and both penetrated by and dependent on foreign actors. Newly independent states found themselves immediately, involuntarily bound by international rules that preceded their independence, rules which their weakness and dependence left them unable to effectively resist or change. Decisions to accept new international rules were often not volitional, self-determined choices. Instead, they were driven by pressure from international actors or were desperate responses to economic crises.[17]

What, then, would it mean to realize self-determination? The goal was not complete autonomy or the elimination of international rules or interdependence in any form. As a practical matter, the conditions limiting the self-determination of post-colonial states – weakness, foreign penetration, a lack of material resources to accomplish their goals, extreme and asymmetric interdependence – also meant that autarky and the complete exclusion of outside authority were not seen as possible, and international cooperation was necessary for realizing state-building goals and economic development. Beyond these practical considerations, many forms of outside involvement and authority were viewed as fully consistent with and even expressions of self-determination.[18] Self-determination projects that involved surrendering sovereign authority included the creation of regional federations, which were attempted or advocated for in Latin America, the Caribbean, Africa, and the Middle East. A very different example was the Lomé Convention, a treaty between the European Economic Community and former colonies in Africa, the Caribbean, and the Pacific. This treaty was expressly intended to transform relations between the two groups by institutionalizing them on the basis of equality and partnership.[19]

---

[16] Anghie 2005; Salomon 2013.
[17] Getachew 2019; Krasner 1985: 4; Wilder 2015.   [18] Getachew 2019: 23–24.
[19] Bengtsson and Elgström 2012; Crawford 1996; Elgström 2000; Oyewumi 1991.

2.1 Self-Determination and International Rules

Rather than complete autarky or independence, self-determined international authority was distinguished from illegitimate domination by whether decisions to cooperate, integrate, or be bound by international rules met two conditions: *domestic affirmation* and *meaningful participation*.[20] Where these conditions were realized to a high degree, international rules and international enforcement of these rules were seen as consistent with self-determination, because domestic interests and beliefs were incorporated into them, and people within a state could, through their leaders, meaningfully and collectively choose whether to be bound by them.

Given the extent of real, material inequality in the international system, international institutions represented a necessary tool for regulating relations between states, creating meaningful equality, articulating new standards of behavior, and, most importantly, getting powerful states to commit to and abide by standards for legitimate relations and the legitimate exercise of power. Concretely, this meant creating and reforming the rules and decision-making bodies of international organizations, creating new international organizations, using treaties to establish equal relations, and extending international legal principles to regulate relations between newly independent states and powerful, developed states.[21] International institutions would provide the structure within which states with less material power and high levels of dependence would be able to domestically affirm international rules and meaningfully participate in their enforcement.

Below, I expand on these two conditions, their importance to political actors in the Global South, and the role of international institutions in realizing them. Before doing so, however, I first address a problem with this understanding of self-determination, the goal of which was to enhance the strength of the state against imperialist pressures. This quality made it vulnerable to abuse by oppressive leaders. Many anti- and post-colonial leaders and thinkers believed in the necessity of democratic governance within states to accompany more democratic global governance.[22] However, at many points, the tension between protecting the post-colonial state from imperialist

---

[20] For discussions on affirmation and participation, see Stilz (2015) and Markell (2008).
[21] Anghie 2015; Getachew 2019; Salomon 2013.
[22] Getachew 2019; Rodney 1972.

pressures and responding to that same state's capacity for violence against its people was resolved in favor of the former.

At the same time, this understanding of self-determination was not limited to authoritarians or to government officials. It overlapped significantly with, drew from, and shared many goals with prominent social and intellectual movements that were also concerned with international forces usurping domestic democratic rule and undermining peoples' rights. These ideas were captured in the Universal Declaration on the Rights of Peoples, adopted in Algeria in 1976 by a group of anti-imperial civil society actors. The declaration defined the right to self-determination as the right of peoples to a democratic government that respects human rights *and* to "determine [their] political status freely and without foreign interference."[23] They were central to Third World Approaches to International Law.[24] Women's rights activists drew a link between imperialist domination and domination of women within post-colonial societies, seeing imperialism as an impediment to women's rights. In Latin America, student groups, intellectuals, and the Catholic Church identified control of the state by global capitalism as the source of domestic oppression. A global movement against anti-Black racism equated white supremacy in the form of control of non-white countries by Western governments with its manifestation in the denial of their rights in the West.[25] These ideas about self-determination formed a shared ideational basis from which many different actors in the Global South engaged with international politics.

2.1.1 Domestic Affirmation

As understood and advocated for by a range of state and non-state actors throughout the Global South, in order for international rules to be self-determined, they must be domestically affirmed. This meant that the decision to accept rules and the international enforcement of these rules should be made and affirmed through domestic decision-making processes, representing an aggregation of domestic interests and beliefs, as determined though domestic political institutions and

---

[23] Universal Declaration on the Rights of Peoples 1976: Preamble, II(5), (7).
[24] Anghie 2005; Bedjaoui 1968, 1979; Chimni 2007; Grovogui 1996.
[25] Armstrong 2016; Beall 2022; Dussel 1981: 106–13, 127–239; Fajardo 2022; Getachew 2019; Marino 2019; Narayan 2019; Sanders 1970; Slim 2002; Tickner 2014.

2.1 Self-Determination and International Rules

processes.[26] In practice, action at the international level should be determined through domestic institutions and domestic contestation within and among the state's citizens and the government. International influences should be "laundered" through domestic institutions and deliberation.[27]

The alternative to domestic affirmation is external imposition. The imposition of a rule could take different forms. In relations of significant inequality or dependence, powerful states can use their power or their control over resources to enforce rules whether or not a weaker state actually accepts them, doing so in ways that the weaker state may be unable to effectively resist, as was the case with rules on property rights and foreign ownership. Another possibility is that the decision to accept and comply with international rules could result primarily, or even exclusively, from external pressures or influences, including the threat or possibility of external punishment or reward.[28] External pressures can be overt, but they can also be less visible, with states driven to accept rules and their enforcement by their reliance on access to resources, the need to maintain positive relations with states on whom they depended for support, and recognition that perceived defiance or non-compliance could elicit retaliation and discipline.[29] As a result, governments might accept international rules that directly conflict with democratically chosen policies.

This distinction between domestic affirmation and external imposition was central to the Cold War policy of non-alignment, according to which the free, non-coerced conduct of a state's foreign affairs was an important consequence of decolonization and an expression of decolonized states' self-determination.[30] Jawaharlal Nehru, India's first prime minister and one of the originators of the concept of non-alignment, emphasized that this was not about "dissociation," but a kind of cooperation that was freely chosen by the state.[31] In laying out this policy, Nehru spoke positively about cooperation, noting that

---

[26] This condition draws from the language of Anna Stilz's (2015) associative theory of self-determination, though Stilz limits her focus to formal colonization and does not develop her theory to address post-independence forms of global governance. See also Moravcsik (1997) on liberal international relations theory.

[27] On the use of international institutions for laundering, see Abbott and Snidal (1998).

[28] Jamal 2012. [29] Korpi 1985.

[30] Muppidi 1999; Životić and Čavoški 2016: 86. [31] Muppidi 1999: 129–30.

India could be influenced through "friendship and co-operation and goodwill," but that if there is "the slightest trace of compulsion, there can be no co-operation."[32]

Regulating economic relations was particularly important, both because of the need for economic development in post-colonial countries and because of the widespread concern that economic dependence allowed former colonial powers to maintain political control over decolonized states. Adebayo Adedeji – who was a prominent Nigerian economist, an advocate for regional integration, and, at the time, the Executive Secretary of the UN Economic Commission for Africa – articulated the importance of self-determined cooperation in pursuing economic development. Writing in 1979, Adedeji rejected autarky as a realistic path for economic development in Africa, suggesting instead that what matters in cooperating with other actors is "the degree and form of interdependence." This should include the ability to "define and implement autonomous decisions *vis-à-vis* other nations."[33] Pan-African activist and historian Walter Rodney similarly wrote in *How Europe Underdeveloped Africa* that "economic independence does not mean isolation," but it does "require a capacity to exercise choice."[34]

Advocacy for domestic affirmation and attempts to realize it took many different forms. Upon gaining independence, one of the most important was institutionalizing, expanding, and enforcing rules on sovereignty and non-interference. Sovereignty was argued to extend to post-colonial states' permanent sovereignty over natural resources. Leaders, legal scholars, and civil society groups throughout the Global South argued that they did not consent to contracts made while colonized that gave ownership of these resources to foreign actors and should not be bound by them. They also argued that, as sovereign states, law over property rights and questions pertaining to compensation for expropriation should be determined by states and respected by foreign actors. This paralleled earlier debates that had taken place in Latin America, with the Calvo Doctrine and the influential 1917 Mexican Constitution representing similar attempts to develop international law to exert domestic control over both resources and decision-making over resources.[35] This was institutionalized in various

---

[32] Quoted in Muppidi 1999: 130. [33] OAU Secretariat 1979: 87.
[34] Rodney 1972: 31.
[35] Anghie 2005: 209–13; Bedjaoui 1968: 115–16; Salomon 2013; Thornton 2018.

2.1 Self-Determination and International Rules

UN declarations and resolutions, as well as in the UN human rights covenants.[36]

The corollary of expanded rules on sovereignty was new rules on non-interference, which would restrict the use of power and the leveraging of inequality or dependence to impose rules. The 1965 UN General Assembly Declaration on the Inadmissibility of Intervention in the Domestic Affairs of States and the Protection of their Independence and Sovereignty was an important example of this. This declaration did two things. First, it expanded the legal definition of interference that was prohibited by international law to include "the use of economic, political or any other type of measures to coerce a State in order to obtain from it the subordination of the exercise of its sovereign rights."[37] Second, it defined these acts of interference as a violation of the right to self-determination.[38] This would enable weaker or dependent states to make foreign policy decisions that accorded with their domestic interests and decision-making processes rather than responding to, as one state representative put it, "open or disguised coercion to make a State do something contrary to its desires and interests."[39] In discussions leading up to the adoption of this declaration, representatives made clear that its content was a matter of realizing the right to self-determination.[40]

One of the aims of this and later declarations was to expand the rules of interference to restrict economic interference, including the use of economic pressure and coercion. Similar prohibitions were included in the 1970 Declaration on Principles of International Law Concerning Friendly Relations and Cooperation among States and the 1974 Charter of Economic Rights and Duties of States, one of the foundational documents of the New International Economic Order.[41]

Attempts to realize domestic affirmation also involved reforming international economic organizations. The IMF and the conditions placed on its development loans were commonly singled out as in need

---

[36] UN General Assembly 1962; United Nations 1966.
[37] UN General Assembly 1965a: Para. 2.
[38] UN General Assembly 1965b: Para. 66–67, 73, 107, 128.
[39] UN General Assembly 1966.
[40] See, for example, UN General Assembly 1965b: Para. 66–67, 73, 107, 128.
[41] UN General Assembly 1970, 1974a. The full title of the 1970 declaration is the Declaration on Principles of International Law Concerning Friendly Relations and Cooperation Among States in Accordance with the Charter of the United Nations.

of reform. Tanzanian Prime Minister Julius Nyerere, while engaged in highly contentious negotiations with the IMF, noted that his government "recognized the [IMF's] legitimate interest in ensuring money was not wasted or pocketed by government officials." However, he objected to the complete "surrender of [Tanzania's] policy determination" through the conditions placed on loans.[42] The 1980 South–North Conference on the International Monetary System and the New International Economic Order, organized by Nyerere and Jamaican Prime Minister Michael Manley and attended by economists, civil society actors, and leaders, was typical in its criticisms. The conference concluded that the "chosen development paths" of countries of the South, which had "the full legitimacy of their popular representation," were being "blocked" by the IMF and replaced with the IMF's imposed terms.[43] Conditionality needed to be reformed to "reflect the sovereign rights of States to choose their own social and economic models and development paths."[44]

2.1.2 Meaningful Participation

The second condition that was seen as necessary for international rules to be self-determined was meaningful participation. All states, through their representatives, should be able to effectively take part in the design and enforcement of international rules to which they are subject.[45] Accepting international authority should not be a one-time surrendering of sovereign control. Instead, having accepted international rules, states should be able to equitably participate in and influence their enforcement on an equal footing with other states. This doesn't mean that states would need to retain complete sovereign control or that they should not be constrained in their actions, but they should have similar influence as other states, even if each states' influence is quite low, as with international courts and tribunals.[46] In fact, creating independent institutions like international courts and arbitration bodies was a common way of restraining the exercise of

---

[42] Nyerere 1980: 7–8.   [43] "The Arusha Initiative" 1980: Para. 11.
[44] "The Arusha Initiative" 1980: Para. 22.
[45] See Markell (2008) on participation.
[46] Meaningful participation here is different from other critiques of democratic deficits in international organizations, which focus on unaccountable judges or bureaucrats making policy.

power by powerful states by distancing international decision-making from state power.

This idea, that self-determination necessitates participation, directly conflicts with the idea that legitimate international authority can take the form of a "benevolent" or domestically constrained hegemon. IR scholarship has argued that hegemons can legitimize their power through things like domestic democratic institutions and commitment to international norms of multilateralism and anti-colonialism, which constrain the hegemon's power in ways that compensate for a lack of participation by those subject to its authority.[47] Yet, even if a hegemon is benevolent or constrained, a lack of participation means that power is exercised arbitrarily from the perspective of the governed, denying them a basic component of self-rule – involvement in their own governance.[48]

Meaningful participation is not met by formal participation or presence, in the form of simply being in attendance during negotiations or discussions over enforcement or possessing formal membership in an international organization in which rules are enforced. Instead, it requires the ability to make substantive contributions to the deliberative process through which decisions about enforcement are made.[49] Otherwise, policies and decisions affecting people within one state would effectively be made by the governments of other states. Julius Nyerere made this criticism of the IMF, asserting that the organization was not "an instrument of all its members," but a "device by which powerful economic forces in some rich countries increase their power over the poor nations of the world."[50]

The denial of meaningful participation was identified by a range of anti- and post-colonial thinkers and leaders as one of the central and irredeemable wrongs of empire that the decolonization movement sought to overcome. It bridged anti-colonial critiques of empire and post-colonial critiques of the international system.[51] Walter Rodney noted the importance of participation, highlighting the "loss of power" under colonialism that deprived colonized peoples of the ability "to participate actively and *consciously* in history."[52] Achieving meaningful political participation was central to the project of decolonizing the

---

[47] Ikenberry 1998; Lake 2009.
[48] See Markell (2008) on the importance of ongoing participation in affairs that affect the governed.
[49] Milewicz and Goodin 2018.   [50] Nyerere 1980: 8.
[51] Getachew 2019: 23.   [52] Rodney 1972: 272, emphasis in original.

French empire via the creation of a French federation, a project advocated for by Aimé Césaire of Martinique and Léopold Senghor of Senegal, leaders of the *négritude* movement. Self-determination would be realized through equal participation in federal decision-making bodies and equal voting rights and citizenship within the federation for French citizens outside of the metropole. By contrast, they rejected an alternative French Union which would give them second-class citizenship and unequal decision-making rights.[53]

In some cases, decisions over the enforcement of international rules fully excluded weaker states, even where they were directly affected by the decisions. For example, decision-making might take place in international organizations or clubs in which weaker states were not members, such as the G7 or the European Community. In other cases, decision-making was seen as dominated by powerful states, even where weaker states had formal decision-making power. Formal decision-making rules in some international organizations might give overwhelming control to some states, leaving others relatively powerless to shape or alter rules or their implementation. Informal processes might allow some states, due to their technical capacity, centrality to networks, or control over resources, to exert control over decision-making. Certain states may be excluded from meaningful participation if they are not regarded by more powerful states as equal partners worthy of having their opinions taken seriously.[54]

Limits on the ability to meaningfully participate in international decision-making were central to calls to reform international institutions. They formed an important part of criticisms that the IMF, the World Bank, and the Security Council were inconsistent with self-determination and demands to reform membership and voting rules.[55] Similar concerns about participation were directed toward the Western-led defense pacts that were pursued in the 1950s and branded by many leaders as imperialistic.[56] At the Bandung Conference in 1955, Nehru criticized these defense pacts by asserting

---

[53] Wilder 2015: 144.
[54] This could be due to pre-existing paternalistic attitudes and racial biases, Hemmer and Katzenstein (2002: 575). See also Búzás (2013).
[55] Bandyopadhyaya 1977: 149–50; Nkrumah 1963: 194–204; "The Arusha Initiative" 1980.
[56] Barnett and Solingen 2007: 201–6; Muppidi 1999; Podeh 1993, Prashad 2007: 39–40.

that "it is the big and powerful countries that will decide matters and not the two or three weak and small Asian countries that may be allied to them."[57] The final communiqué adopted by the conference proposed a set of principles on which international relations should be based, which included "Abstention from the use of arrangements of collective defense to serve the particular interests of the big powers."[58]

Latin American leaders, too, had long viewed participation as an essential part of the full realization of sovereignty and self-government. This was a core idea behind their campaign in the late nineteenth and early twentieth centuries to articulate standards according to which equal participation in international conferences and organizations by small states was a fulfillment of their rights as sovereigns. This advocacy carried over into debates over the design of the League of Nations, through the inter-war World Economic Conference and the development of post-WWII institutions, and into the post-war era. Latin American leaders pushed for greater involvement in the meetings at which these issues were debated and for a greater role and voting power in the institutions that were formed.[59]

Economic relations were again important. In the 1973 African Declaration on Co-operation, Development and Economic Independence, African heads of state articulated that "ensur[ing] effective and equitable African representation in international organizations" was an important component of economic independence.[60] A 1979 report released by the secretariat of the Organization of African Unity expressed a "refus[al]" for Africa "to become integrated into a world of vassals" and declared their intention to "take over the management of all [their] own affairs and not merely participate to the extent dictated by others."[61] Reform of international economic organizations to increase participation of developing states became an important aim of the NIEO.[62]

2.2 Self-Determination Through Regional Authority

Expanding the scope and authority of regional organizations is one of the principal ways that leaders in the Global South have used

---

[57] Quoted in Prashad 2007: 40.
[58] First Asian-African Conference 1955: G(6(a)).
[59] Finnemore and Jurkovich 2014; Thornton 2018.
[60] OAU Assembly of Heads of State and Government 1973: A.6.
[61] OAU Secretariat 1979: 28.   [62] UN General Assembly 1974a: Article 10.

international institutions to increase self-determination. Leaders expand the types of activities carried out by their regional organization while articulating the right of regions to manage their own affairs. I refer to this strategy as establishing their regional organization as an authority or, more succinctly, establishing regional authority.

There have been many examples of regional organizations being used for this purpose. As discussed in the previous chapter, during the drafting of the UN Charter, Latin American and Middle Eastern states argued that the charter should recognize regional "arrangements" and give them priority over dispute settlement within their regions, doing this alongside the creation or reconstitution of regional organizations to deal with regional conflict. Latin American states also argued for the primacy and autonomy of regional "agencies" in the World Health Organization,[63] and Latin American and Middle Eastern states supported regional preferential trade during the drafting of the General Agreement on Tariffs and Trade.[64] Regional development banks were, in part, an attempt by states to increase their influence over the provision of development aid.[65] The norm of regional solutions to regional problems was used to limit great power intervention in African conflicts through the dual directives for African states dealing with a conflict to "try [the] OAU first" and for those outside of the continent to allow African solutions to African problems.[66]

This strategy is a subtle way of pushing back against international pressure, often in recognition of the limits of open resistance. For materially weak or externally dependent states, open resistance or contestation might not only fail, but it may also elicit retaliation or discipline from more powerful actors. This is especially likely where those powerful actors are invested in certain rules or institutions or view certain kinds of non-cooperative behavior with suspicion. In fact, many of the initiatives described in the previous section, particularly the NIEO, attracted condemnation from Western governments. For a norm like human rights, which has a strong moral quality, even principled resistance to enforcement can attract suspicion.

Establishing regional authority is intended to come across as positive cooperation rather than resistance. Leaders in a region assert leadership over rules and their enforcement rather than opposing

[63] Hanrieder 2016.   [64] Chase 2006: 23, 25; Kim 2010: 51.
[65] Krasner 1981; Thornton 2018.   [66] Duursma 2020; Mathews 1977.

2.2 Self-Determination through Regional Authority

them.[67] Given the constraints that leaders face, this can be a less costly and more effective approach for resisting attempts to impose rules and ensuring voice and influence over enforcement. The aim of this strategy is to persuade a range of different actors, including powerful states and global civil society, to alter their approaches in recognition of the authority of regional organizations.

Why would this strategy be an effective way to constrain powerful states? The reason is that it appeals to the beliefs and expressed commitments of the governments of those states and, indirectly, the domestic audiences to whom they account for their policies. It does so by combining their belief in the normative desirability of self-rule with a second value to which Western governments have committed themselves: that international institutions are an especially legitimate forum for international action.

For both the US and Western European governments, an important part of the post-World War II and post-decolonization international order has been the belief that domination of weak states is illegitimate and an expressed commitment to the idea of local self-rule. Despite the US government's own history of imperial expansion, opposition to imperial rule and support for self-government has been an important part of the United States' self-conception and of the values it advanced for the post-WWII international order. For Western European governments, it became important in the wake of decolonization to establish relations with former colonies on the basis of equality, partnership, and respect for self-determination.[68] International institutions were an important way for Western governments to legitimize their relations with the Global South.[69]

These two beliefs, in the legitimacy of self-rule and the legitimacy of international institutions, were combined in advocacy for self-rule through regional organizations. Where states in a region take matters into their own hands, and where they do so through international institutions, it can be difficult for those outside of the region to reject requests to defer to these regional organizations, follow their lead, or give them a voice in decisions affecting the region.[70]

---

[67] Fioretos 2020; Goddard 2015; Goddard and Larkin 2023.
[68] Elgström 2000: 175–76; Ikenberry 1998; Ikenberry and Kupchan 1990; Lake 2009: 14–15; Marantis 1994: 5; Moore 2012; Oyewumi 1991.
[69] Ikenberry 1998; Ikenberry and Kupchan 1990; Lake 2009.
[70] Goddard 2015: 108–9; Mitzen 2006.

Because this is a strategy of resistance through cooptation, it can require empowering regional organizations in ways that leaders would not have done had rules not been imposed. This was the case with the decision to accept regional enforcement that compromised on the norm of non-interference. Where leaders lack the ability to resist the imposition of rules – to compel more powerful actors to stop demanding compliance or carrying out enforcement – they can instead persuade powerful actors of the appropriateness and utility of a regional approach.[71]

The logic behind this approach is that the imposition of rules presents the rules and their enforcement as the new status quo. If rules will be enforced one way or another, establishing regional authority over rules can create forms of enforcement that members of the regional organization can domestically affirm and meaningfully participate in, relative to this new status quo.[72] It expands the voice and influence of the regional organization's member states over decision-making and allows for regional influence over outside actors that involve themselves in the region.

What about regional organizations makes them more consistent with self-determination? Regional cooperation, in general, and regional organizations, in particular, provide a form of international organization that is consistent with and can help to realize self-determination. A representative of Trinidad and Tobago articulated this perspective on regional cooperation during a speech to the UN General Assembly shortly after Trinidad's independence. The representative stated, "We do not accept that regional collaboration is inconsistent with self-determination…We are firmly of the view that it is through such associations that small nations are afforded the best opportunity to contribute to the solution of the world's problems."[73]

This is not about regional organizations being seen as inherently legitimate by their members. Instead, these organizations are designed to enable meaningful participation and domestic affirmation by all members. They tend to use equal decision-making rules that give member states equal voice. They often have mechanisms for prohibiting the imposition of the policy preferences of more powerful states

---

[71] Finnemore 1996.
[72] See Gruber (2000) for a similar discussion of powerful states imposing a new, worse status quo on weaker states.
[73] UN General Assembly 1967: Para. 44 and 55.

2.2 Self-Determination through Regional Authority

onto weaker members. The expansive non-interference rules and the consultation mechanisms of the Organization of American States, directed at constraining the US, are important examples of this. The Organization of African Unity's norm of consensus decision-making ensures that the preferences of the majority were not imposed onto the minority.

Meaningful participation is institutionalized through equal, one-state, one-vote decision-making. Where decision-making bodies within a regional organization do not have universal membership, meaningful participation is guaranteed by things like rotating membership and quotas for equitable representation. This is an important difference between the UN Security Council and the African Union's analogous Peace and Security Council, as the latter has no permanent members or veto holders. Meaningful participation can also be realized in institutional bodies with high levels of independence from state power. Equal decision-making rules allow each state greater ability to participate in the design of such bodies, decisions to re-contract with them, and the appointment of individuals that serve in these bodies, while independence keeps any one state from dominating decision-making by the body itself.

This strategy allows for more self-determined enforcement of rules in at least three ways. First, it creates an international institution to enforce, elaborate on, and implement rules that is more responsive and accountable to actors in a given region. Second, it can limit attempts to impose rules and the enforcement of rules by outside actors. It does so by persuading those actors to accept and even defer to the authority of the regional organization, where the pre-existing decision-making rules, membership composition, and norms increase the likelihood that states will be able to exercise voice and influence on an equal basis. This can include limiting the involvement of outside actors to supporting, cooperating with, or following the lead of the regional organization. More importantly, it can limit enforcement in contexts that are dominated by other states and where their voice is crowded out by others. It can also create a more level playing field within the region when there are significant power inequalities.

Finally, by establishing their regional organization as an authority over rules and their enforcement, states can create normative expectations that the regional organization *ought* to be consulted and that its opinions *ought* to be listened to and respected when it comes to policymaking that affects the region. A recent manifestation of this appears in the norm in the UN Security Council to give the African Union a special voice with respect to matters pertaining to Africa, which it exercises through the African members on the Council and through annual formal consultations. States thus increase their influence over policy at the global level via their collective voice within the regional organization. This establishes regions not as autonomous from outside involvement, but as possessing special knowledge, expertise, and legitimacy and, accordingly, entitled to exercise voice over and participate in decision-making that affects the region.[74]

2.2.1 Steps to Establishing Regional Authority

Establishing regional authority over an issue area involves establishing authority in two senses. First, the authority of regional organization is established outwardly, with respect to others that have an interest in or claim to authority over the rule, who must be convinced to accept that the regional organization has a right to be listened and deferred to. Two, it is established internally, with the members accepting for themselves the regional organization's legitimate "right to rule" and their own duty to comply.[75] The internal and external sides of establishing regional authority are linked, as the willingness of other actors to accept the regional organization's authority is contingent to some degree on the design of regional institutions. To be accepted as an authority, these institutions must be designed to meet minimal expectations of legitimacy and effectiveness held by actors outside of the region, as well as by global, regional, and domestic non-state actors.

The strategy of establishing regional authority involves two non-sequential – often simultaneous – steps that correspond to these two ways in which authority must be established. First, leaders assert the authority of their regional organization over an issue area and its enforcement and, second, they themselves accept the authority of the regional organization, including through institution-building and increased cooperation within the regional system.

The first step, asserting regional authority, involves persuading other actors to accept that the regional organization, and regional

---

[74] Acharya 2011.
[75] Barnett and Finnemore 2004: 20; Blau 1963: 306–7; Lake 2009: 17–18.

2.2 Self-Determination through Regional Authority

organizations in general, should be regarded as an authority over rules and the enforcement of rules within a given issue area. The authority of regional organizations over their regions, their competence over a given issue, and the nature of their authority vis-à-vis existing authorities – e.g. whether they are super- or subordinate or complementary to them – are all contestable.[76] As I illustrate in Chapter 4, this was especially the case with human rights, an issue defined by the importance of universality and thus less obviously well-suited to an approach in which authority is devolved to the regional level.

Getting actors outside of the region to accept the organization's authority means persuading them that they should "defer to [its] judgment" and grant the organization "a right to speak and to have those statements conferred credibility"[77] when it comes to issues within its purview. Other actors and organizations, including those with a claim to authority over the region or the rule, must be persuaded to accept the regional organization as an authority, meaning that it has the right to speak and be listened to in cases where their authority overlaps or where an outside actor has a strong interest in the issue. A regional organization's authority is likely to be contested where it is being expanded into a new domain.

Establishing regional authority is a strategy aimed at persuading a range of actors, including Western governments and their publics, bureaucrats of international organizations, and non-state actors such as multinational corporations and civil society, to either demobilize or to limit their mobilization to supporting regional approaches.[78] As noted above, it does so by drawing on and appealing to their beliefs about legitimate international relations, particularly their beliefs about international institutions and self-rule. It also draws from concerns about interference in and domination of the weak by the strong. Chapter VIII of the UN Charter, itself a product of efforts to establish regional authority, is an important resource for this strategy. It articulates the primacy placed on regional organizations to handle matters within their own regions within one of the foundational institutions of the post-WWII order.

Non-state actors like domestic, regional, and international civil society and the staff and leadership of international organizations also

---

[76] Avant et al. 2010; Bebr 1955; Hettne and Söderbaum 2006.
[77] Barnett and Finnemore 2004: 20.
[78] On legitimation strategies, see Goddard (2015), Goddard and Krebs (2015).

play an important role, monitoring the actions of governments, pressuring states to act, and demanding changes in behavior. Establishing regional authority is also effective at responding to their demands for action, as well as appealing to their beliefs about legitimacy. Civil society is sensitive to criticisms that they are inviting in domestic interference by Western actors engaged in "civilizing" missions or that they themselves are engaged in such missions.[79] For this reason, they have incentives to favor the creation of *effective* regional institutions, which are far less likely to face these kinds of accusations. Civil society and international bureaucrats may believe that there is value in "local ownership."[80]

In fact, when states within a region respond to outside advocacy by creating and using regional institutions, this can be seen as the product of successful advocacy, and civil society and global organizations may be open to supporting these efforts. The International Commission of Jurists, an international human rights NGO, expended a great deal of effort advocating for the creation of African human rights institutions, and once these were created, made efforts to channel their human advocacy through the regional system.[81] Finally, international bureaucrats in global organizations may benefit from burden-sharing with regional organizations, an idea that received significant attention in the context of peacekeeping after the end of the Cold War.[82]

In the second step, member states of the regional organization accept the authority of their regional organization over themselves. This involves building, expanding, or finally accepting the regional organization's engagement in the issue area and enforcement of rules, as well as offering their own compliance and cooperation. An issue area may already be part of a regional organization's mandate, as was the case with human rights in both the OAS and the Arab League. However, leaders need to actually accept and engage with this authority and possibly expand it further. In other cases, the issue area may be outside of the regional organization's existing competence, and members of the regional organization must delegate new authority to the organization. In either case, having created institutions that can act as an authority,

[79] Keck and Sikkink 1999.
[80] An-Na'im 2001; Autesserre 2016; de Waal 2003: 485; Ejdus 2017; Mutua 2004.
[81] Tolley 1989.   [82] Barnett 1995a; UN Secretariat 1992: Para. 60–65.

they also have to engage with these institutions if they want to persuade outside actors to defer to or support the regional organization.

One of the primary goals of this strategy is to persuade others to accept the regional organization as an authority. Whether members of a regional organization are able to do this depends, in part, on whether regional mechanisms fit with other actors' beliefs about what constitutes effective and legitimate enforcement and whether these other actors can expect regional mechanisms to actually function. These expectations form a baseline for how outside actors will conceive of what an authority, and legitimate action, look like. They constrain leaders' efforts at persuading other actors to accept and defer to regional action.

Because of this, regional mechanisms must be designed to meet minimal expectations as to what constitutes appropriate and effective enforcement, and leaders must accept the regional organization's authority and cooperate with it to some extent. Even where a regional organization has existing competence, states may need to expand the organization's authority and increase their cooperation within it in order to meet these expectations.

External expectations pertain to both the content of rules and the form that enforcement takes. In terms of content, this strategy may occur alongside or sit in tension with norm localization, in which states within a region adapt and alter global norms to make them cohere better with local or regional norms.[83] In fact, where states are attempting to establish regional authority over an issue, regional rules may look *more* like global versions than might be expected if the primary goal were norm localization.

With respect to the form of rule enforcement, both the design of the enforcement bodies within regional organizations and the kinds of actions that they are empowered to carry out matter. These design questions vary based on the issue area. Do enforcement bodies need to be independent, or can they be composed of state representatives? Should their members consist of individuals with particular kinds of expertise? Are there specific decision-making rules they should abide by? Are there certain activities that are seen as particularly central or important to enforcement? One design question that is central to this book is whether regional organizations should be empowered to interfere in member states' domestic affairs.

[83] Acharya 2004, 2009.

2.2.2 Regional Authority and Human Rights

The strategy of establishing regional authority can be (and often has been) used to support the norm of non-interference. Actors outside of a region have been encouraged to defer to regional organizations, while within the region, strict rules of non-interference are observed. However, by the time leaders in Africa and Latin America were facing the imposition of human rights enforcement, shared expectations surrounding the enforcement of human rights required international interference. Leaders within these regions were themselves involved in shaping these expectations, although many also remained reluctant to accept authority themselves. However, in the face of imposed enforcement and in attempts to meet external expectations, they became willing to compromise on the norm of non-interference.

Establishing regional authority sometimes involves delegating authority toward which governments are ambivalent or even actively opposed. This was the case with accepting interference, which many leaders that supported human rights remained concerned about doing because of the important role that strict rules against interference played in protecting them from pressure and interference from more powerful states.[84] However, where enforcement was being imposed (here, interventionist enforcement of human rights), or where there was a credible threat of imposition, leaders faced a situation in which they now expected to be made subject to enforcement one way or another. Given this reality, establishing regional authority could help to ensure enforcement that was more consistent with self-determination.

Through this strategy, leaders sought to create enforcement institutions that they could domestically affirm and over which they could have more voice and influence. To persuade other actors to accept their regional organization as an authority over human rights, they had to meet these actors' minimal expectations of appropriate and effective enforcement. In the case of human rights, this meant accepting enforcement that compromised on traditional conceptions of sovereignty and, most importantly, on the norm of non-interference.[85]

This is because, by the 1970s, interference had become central to human rights enforcement. This included things like commenting on, criticizing, or making recommendations regarding states' domestic

---

[84] See Chapter 3.   [85] I discuss the emergence of this expectation in Chapter 3.

human rights practices. It also included mechanisms to receive accusations of human rights violations from people within states, conduct adversarial investigations against states or state agents suspected of violations, as well as requirements for states to themselves produce potentially damaging information regarding their own failure to comply with human rights.[86]

In regions experiencing it, the imposition of human rights enforcement shifted the preferences and incentives of leaders within the region such that they became willing to accept interference. As I discuss more in Chapter 3, this imposition consisted of the introduction by Western governments of economic enforcement of human rights. Bargaining within the region over the design of regional institutions then took place between leaders that supported human rights, autocrats and leaders of states in which human rights were being violated on a widespread basis, and leaders that regarded human rights as an ideological tool in the Cold War. However, it occurred in the shadow cast by the imposition of enforcement and by the attention and pressure of non-state actors, who monitored how states within regions designed and engaged with regional institutions. In both Africa and Latin America, many democratic leaders and governments that were otherwise supportive of human rights had remained ambivalent about accepting human rights enforcement that involved interference. They, too, were pushed to accept regional interference by the imposition of human rights enforcement.

Leaders of states facing these new enforcement policies had reason to be distrustful and even resentful of human rights enforcement by former colonial powers and governments they regarded as imperialist or neo-colonial. They rejected as illegitimate the underlying inequalities that made such enforcement possible. Western governments also had histories of undermining democratic governments throughout the Global South. They were not seen as trustworthy stewards of human rights policy but as exercising power in ways that were arbitrary and capricious. In response, leaders of democratic governments and leaders that supported human rights in the Global South played a crucial role in establishing regional authority over human rights. This included pushing for regional institutions to be designed with real teeth and helping to ensure that real enforcement took place.

---

[86] Hawkins 2004: 781.

Many leaders that supported human rights did not have a preference between regional enforcement versus enforcement within the UN or other international institutions, though they viewed regional enforcement as having the potential to be at least as good. However, it was often easier to convince authoritarian leaders in the region to accept regional enforcement, for reasons I discuss more below. In some cases, leaders within a region preferred regional organizations because they wanted to exclude states from outside the region from involvement in enforcement, including former colonial powers. Finally, regional enforcement allowed leaders in the region to claim a leadership role for themselves in the enforcement of human rights.

Authoritarian leaders, repressive governments, and those that were deeply skeptical of human rights were pushed to delegate more authority than they otherwise would have and to cooperate within regional systems by the imposition of enforcement. Some of the motivation for this was basic regime survival. Leaders that were directly targeted saw in regional systems the opportunity for greater voice and influence, as well as the possibility for an easier or more sympathetic audience.

However, the hope of easier enforcement was greatly limited by the need to delegate sufficient authority to persuade other audiences to accept regional authority and defer to regional enforcement. The targeting of their region led leaders to expect a high likelihood of being targeted themselves. Because of this, governments that were abusing human rights but had not yet been singled out for scrutiny or enforcement also faced incentives to accept regional authority. Some leaders faced behind-the-scenes pressure and threats from Western governments, while others tried to pre-empt enforcement by demonstrating cooperation with the regional system.

It may not seem like self-determination would be a relevant concept for talking about dictatorships or states committing significant human rights abuses. Nevertheless, this principle was an important motivation for these governments. Irrespective of how others saw them, these leaders tended to see themselves as legitimate representatives of their people's interests and as the legitimate holders of sovereign authority. They resented having their authority usurped or undermined through enforcement that exploited their weakness or echoed colonial or imperial dynamics. They also objected to forms of enforcement that they viewed as unfair, selective, and hypocritical. Finally, these leaders sometimes saw human rights abuses as unavoidable collateral damage that occurred in pursuit of legitimate state-building and development goals or security interests.[87]

In Latin America, right-wing dictatorships believed themselves to be facing a real threat of domestic terrorism and communist infiltration and bristled against their efforts to respond to these threats being undermined by outside actors. In regions that had been decolonized recently, many dictators saw themselves as continuing the anti-colonial struggle in the post-independence period; many had come to power as a result of decolonization and were sensitive to forms of influence that they regarded as neo-colonial. One might disagree with these leaders' interpretation of their situation, but that is separate from whether it formed a genuine and distinct motivation for them.[88]

Non-state actors, both within and outside the region, also played important roles. Norm entrepreneurs within regions pushed for the creation of and engagement with regional institutions. These included high-level officials within regional organizations and prominent members of the legal and advocacy community. Domestic, regional, and global activists and civil society played an important role in drawing attention to human rights violations and insisting that action be taken in response to them. High-level bureaucrats within the United Nations used their positions to keep attention focused on human rights abuses. In creating regional institutions, one thing leaders could hope to accomplish was to facilitate a "boomerang pattern" which operated through regional rather than global regimes.[89] Non-state actors had their own incentives to support the creation of effective regional human rights mechanisms. However, they had to be at least minimally persuaded that these were real mechanisms with real authority with which states would actually engage.

2.3 Authority in an Unequal World

The anticipation of coercive or punitive actions by a stronger actor, or one with which there is a relationship of dependence, is a powerful force in a world that is deeply unequal. The nature of international relations – characterized by inequality, extreme asymmetric

---

[87] Arguments about responding to domestic terrorism and developmental authoritarianism were two common examples of this argument.
[88] For evidence that this is a motivation of leaders, see Powers and Altman (2023).
[89] Keck and Sikkink 1998.

interdependence, and a history of powerful states using these to get what they want – means that, counter to much theorizing on international authority, powerful actors often do not need to rely on legitimacy, "soft power," or even occasional carrots and sticks to induce compliance from weaker states.[90] Instead, all that is required is for weaker states to anticipate negative consequences from not complying.

One consequence of inequality and dependence is that states may become subject to rules in ways that are formally voluntary but not self-determined. Powerful states can issue rules and punish noncompliance in ways that are cheap for themselves but devastating for their targets. This can involve simply rescinding vital support or redirecting essential resources to another, more compliant state. In this strategic environment, overt acts of resistance, contestation, and defiance may not only fail, but they may elicit costly retaliation, and leaders of weaker states often try to avoid such confrontations.[91] Because of this, what looks on the surface like the acceptance of authority may instead be a rational calculation that contestation will be costly and unsuccessful.[92]

This is not to say that real, legitimate international authority does not exist, only that, on the surface, acceptance of authority as legitimate, reluctant acquiescence, and quiet resistance may look very much alike. Are compliant acts "symbolic obeisance," demonstrating respect for the authority of a dominant state?[93] Are they reluctant acquiescence done in recognition that power differentials make resistance futile?[94] Or are they "everyday resistance," in which weaker actors placate the powerful by telling them what they want to hear while quietly subverting their authority?[95]

Answering this question requires looking at the motivation behind compliant acts, which is what I turn to in the following chapters. I explore the empirical evidence in support of my argument that the

---

[90] Nye (1990) discusses the concept of soft power. See also Ikenberry (2001) and Lake (2009).
[91] Gruber 2000; Hurrell 2005; Korpi 1985; Moe 2005; Pierson 2015. On the effect that these expectations have on populations in the Middle East, see Jamal (2012).
[92] See Pouliot (2017) for a similar discussion of how subordinate states operate within and experience hierarchy.
[93] Lake 2009: 12.   [94] Pouliot 2017.   [95] Scott 1985, 1990.

2.3 Authority in an Unequal World

creation, acceptance, and expansion of regional human rights institutions in Latin America and Africa represented an attempt to quietly resist the imposition of human rights enforcement in recognition that more open forms of contestation would be ineffective, while an absence of this imposition helps to account for the absence of similar outcomes in the Middle East and Southeast Asia. As detailed in this chapter, regional organizations are an important means of navigating, resisting, and transforming international hierarchies to increase space for self-rule. Accepting regional interference was a way for leaders to create more legitimate forms of enforcement in the face of what they regarded as illegitimate domination.

3 | The Imposition of Human Rights Enforcement

In 1977, Amnesty International was awarded the Nobel Peace Prize for its advocacy for prisoners' rights and against the use of torture. Introducing the prize at that year's award ceremony, the head of the prize committee, Aase Lionaes, placed Amnesty's work in the context of the dramatic changes that had occurred in global understandings of sovereignty. Lionaes contrasted views that had been espoused at the Belgrade Conference – the 1961 meeting of governments where the Non-Aligned Movement was formed – with prevailing public opinion then, in the late 1970s.

At Belgrade, "[a] number of nations maintained ... that for one country to call attention to a violation of human rights in another country constituted interference in the internal affairs of that country." By contrast, she continued, "I cannot believe that a ruse of this nature aimed at glossing over injustices perpetrated in one's own country will be countenanced by international opinion today. On the contrary, the view is now gaining ground that no state can lay claim to absolute national sovereignty where human rights that are universally recognised are involved."[1]

This view, that the protection of human rights justifies international interference and that saying otherwise is cynical and self-serving, would likely not strike many today as controversial. In scholarship, sovereignty has been theorized as a "barrier" to human rights,[2] or alternately, as a "pathology"[3] or "flaw"[4] of the international order that human rights help "disable."[5] The contemporary practice of human rights centers around the idea that legitimate and effective action necessitates international involvement in states' domestic politics. It is widely accepted that international action to reduce abuse by

---

[1] "Award Ceremony Speech" 1977. [2] Henkin 1995: 31.
[3] Macklem 2015. [4] Buchanan 2013: 125. [5] Cohen 2012: 14.

the state against those within its borders is what human rights enforcement *is*.

Though this understanding of human rights and sovereignty is now largely taken for granted, at the time Lionaes gave her speech, an interventionist human rights regime had just recently emerged.[6] Economic enforcement quickly became one important piece of this regime. This form of enforcement involves things like cutting off aid or trade relations in response to non-compliance and adding formal conditionality to treaties, as well as the lingering threat that positive relations and economic support require positive engagement with human rights.

The incorporation of human rights into economic relations between the developed and developing world was enabled by the new understanding that protecting human rights is a legitimate reason for interference and that any actor with the means to do so is justified in demanding compliance with human rights standards and punishing non-compliance. When Western governments began to employ economic pressure to enforce human rights in the 1970s, it was part of a new normative environment that demanded, enabled, and legitimized interference by Western governments to protect human rights in the Global South.

In this chapter, I trace the rise of economic pressure as a tool used by Western governments to enforce human rights and the uneven application of this pressure by region. These policies emerged as *ad hoc*, targeted responses to the most flagrant and widespread violations of human rights. However, they soon grew to encompass improving respect for human rights in any state that benefited from development assistance or that traded with the West. Their broad institutionalization created a set of policies to which all states that were dependent on or recipients of things like aid and preferential trade access were vulnerable. This included states whose leaders could recognize the targeting of their region and their own vulnerability to enforcement policies. Leaders that supported human rights, respected them domestically, and were democratically elected also became subject to these

---

[6] Anghie 2019; Borstelmann 2013; Brier 2015; Burke 2015; de Waal 2003; Eckel 2019; Eckel and Moyn 2013; Kelly 2013a, 2013b; Lorenzini et al. 2022; Mohandesi 2017; Morgan 2011; Moyn 2010.

policies through the widening and institutionalizing of this system of carrots and sticks.

The decision-making of Western leaders over where to apply economic pressure to enforce human rights was strongly impacted by their own economic and security concerns. In trying to balance human rights with other priorities, Western governments deployed these policies unevenly, and regions that were more strategically important and less economically vulnerable were spared costlier forms of enforcement. Latin America was targeted first, followed soon by Africa. By contrast, the Middle East and Southeast Asia were actively excluded from a proactive human rights policy and, in some cases, even aided by Western governments in addressing international pressure on their human rights violations.

Some leaders from the Global South supported economic pressure in response to the most egregious violations of human rights.[7] However, the widening of these enforcement policies conflicted with their ideas about self-determination as it applied to legitimate relations between states and legitimate exercises of power. The policies were designed in contexts in which Western states had nearly complete control, such as international financial institutions (IFIs), the European Economic Community, and their own bureaucracies and legislatures. They worked by leveraging the dependence and material weakness of developing states, and their decision-making processes set the West up as judge of human rights in the Global South.

Though leaders throughout the Global South objected to these policies, the same changes in the normative environment that had encouraged the use of economic pressure by Western governments also altered the strategies that were available to leaders in the Global South for responding to them. In particular, it delegitimized appeals to state sovereignty and non-interference, rendering ineffective their strategy of demanding more and more expansive rules of non-interference and elaborations of sovereignty that, as described in Chapter 2, had formed an important part of how these leaders had used international institutions to realize self-determination.

These new policies emerged into a contested space, setting up a clash between these two conceptions of global justice. They appeared at a moment when the Global South was demanding far-reaching changes

---

[7] *FRUS* 2013: Document 42; King 1997: 56.

3.1 The Changed Normative Landscape for Human Rights and Interference

to the global order, most importantly in the launching of their campaign for a New International Economic Order (NIEO) in 1974. Through this, leaders of developing states argued that development assistance was an entitlement, not charity that developed states could offer and withdraw at their discretion. It was in this contested space that leaders encountering economic enforcement began to establish regional authority over human rights.

3.1 The Changed Normative Landscape for Human Rights and Interference

The 1970s represented a significant and dramatic break in the global human rights regime. As has been extensively documented, it was at this time that human rights enforcement began to take on its modern form.[8] In fact, the extent to which human rights enforcement prior to the 1970s differed from its modern form has led some scholars to question even categorizing it as human rights activity.[9]

The term "human rights" became central to the language of global justice in the 1940s via its incorporation into the charter of the newly formed United Nations, in 1945, and the drafting and adoption of the Universal Declaration of Human Rights (UDHR) in 1948.[10] From these first years through the early 1970s, advocacy for and implementation of human rights was characterized by forms of action that largely respected and even bolstered the sovereignty of the Global South, namely by tackling global inequality and human rights violations that were international in nature.[11]

After the adoption of the UDHR, divisions had quickly emerged between the Global South and the West, with the priorities of the

---

[8] Borstelmann 2013; Brier 2015; Burke 2015; de Waal 2003; Eckel 2019; Eckel and Moyn 2013; Keck and Sikkink 1998; Kelly 2013a, 2013b, 2018; Lorenzi et al 2022; Mohandesi 2017; Morgan 2011; Moyn 2010; Sikkink 1993, 2004. There are some debates over this claim, but these relate to questions regarding how to understand the changes that took place in the 1970s (Anghie 2013), the degree to which there is continuity between the 1970s and earlier periods (Hoffmann 2016: 280–81), and whether or not later periods were more significant (Hoffmann 2016).

[9] Anghie 2019; Moyn 2010. See Moses et al (2020) and Slaughter (2018) disputing this.

[10] Evans 1996: 2; Henkin 1990.

[11] Beall 2022; Burke 2011; Dehm 2019; Jensen 2016; Tolley 1983.

Global South coming to dominate human rights activity in the UN. This dynamic became even more pronounced in 1967, when the membership of the UN Commission on Human Rights (UNCHR), then the main UN body mandated with addressing human rights, was amended to give the Global South a majority.[12] Western governments, by contrast, demonstrated little interest in addressing human rights within the UN at this time. They had been ambivalent about including human rights in the UN Charter in the first place, and they remained more concerned with controlling the agenda in the General Assembly's First and Second Committees, where security and economic issues were dealt with.[13]

The specific priorities that became the focus of human rights activity at this time were racial discrimination and apartheid, the right to self-determination, and economic and social rights in the Global South. For each of these priorities, much of the emphasis was on the responsibility of Western governments to realize and cease violations of these rights or the West's complicity in violations. Advocacy for self-determination focused on both decolonization and the self-determination of independent states. Self-determination had not been included in the Universal Declaration, and one product of this advocacy was to establish it as a human right in the 1960 Declaration on the Granting of Independence to Countries and Peoples and as Article 1 of both UN human rights covenants. During the drafting of the UN human rights covenants, there was broad support from the Global South for language on self-determination that would apply to independence for colonized territories and non-interference for independent states.[14]

With respect to economic and social rights, one important focus was establishing that Western governments had an obligation to assist developing states in realizing these rights. In debates in the UNCHR, representatives from the Global South emphasized the West's responsibility for the underdevelopment of the rest of the world, pointing to colonialism and the upholding of international structures that inhibited states' development. They also emphasized that it was impossible for developing states to realize economic and social rights without international assistance.[15] Hernán Santa Cruz of Chile, one of the original

---

[12] Tolley 1983, 1984.   [13] Burke 2011: 8; Lauren 1983.
[14] Cassese 1995: 55–57; Lauren 1983.
[15] Alston and Quinn 1987: 189; Dehm 2019.

drafters of the UDHR, was among the most emphatic in arguing for the responsibility of developed states to realize economic and social rights in developing states and to respect the right to permanent sovereignty over their natural resources.[16]

By contrast, there was very little activity that involved interference in the Global South. The main exception was the campaign against *apartheid* South Africa, which was framed as a special case of incomplete decolonization.[17] In 1967 and 1970, two important expansions were made to the UNCHR's authority with the exclusive purpose of enabling greater pressure on apartheid governments.[18] Its mandate was amended in 1967 to create procedures to allow the commission to receive and act on individual complaints of human rights violations. In 1970, states gave the commission authority to investigate human rights violations.

The drafting and adoption of the UN human rights conventions also took place during this time, between 1950 and 1966. The International Covenant on Civil and Political Rights (ICCPR) established an enforcement body that could comment on states' self-reporting, receive complaints of human rights violations from individuals within states, and issue non-binding decisions on these complaints. This authority to receive and make decisions on petitions from individuals has come to be one of the core tasks of international human rights institutions, but to accept this authority, states had to ratify a separate Optional Protocol. By the end of 1972, only eight states had ratified this Optional Protocol,[19] and the ICCPR itself didn't come into effect until 1977.

The character of human rights advocacy changed dramatically in the 1970s, triggered in large part by the overthrow of Salvador Allende in Chile on September 11, 1973. One significant part of this change was in beliefs about how sovereignty and human rights should be weighed against one another and the circumstances under which violating a strict conception of sovereignty was permissible. A human rights lawyer for Amnesty International noted this change during human rights hearings being held by the US Congress in 1973, asserting that

---

[16] Boilard 2019: 122–27; Humphrey 1983: 412; Quiroga-Villamarín 2019: 83, 92; Santa Cruz 1995.
[17] Klotz 1995; Tolley 1983, 1984. [18] Tolley 1983; Weinstein 1976.
[19] Those states were Costa Rica, Colombia, Ecuador, Uruguay, Madagascar, Sweden, Denmark, and Norway. Barbados and Mauritius ratified in 1973.

governments "can no longer say, 'It's none of your business.'"[20] This new logic of sovereignty and human rights was also reflected in the above remarks introducing Amnesty International's Nobel Peace Prize in 1977, by which time this new logic had taken hold to a significant degree.

An emerging transnational human rights advocacy network that linked together global organizations and domestic civil society was an important driving force behind these changes.[21] Amnesty International was among the most significant international NGOs in this network. It had grown rapidly since the late 1960s and expanded its focus from campaigning for individual prisoners of conscience to carrying out global campaigns against torture and the practice of "disappearances." Amnesty International's leadership seized on the events in Chile in a campaign that was hugely impactful, for which the organization was awarded the Nobel Peace Prize.[22]

An important reason why the events in Chile so fully reoriented attitudes toward human rights and sovereignty was the situation's unique ability to unite a wide range of actors.[23] Salvador Allende was a democratically elected socialist leader who was popular and highly respected in the Global South and in international socialist circles. Non-aligned countries, democratic socialist leaders in Europe, and Soviet governments reacted strongly to the violent overthrow of Allende's democratic socialist government, his death, and his replacement by a right-wing, US-aligned military dictatorship. An unlikely coalition of Global South, Soviet, and Western European governments helped to put Chile's human rights violations on the international agenda and keep them there, pushing for investigations and issuing condemnations that violated a strict conception of sovereignty.

Chile also united civil society actors, both within and outside of Latin America. There was ambivalence from certain corners, particularly from leftist, anti-Marxist, and anti-imperialist groups, about rich, Western states enforcing human rights in the poor states of the Global South. At the same time, the right-wing dictatorship in Chile, along with those in other Latin American countries with similar governments, were seen by many as a manifestation of US imperialism and of the domination of the people by global capitalism. The consequence

---

[20] Kelly 2018: 152.   [21] Keck and Sikkink 1998; Sikkink 1993.
[22] Kelly 2018: 152–53; Moyn 2010.   [23] Kelly 2018: 152.

was a high level of agreement on taking action against Pinochet, in spite of differences in how different actors understood the nature of the problem.[24]

Leaders in the Global South were simultaneously affected by and part of creating these changing understandings and beliefs about human rights and sovereignty, including through their response to Chile, their ratification of human rights treaties, and their growing support for expansions of the UN's human rights institutions. Beginning in 1977, proposals to expand the UN's power to enforce human rights came from, or received important support from, Global South delegations. In 1965, Costa Rica had taken up the cause of setting up a UN High Commissioner for Human Rights, an independent and impartial office that would carry out a wide range of enforcement functions. In 1977, in the context of the increased interest in human rights enforcement, the idea gained new interest, and a new proposal to create the office was co-sponsored by ten African and Latin American states.[25] A proposal for all states to permanently give consent for visits by UNCHR was made by Senegal in 1977.[26] Representatives of some Global South states also supported a proposal by Italy in 1978 to expand the use of ad hoc groups for investigating human rights in any state in which human rights abuses were taking place.[27] In 1977, Nigeria proposed to expand the mandate of the Economic and Social Council to allow it to monitor human rights and act on violations.[28]

These proposals for reforming the UN were unsuccessful at the time, in part because of divisions within the Global South over the question of whether to allow interference. A statement by a representative of Senegal, a country that consistently supported human rights initiatives, captured the concerns created by this more interventionist enforcement. Addressing the UN General Assembly in 1979, the representative stated that "the sovereignty of States should not serve to conceal human rights violations." At the same time, "the protection of human rights cannot be used as an excuse to disregard the sovereignty of States and to interfere in their internal affairs."[29]

---

[24] Chomsky and Herman 1979; Kelly 2013b; Tulli 2021.
[25] UN General Assembly 1977a.   [26] UN General Assembly 1977c.
[27] UN General Assembly 1978a: 1601–2.   [28] UN General Assembly 1977g.
[29] UN General Assembly 1979a: Para. 143.

3.2 The Rise of Economic Enforcement

Western governments were greatly affected by these changing beliefs about legitimacy and the shifting costs and benefits of interfering in other states in the name of human rights. These governments had generally made human rights a low priority in the UN, and human rights had not been an important factor in their relations with developing states. This changed in the 1970s, when Western governments began to face demands to act on human rights violations, along with criticism for providing support to governments that violated human rights.[30]

There were new political costs to Western leaders for being seen as taking a permissive stance toward – or actively assisting – governments that were violating human rights, along with new political rewards for those that took a strong, principled stance on human rights. Many leaders were individually influenced by these shifting beliefs about what constituted legitimate interference and legitimate relations between states, and they began to pursue human rights of their own initiative. With decolonization mostly complete by this time, human rights were also less of a political problem for the West and, instead, had become an area in which they could assert moral leadership in the context of their Cold War rivalry with the Soviet Union.

When Jimmy Carter spoke in front of the UN General Assembly in March 1977, several months after his inauguration, he articulated this new understanding of human rights and sovereignty, asserting that all members of the UN, by ratifying the UN Charter, "ha[d] pledged themselves to observe and respect basic human rights. Thus, no member of the United Nations can claim that mistreatment of its citizens is solely its own business." This also implied a duty for other states to act. "[N]o member can avoid its responsibilities to speak," Carter asserted, when human rights violations occur elsewhere.[31] In other words, it was not only permissible for the US government to enforce compliance with human rights, it was required of them. These words matched his administration's approach as it was laid out internally. Secretary of State Cyrus Vance circulated a telegram to all embassies and consulates later that month stating members of the UN "may not, of course, legitimately complain that the practice [of

[30] Arts 2000: 223–24.   [31] FRUS 2014: Document 29.

3.2 The Rise of Economic Enforcement

violating human rights] is an internal affair on which others may not comment."[32]

One immediate result of these changes in the normative environment was that Western governments began to reduce or cut off aid to states that were identified as being especially egregious violators of human rights.[33] These policies began as ad hoc responses to the worst human rights violations, but they were quickly widened and institutionalized to cover relations with a larger swath of states, forming a new body of economic enforcement policies.

In the United States, congressional Democrats were the first to push for human rights to be incorporated into economic relations with developing states.[34] In 1973, Congressman Donald Fraser, the chair of the International Organizations and Movements subcommittee, began holding public hearings on human rights violations in other states. In 1974, Congress began to pass increasingly restrictive legislation mandating that aid be withheld and trade limited to countries that engaged in a "consistent pattern of gross violations of internationally recognized human rights." It also mandated that the State Department prepare human rights reports on all countries that received US security assistance. In 1975, Chile became the first country to have its security assistance cut off under the new legislation,[35] and in 1976, security assistance was cut off to Uruguay.[36] That year, the US also voted against a development loan for human rights reasons for the first time, denying a loan to Chile.[37] These laws were, in part, aimed at forcing the hand of Republican president Gerald Ford who, along with Secretary of State Henry Kissinger, objected to incorporating human rights into US foreign policy.[38] In 1975, Ford created the Bureau of Human Rights and Humanitarian Affairs within the State Department in the hope that this would deter further congressional pressure, further institutionalizing human rights in US foreign policy.[39]

The pressure from the United States on human rights expanded considerably after Jimmy Carter became president in 1977, with Carter's administration embracing human rights as a foreign policy goal. Early in his presidency, Carter issued a Presidential Directive outlining a plan to use "the full range of [the US's] diplomatic tools"

---

[32] *FRUS* 2013: Document 28.   [33] Keck and Sikkink 1998.
[34] Eckel 2019: 192.   [35] Binder 1975.   [36] *FRUS* 2015: Document 348.
[37] Weissbrodt 1977: 259.   [38] Keys 2010; Weissbrodt 1977: 238–59.
[39] Keys 2010: 823.

to encourage respect for human rights and punish violations.[40] Carter also encouraged cooperation among Western governments on using economic measures to respond to human rights violations, raising the issue at the G7's 1977 London Summit.[41]

When Ronald Reagan became president of the United States in 1981, he did so in part on a platform that was openly antagonistic toward Carter's human rights foreign policy. Upon taking office, Reagan appointed a Secretary of State, Alexander Haig, who referred to human rights as "sissy ... fancy pants stuff."[42] However, Reagan's administration could not escape the new demands to act on human rights or the new beliefs that US foreign policy should be consistent with and serve to further human rights. In a 1981 memo on human rights policy from two high-level State Department officials to Secretary of State Haig, the officials cautioned Haig (in all italics) that *"We will never maintain wide public support for our foreign policy unless we can relate it to American ideals and to the defense of freedom."*[43] In 1982, Haig circulated a memo with the directive that human rights should "occupy a prominent place in the formulation and conduct of our foreign policy."[44]

Rather than going away, the US government's human rights foreign policy simply changed form. Reagan found human rights language to be useful to his administration's Cold War policies, using it to target leftist rebel groups and left-wing totalitarian governments, which he labeled as qualitatively worse for human rights than right-wing authoritarians.[45] Jeanne Kirkpatrick, a political scientist who had helped develop the idea that human rights violations in leftist "totalitarian" governments were worse than those in right-wing "authoritarian" governments, was appointed as Reagan's ambassador to the UN. As ambassador, she argued that the human rights movement was guilty of "exculpat[ing]" terrorist or revolutionary groups, justifying a shift in US human rights policy to focus on leftist rebel groups.[46]

---

[40] *FRUS* 2013: Document 29; Presidential Directive NSC-30: Human Rights 1978.
[41] *FRUS* 2013: Document 24; Kaufman 1998; Rowen 1977.
[42] Weinraub 1982.   [43] *FRUS* 2017: Document 54 (Emphasis in original).
[44] *FRUS* 2017: Document 56.
[45] "Administration Said to Follow Double Standard on Human Right" 1982; Jacoby 1986: 1068; Kirkpatrick 1979.
[46] Kirkpatrick 1986.

3.2 The Rise of Economic Enforcement

The US government under the presidency of Jimmy Carter is perhaps the most well-known actor in establishing and promoting a strong human rights foreign policy, and the addition of human rights to the foreign policy of a superpower was certainly significant. However, over the course of the 1970s, leaders of Western European countries, most importantly the United Kingdom, the Netherlands, and Nordic states, also began to pursue human rights as part of their foreign policies.[47] Many European governments became heavily involved in the international response to Chile, and socialist political parties throughout Europe advocated against Pinochet's government.[48] Human rights also became part of European foreign policy within the European Economic Community (EEC) at this time.[49]

As with the US, Europe's approach to human rights began with a narrow focus that quickly expanded. In response to Chile, European politicians joined "solidarity groups," which investigated and lobbied support against the Chilean government's human rights practices.[50] European governments reduced economic assistance, voted against loans in IFIs, refused to reschedule existing debts, and reduced or severed diplomatic ties.[51] The United Kingdom sanctioned Uganda for expelling migrants in 1972 and again in 1976 as knowledge of Idi Amin's brutal regime became more widespread. The United Kingdom, the Netherlands, and the Nordic countries began to institutionalize human rights in their domestic bureaucracies, and some European governments expressed interest in incorporating human rights into their voting in IFIs.[52]

A major development in Western Europe's economic enforcement policies occurred in 1977, following a burst of attention on the human rights abuses of Idi Amin's government in Uganda. Uganda was a major recipient of European aid through the Lomé Convention (Lomé), an association agreement governing development assistance and preferential trade between the EEC and their former colonies, the

---

[47] Eckel 2019: 190–242.
[48] Eckel 2019; Kelly 2018: 94–133; Lorenzini et al. 2022.
[49] Arts 2000; Fierro 2003; King 1997; Lorenzini et al. 2022: 6.
[50] Kelly 2013b: 178.
[51] Crittenden 1976; "Economic Measures Set" 1975; *FRUS* 2013: Document 4, 105; "The British Cabinet's 'New Approach' to Chile" 1979; "U.S. Cuts Back Ties" 1979; Vogelgesang 1978: 824; Young-Anawaty 1980: 72.
[52] Eckel 2019: 190–242; *FRUS* 2013: Document 4.

African, Caribbean, and Pacific (ACP) states. The attention on Uganda, a recipient of aid through Lomé, was an embarrassment to the EEC and its member states. They responded to the situation by issuing the "Uganda Guidelines," which stated that any assistance going to Uganda through the Lomé Convention should "not in any way have as its effect a reinforcement or prolongation of the denial of basic human rights."[53] These guidelines were used to substantially reduce economic assistance to Uganda.[54]

European leaders quickly moved to generalize the Uganda Guidelines to apply to all beneficiaries of Lomé assistance. In June 1977, EEC states announced their intention to add human rights provisions to the Lomé Convention during scheduled renegotiations for the convention,[55] and they applied the guidelines to several other African states over the next few years.[56] In November 1979, despite their failure to add human rights to Lomé during renegotiations, they adopted an internal policy announcing their intention to apply human rights considerations anyway.[57]

The French government held out longer against a human rights foreign policy, pointing to concerns that such policies were neo-colonial and would negatively affect their Cold War strategies. This changed when, in May 1979, Amnesty International released a report detailing the mass killing of children in the Central African Empire in which the dictator, Jean-Bédel Bokassa, was alleged to have been personally involved. France was a major patron of Bokassa and France's then-president, Valéry Giscard d'Estaing, was known to be a personal friend and golf buddy of Bokassa's. Within several months after the release of the report, the French government lent its support to an *ad hoc* African investigation into the killings, cut off assistance to the Central African Empire, and provided support to a coup that overthrew Bokassa.[58] In 1981, Francois Mitterrand was elected president of France on a pro-human rights foreign policy platform.[59]

These policies had been brought into existence, in large part, by socialist and liberal governments. When conservative European

---

[53] King 1997: 55.   [54] Fierro 2003: 45; Moravcsik 1995: 166.
[55] Moravcsik 1995: 168.   [56] Arts 2000: 324–25.
[57] European Commission 1979: 4; Young-Anawaty 1980: 94.
[58] "Papa Bok is a Millstone to France" 1979; "Vive la France?" 1979; Welch 1981: 406–8.
[59] Randal 1982.

governments came to power in the 1980s, there was a transformation similar to what had taken place in the US in the transition from Carter to Reagan. Human rights policy simply took on a new shape that was more consistent with the priorities of the new conservative governments. This included drawing a link between human rights, domestic stability, and economic development outcomes, a link which justified making human rights a consideration in the distribution of development assistance.[60]

Within the EEC, European leaders and commissioners continued to push to add human rights to Lomé, and in the second half of the 1980s, human rights became a regular consideration in EEC decision-making.[61] In 1986, the European Community Foreign Ministers issued a formal policy statement on human rights, naming them an "important element" in the "development of their relations with non-member States as well as in the administration of aid."[62]

Finally, the European Parliament became an important driver of Europe's human rights foreign policy, including by pressuring member governments to act on human rights. The parliament had adopted human rights promotion as a cornerstone of its "democratic legitimacy" in the 1970s. Pressure from the parliament on European states became even stronger after the parliament's first direct elections in 1979, in which many successful candidates campaigned on human rights.[63] Parliamentarians regularly demanded greater consideration of human rights in decision-making over development assistance and questioned European leaders on the human rights violations of aid recipients.[64]

Western governments, having adopted these policies in response to shifting norms, were subsequently enabled in their use of pressure against weak and formerly colonized states by an international environment that had become much more permissive of coercive action where it was undertaken in the name of human rights. This included domestic publics that did not want to see their money supporting governments that abused their people. Shifting beliefs on the part of Western leaders, their publics, and global civil society legitimized concern with human rights in weaker states and former colonies.

[60] Eckel 2019.
[61] European Parliament 1993: 4; Kamminga 1989: 33; Marantis 1994: 7 n30.
[62] Arts 2000: 119–20.   [63] Arts 2000: 251; Boumans and Norbart 1989: 137.
[64] European Parliament 1983a: 7–8.

As a result, in instituting these policies and demanding and enforcing compliance with them, governments in the West were largely unconstrained by concerns about the legitimacy of interference in weaker states. Western leaders registered the complaints from leaders in the Global South that their human rights policies were inappropriate interference, but they were undeterred.[65]

3.3 Patterns of "Regional Discrimination"

Though Western governments were now empowered to use economic pressure to enforce human rights, they did not apply these pressures evenly. Human rights had to compete with other foreign policy priorities, and Western leaders, politicians, and bureaucrats faced domestic pressure to act on human rights alongside the need to deal with other pressing economic and national security priorities. As a result, where they actively incorporated human rights into their foreign policy decision-making, they did so where it was relatively cheap, meaning there were few tradeoffs or chances of it damaging other important priorities, and easy, in the sense that there were pre-existing relationships and institutions into which human rights could be introduced.[66]

This tendency by Western governments to subsume human rights to other strategic concerns in devising their foreign policies has been extensively documented in existing scholarship.[67] It has also been noted with dismay by civil society. In a 1994 report by Amnesty International, the group alleged that throughout the Cold War, Western governments "found it expedient to ignore clear evidence of systematic human rights violations" for states of "strategic importance."[68] Aryeh Neier, the co-founder of Human Rights Watch and, at the time, the president of the international NGO the Open Society Institute, wrote in 1996 that "geopolitically or economically significant" states were frequently spared extensive human rights pressures.[69] Neier outlined a situation in which, "[t]ime and again," human rights organizations have noted the "disjunction between what

---

[65] *FRUS* 2013: Document 13, 29, 42, 193, 196.   [66] Levitsky and Way 2006.
[67] Alesina and Dollar 2000; Carleton and Stohl 1985; Chayes and Chayes 1995: 106–7; Dietrich and Murdie 2017; Dunning 2004; Grigoryan 2020; Krasner 1999; Lebovic 1988; Lebovic and Voeten 2009; Neumayer 2003a, 2003b; Nielsen 2013; Poe 1991; Sandholz 2016.
[68] Amnesty International 1994: 9–10.   [69] Neier 1996.

3.3 Patterns of "Regional Discrimination"

is said in [the State Department human rights] country reports and US policies toward those countries."[70]

This was no less the case for governments that were led by individuals with a real desire to incorporate human rights into their foreign policies, such as Jimmy Carter's administration in the United States and James Callaghan's Labour government in the United Kingdom. In fact, both were clear about the need to be "pragmatic" in their approach to human rights.[71] Governments accepted the limits of what they could accomplish with their human rights policies and the need to avoid jeopardizing other policy areas.[72]

As early as March 1977, just months after Carter took office, his Director of Policy Planning for the State Department, Anthony Lake, clarified in a classified memo that the US government's human rights policy would "inevitably focus on some nations more than others." Specifically, it would avoid "those cases where US action on human rights *per se* could endanger other objectives (such as disarmament) which, in fact, serve or complement the cause of human rights." In general, Lake concluded that there was a need to "limit engagement on human rights with economically or political important governments in order to maintain the cooperation of these governments on 'vital' interests."[73] By contrast, he noted that "with some [countries] ... our bilateral interests are so modest that our prime interest is human rights."[74] These kinds of references to balancing human rights with other interests were common.[75]

This was also true for the British Labour government that had come to power in the United Kingdom in 1974 on a platform of promoting human rights. Foreign Secretary David Owen, one of the most important actors in moving Britain and Europe toward a robust human rights foreign policy, was open about the fact that the government would need to "balance morality with reality" in pursuing these goals.[76]

These decisions were not made on an individual, state-by-state basis, but with the larger region in mind, resulting in what Anthony Lake

---

[70] Neier 1996: 99.   [71] Carleton and Stohl 1985; Kaufman 1998.
[72] Bloomfield 1982. For similar assessments on the pragmatism of the Carter administration's approach, see Kaufman 1998; Pflüger 1989: 709; Rubner 2011: 186; Schmitz and Walker 2004: 114–15.
[73] *FRUS* 2013: Document 29.   [74] *FRUS* 2013: Document 105.
[75] Kaufmann 1998; Rubner 2011: 186; Schmitz and Walker 2004: 124.
[76] Rubner 2011: 196.

referred to at the time as "regional discrimination."[77] Regions were treated as systems, with policies toward one state affecting policy in other states. In Latin America and Africa, it was much easier to make human rights a priority. These two regions were targeted extensively while, for the Middle East and Southeast Asia, human rights remained subsumed to Western governments' security and economic goals.

3.3.1 Pressure emerges in Latin America and Africa

Latin America emerged as the first and most intense target for international attention and enforcement in the aftermath of the overthrow of Salvador Allende in 1973. This was, in part, the product of media and transnational advocacy attention on Chile and, eventually, other Latin American governments.[78] However, just as important was the fact that Latin America was, in the words of Anthony Lake, "the best theater for [US] human rights activity, at little risk to other ... interests." According to Lake, the US had "a good deal of leverage" in Latin America. Additionally, Latin American governments were "ideologically disinclined to turn to Moscow,"[79] meaning that the US did not need to worry about pushing them too hard.

As discussed above, this pressure focused on Chile first, resulting in US action to cut off security assistance and vote against development loans. Additional cuts in economic assistance were debated by Congress.[80] Pressure expanded to the rest of Latin America when Jimmy Carter became president in 1977. At the meeting of the General Assembly of the Organization of American States in June of that year, Secretary of State Cyrus Vance announced the US government's intention to link human rights with regional aid,[81] and the US broached the issue of human rights at an Inter-American Development Bank meeting that same month.[82] By 1978, US assistance had been restricted to Argentina, Brazil, Uruguay, Nicaragua, and El Salvador,[83] and the US had enacted new trade barriers with a number of these countries.[84]

---

[77] FRUS 2013: Document 105.
[78] Hafner-Burton and Ron 2013; Kelly 2013b: 165.
[79] FRUS 2013: Document 105.   [80] FRUS 2015: Document 217, 218, 220.
[81] US House of Representatives 1977.
[82] "Kidnapping Mars IDB Meeting" 1977.   [83] FRUS 2013: Document 62.
[84] Benham 1977.

3.3 Patterns of "Regional Discrimination"

The region's weakness and the absence of countervailing geostrategic priorities made enforcement easy and cheap, while Latin America's high levels of economic dependence created easy avenues for enforcement.[85] One US State Department official articulated the reasons for the outsized focus on Latin America in a confidential memo. The official noted that "we have a good deal of leverage in Latin America; more countries there are traditional recipients of our economic and military assistance than in, for instance, East Asia; our security and economic stake is less than in East Asia or the Middle East."[86] The pressure on Latin America was so disproportionately intense that, in one memo, an unnamed official from the State Department was said to have "expressed particular concern that Latin America is being singled out because there are so few conflicting US interests and the decision therefore seems so easy."[87]

This affected even states in Latin America that were more strategically and economically important to the US. Argentina was an important trade partner, and its right-wing dictatorship was an ally in the United States' anti-communism efforts. It was nevertheless targeted extensively with economic pressure that was aimed at altering its human rights practices. In August 1978, a member of Carter's National Security Council noted that he was "absolutely astounded by the sheer quantity of trade" that was being embargoed against Argentina.[88] As I show below, strategically important states in the Middle East and Southeast Asia were treated very differently.

Early on, Western and Northern European states also showed outsized attention to Latin America. The Western hemisphere had long been accepted as the United States' sphere of influence, and European relations with Latin America had been much more limited. One effect of these limited relations was that European states faced relatively few countervailing political concerns in pursuing human rights in the region.[89] European politicians joined "solidarity groups" targeting the Chilean government.[90] In 1975, the Paris Club of creditors refused to reschedule Chile's debts, and European governments voted against a World Bank loan to Chile.[91] Their attention widened to other states in the region, including other Southern Cone countries, Nicaragua, and

---

[85] Levitsky and Way 2006.   [86] *FRUS* 2013: Document 105.
[87] *FRUS* 2013: Document 7.   [88] *FRUS* 2018b: Document 89.
[89] Beti 1981.   [90] Kelly 2013b: 178.   [91] Crittenden 1976.

El Salvador. Western European governments reduced economic assistance, voted against loans in IFIs,[92] reduced or severed diplomatic ties,[93] and provided support and legitimation to domestic opposition movements of repressive leaders.[94]

Africa was the next region to face the West's economic enforcement policies. For the US government, the fact that it had few interests in Africa initially resulted in less attention on the region.[95] A 1977 memo from an official in the US State Department remarked that Congress, the main driver of US human rights policies up to that point, "still has a certain myopia as far as African human rights are concerned, and this has protected Africa from the sort of attack faced in Latin America."[96] This changed after a 1977 report by Amnesty International on the execution of an archbishop and two former government ministers in Uganda. This, alongside Ugandan dictator Idi Amin's targeting of Americans living in Uganda, drew a swift reaction from the US.[97]

At this point, a lack of competing interests left US policymakers relatively free to prioritize human rights over other issues in Africa. Aid and trade was blocked to Uganda in 1978.[98] Following the explosive report on the Central African Empire released in 1979 by Amnesty International, Carter's administration was quick to put pressure on its government, and the legislature removed funding for a rural health project from the budget.[99] Aid to the Central African Empire was suspended for human rights reasons in 1978, followed by Mozambique, Angola, Zambia, and Tanzania in 1979.[100]

Because of economic relations built during the colonial period, Western European governments had far more extensive pre-existing ties with Africa. Europe was Africa's largest source of development assistance and the most important market for the continent's commodity exports. Their relationship was institutionalized most importantly in the Lomé Convention, and African states made up 47 out of 56 Lomé recipient states in 1978. Because of Lomé, the

[92] FRUS 2013: Document 4, 105; Vogelgesang 1978: 824.
[93] "The British Cabinet's 'New Approach' to Chile" 1979; "U.S. Cuts Back Ties" 1979; Young-Anawaty 1980: 72.
[94] Tomayo 1981.
[95] Rubner 2011: 189–94. By contrast, apartheid Africa received attention from the public and the US Congress.
[96] FRUS 2013: Document 62. [97] Gertzel 1980: 464; Oberdorfer 1977.
[98] Fredman 1979; Rubner 2011: 196. [99] FRUS 2018c: Document 119.
[100] FRUS 2013: Document 53, 105; Rubner 2011: 187.

3.3 Patterns of "Regional Discrimination"

EEC's relationship with Africa was far more institutionalized than their relations with other parts of the Global South, providing both opportunity and leverage for enforcing human rights.

There was a great deal of emphasis on Africa from individual European governments. For the United Kingdom under the pro-human rights Labour government that was in power from 1974 to 1979, their primary emphases regarding human rights were on Uganda and adding human rights to Lomé.[101] Because of their prior colonial relationship with Uganda, the situation there elicited attention from the UK earlier than other countries, with Britain breaking off diplomatic relations with Uganda in 1976.[102] When David Owen became UK foreign secretary in 1977, he pushed to expand the country's attention to human rights.[103] Under the British presidency of the EEC in 1977, Britain worked to make human rights a part of the Lomé Convention.[104]

The existence of Lomé and the leverage it provided over African states provided a clear path to incorporating human rights into their economic relations. Following the 1977 reports on Uganda, members of the EEC issued the abovementioned "Uganda Guidelines." Aid to Uganda was substantially reduced, and the aid that continued was redirected to ensure it went to only humanitarian causes.[105] The EEC immediately began to push to add human rights to Lomé, and they applied the Uganda Guidelines to Equatorial Guinea in 1978, to the Central African Empire in January and April 1979, and to Liberia in 1980.[106]

3.3.2 An Absence of Pressure on the Middle East and Southeast Asia

In these same years, the foreign policies of Western governments toward the Middle East and Southeast Asia developed along a very different path, with human rights consistently subsumed to other priorities. Throughout the Cold War, both regions were strategically important theaters for superpower rivalry, with the Soviet Union and the United States supporting and propping up different repressive authoritarian governments.[107]

---

[101] Rubner 2011: 198.   [102] Lowman 2022: 13.
[103] Grealy 2022b; Lowman 2022: 14–15.   [104] Grealy 2022a: 125, 129.
[105] Fierro 2003: 45; Moravcsik 1995: 166.   [106] Arts 2000: 324–25, 423.
[107] Baxter and Akbarzadeh 2012; Jamal 2012; Khalidi 2009: 9–21; Podeh 1996; Sneh 2008.

With the Middle East, oil politics and attempts to broker peace between Israel and the rest of the region were the main priority. In fact, just as human rights were entering into Western states' foreign policies, several major global events made the Middle East an especially unattractive target for attempting to enforce human rights using costlier methods. The 1973 Yom Kippur War, in which a coalition of Arab states was defeated by Israel, and the subsequent OPEC oil boycott, which the Arab members of OPEC organized to punish supporters of Israel, made Middle Eastern peace and retaining access to Middle Eastern oil priorities for both Europe and the United States. There was also an increase in terrorism originating from the Middle East with which European governments were preoccupied.[108]

Jimmy Carter made achieving peace in the Middle East a centerpiece of his administration's foreign policy this goal ultimately took priority over pressing for improvements in human rights.[109] Anthony Lake noted in 1978 with respect to US human rights policy that "our desire to move Arabs and Israelis toward a peace settlement and the importance of Mideast oil have kept arms sales high."[110] He continued to explain that "we have not put primary emphasis on human rights considerations, in view of our other pressing interests, when deciding on arms sales or determining our approach to the area generally."[111] In 1979, the overthrow of the Shah of Iran resulted in another jump in oil prices and the loss of a reliable US ally and friendly source of Middle Eastern oil.[112]

This increase in countervailing costs for pursuing human rights in their foreign policy with the Middle East was coupled with diminishing economic vulnerability of states in the region, with the wealth of some states increasing by as much as 1,000 percent during the 1960s and 1970s.[113] Anthony Lake noted that, among Middle Eastern states, "few of them are recipients of our economic assistance," eliminating what was in other regions an important source of leverage.[114]

Western European states were similarly dependent on Middle Eastern oil, and they had also become increasingly concerned with terrorism in the region after several high-profile hijackings.[115] In the 1970s, the EEC initiated efforts to create a Lomé-style system with

[108] Bicchi 2002. [109] Schmitz and Walker 2004: 128; Sneh 2008.
[110] *FRUS* 2013: Document 105. [111] *FRUS* 2013: Document 105.
[112] Jones 2012; Sneh 2008: 171, 178. [113] Alnasrawi 1987; Owen 1981.
[114] *FRUS* 2013: Document 105. [115] Bicchi 2002.

3.3 Patterns of "Regional Discrimination"

what they referred to as the "Mediterranean Group," which consisted of southern Europe, the Middle East, and North Africa. However, this policy never got off the ground, due in part to the bargaining power that control of oil provided the "Mediterranean" states. In a separate initiative, 1974 saw the beginning of the Euro-Arab Dialogue between the EEC and the Arab League, which was intended to establish political cooperation between the groups, though it ended up focusing only on discussions of economic development, and Arab states abandoned it in 1979.[116] In both of these forums, human rights never entered into discussions, even while the EEC was simultaneously pushing for the incorporation of human rights into Lomé.[117] I discuss relations between the West and the Middle East, and how this impacted the development of regional human rights institutions, in more detail in Chapter 6.

A similar situation prevailed in Southeast Asia, where states' economies during the 1970s grew faster than any other region in the Global South[118] and Southeast Asian countries emerged as important markets for Western exports.[119] There were also a number of overriding national security considerations for Western states, most notably the conclusion of the Vietnam War and the threat of Southeast Asia falling to communism. This concern motivated a great deal of strategic activity and intervention in the region.[120] In the immediate aftermath of a communist government coming to power in Vietnam in 1975, the US was concerned about expanded Soviet influence in the region and prioritized its partners there.[121]

As with the Middle East, strategic considerations led the US and Western Europe to downplay human rights violations.[122] Anthony Lake noted that the "greatest risk to other US interests from the human rights policy may be in East Asia."[123] In the Philippines, a US military base that served as an important access point to the region was up for renegotiation, and the White House deliberately downplayed human rights violations being committed under the authoritarian Ramos Marcos government in order to facilitate the negotiations.[124]

---

[116] Albinyana and Fernández 2018.
[117] Albinyana and Fernández 2018; Tsoukalis 1977; de la Serre 1980.
[118] Phung *et al* 2014.   [119] Hurst 1997: 84.   [120] Buszynski 1981: 287.
[121] Adesnik and McFaul 2006: 12–13; Hawes 1986: 20–22.
[122] Adesnik and McFaul 2006: 9; Kaufman 1998.
[123] *FRUS* 2013: Document 105.
[124] *FRUS* 2013: Document 105; Hawes 1986: 20–21.

In Indonesia, the US consistently sought closer ties with the repressive Suharto government because of the country's growing economic importance and its role as a consistent opponent of communism in the region.[125] American officials responded to reports of massive violations of human rights in East Timor by asserting publicly that the reports were "greatly exaggerated" and attempting to downplay the violations to Congress.[126] In a telegram to the US embassy in Jakarta, the State Department suggested ways that Indonesia could improve its image and "deflect UN interest."[127] Where the US engaged with human rights, it tended toward forms of engagement aimed at nudging countries toward reforms, such as quiet, behind the scenes pressure, the use of public statements, or support for resolutions in international organizations.[128]

Efforts to keep human rights issues from interfering with their relations with East Asian states showed up in the annual US State Department human rights reports. In 1979, a member of the National Security Council noted "striking inconsistencies" between the reports of different countries in 1979, which the official suggested was due to these countries' "political importance." The memo noted that:

"[T]he problems between competing interests were solved by balancing every negative statement with a positive statement, resulting, particularly in the East Asian reports (Korea, Philippines, and Indonesia) in extraordinary length."[129]

Similarly, relations between the EEC and Southeast Asian states included no discussion of human rights. This was despite the fact that there were several attempts to institutionalize relations between the two regions during the 1970s, with ASEAN states seen as a good, underexploited market for European trade.[130] In 1972, a Special Coordinating Committee of ASEAN Nations was established to coordinate and enhance trade, along with the ASEAN Brussels Committee that same year. Their interactions were regularized in EC-ASEAN Ministerial Meetings.[131] In 1980, the EEC signed the Cooperation Agreement between Member Countries of ASEAN and the European

---

[125] Simpson 2009: 798–99; Simpson 2019.   [126] Simpson 2009: 806, 809.
[127] Simpson 2009: 807.   [128] Adesnik and McFaul 2006; Burns 1982: 101.
[129] FRUS 2013: Document 180.   [130] European Commission 1979.
[131] Doidge 2004: 46.

Community.[132] With each of these, European governments did not introduce human rights, either as a condition for cooperation or a topic for discussion. It was only after the Cold War that human rights entered their inter-regional relations.[133] Even then, it was limited by geopolitical concerns.[134]

One consequence of the fact that these policies were designed by region was that even countries that were themselves relatively unimportant but were located within important regions were spared significant economic pressure. Cambodia was not individually important, but human rights in Cambodia were nevertheless de-emphasized on account of larger regional efforts to oppose Soviet influence in the region. Carter's administration was aware of the extent of the Khmer Rouge's violence in Cambodia. His administration was frequently criticized by Congress for its lack of attention to the problem and pressured to take stronger action. This pressure had little effect. The Khmer Rouge were eventually driven from power by the Vietnamese government in December 1978, and the US government responded by condemning the intervention, exerting pressure to get Vietnam out of Cambodia, and supporting a Chinese invasion of Vietnam in 1979.[135]

3.4 Economic Enforcement and Clashing Views on Legitimacy

The new economic enforcement policies described in this chapter emerged into a contested space. The environment in the 1970s and 1980s was marked by debates over the legitimacy of respecting sovereignty where human rights were concerned. On the one hand, there were new ideas about the importance of responding to human rights violations and rapidly changing beliefs about the conditions under which it was acceptable to interfere to protect human rights. On the other hand, concerns remained about the principle of self-determination in relations between states, and beliefs persisted regarding the importance of non-interference for guarding against illegitimate domination.

The new assertiveness of Western governments, who now wielded their control of resources to reward and punish human rights practices,

---

[132] Association of Southeast Asian Nations 1980; European Commission 1980b: 101–4.
[133] Association of Southeast Asian Nations 1980; European Commission 1980b: 101–4; Wang 2012.
[134] Wang 2012: 19–20.   [135] Clymer 2003: 248–57.

competed with rather than replacing their concerns about appropriate relations with the Global South. Western leaders continued to worry about the Global South's legitimate demands for self-rule, and leaders faced lingering concerns about provoking accusations of "Yankee imperialism" or neo-colonialism.

For governments in the Global South, support for interventionist enforcement of human rights did not displace the value that they placed on the right to self-determination, including economic self-determination. In 1974, as Western governments began to pursue economic enforcement of human rights, the Global South's own advocacy entered a new, more assertive phase with the launching of the campaign for a New International Economic Order. The NIEO conceived of economic conditions and pressure as violating the rights to development and economic self-determination and as a derogation of the duty of developed states to realize these rights. This campaign received significant support from leaders who also supported interventionist enforcement of human rights.

Representatives from the Global South who supported both kinds of rights argued for their inter-relatedness and interdependence. In 1977, a representative of Costa Rica, an important regional and global advocate for human rights, asserted at the UN General Assembly that "only when rich States really comply with their obligation to co-operate with the poor in their efforts to overcome under-development can they rightfully call for the full observance of human rights."[136] These projects were rejected by Western governments.[137]

As I develop in the next two chapters, in Latin America and Africa, leaders in these regions objected to being made subject to economic enforcement policies. However, they could not compel Western government to stop, and shifting beliefs and attitudes toward human rights and sovereignty meant that the norm of non-interference was no longer an effective response. When representatives of the African, Caribbean, and Pacific states argued that the addition of human rights conditions to the Lomé Convention constituted inappropriate interference, the director of one international NGO characterized this as "an argument now regarded as the last resort of scoundrels."[138] Appeals to non-

---

[136] UN General Assembly 1977d: Para. 174.   [137] Beall 2022.
[138] Young-Anawaty 1980: 96.

3.4 Economic Enforcement and Contested Legitimacy

interference were increasingly treated as a sign that governments were acting in bad faith and had something to hide.

The regionalization of human rights occurred in this contested space. Establishing regional authority over human rights represented an attempt to reshape beliefs about appropriate enforcement by grafting together concerns about self-rule with beliefs about the legitimacy of international institutions. Latin American and African leaders reconciled themselves to the inefficacy of appealing to the norm of non-interference. They worked within the space opened up by the ongoing contestation over appropriate relations between the Global North and Global South, developed and developing states, and former colonizers and the formerly colonized. Western leaders held lingering concerns about the legitimacy of their relations with the Global South, and because of this, they were open to appeals to defer to regional human rights enforcement, provided that they judged regional institutions to be minimally acceptable.

4 | Latin America and the Emergence of Regional Authority over Human Rights

After the overthrow of Salvador Allende and the new dictatorship's brutal consolidation of power in 1973, Chile became the first and most intense target of the modern human rights movement. An extensive body of research points to the case of Chile as not just a target of advocacy, but as an important arena in which modern human rights advocacy took shape. New means of enforcement emerged, new advocacy groups gained prominence, and new networks formed, linking together international and domestic human rights activists around the globe.[1]

In response to the events in Chile, Western governments first began to widely and systematically use economic pressure to shape the human rights practices of states that relied on them for things like development and security assistance and preferential trade. Though these policies began with the ad hoc targeting of Chile, they quickly expanded into a broad, institutionalized system of carrots and sticks intended, as laid out in a presidential directive issued by Jimmy Carter, to "promote the observance of human rights throughout the world."[2] Over the course of a few years, human rights became a major issue in economic relations between the US and all of Latin America.

It was out of this pressure on Chile, and in the process of responding to the widening and transformation of this pressure, that the strategy of establishing regional authority over human rights emerged and took shape. Though this strategy had been used before in other issue areas, with human rights, it changed from being consistent with and strengthening the norm of non-interference to accepting interference as legitimate, provided that it gave sufficient voice to regional organizations.

---

[1] Eckel 2019; Eckel and Moyn 2013; Keck and Sikkink 1998; Kelly 2018; Moyn 2010; Sikkink 1993.
[2] Presidential Directive NSC-30: Human Rights 1978.

A central part of this effort was developing the idea that regional organizations had special authority with respect to human rights within their regions, which by the early 1970s, was not at all taken for granted. The idea that human rights are universal, and thus cannot be localized, worked against viewing regions as authorities over this issue. In 1968, a UN study group, convened to consider the possible role for regional human rights commissions in the promotion and protection of human rights, expressed skepticism over whether a regional approach was appropriate or desirable. The group's final report included assertions that human rights were a "universal problem,"[3] and that "United Nations activities alone could ensure a uniform application of accepted norms."[4] In contrast to economic development, where effective implementation "depended on local conditions, climate and resources, with each region calling for a different approach," human rights "were subject to universal rules which allowed of no derogations."[5] Regional commissions, the report noted, offered "no tangible advantages" relative to the UN.[6]

In 1976, once Latin American representatives had begun to argue for the idea of regional authority over human rights, a Yugoslav diplomat dismissed the idea that "the question [of human rights] should be dealt with by the corresponding regional group," which "implied that the mass violations of human rights was not a concern to the United Nations in general."[7] In 1978, a Dutch representative cautioned against regional institutions that "claim precedence over the United Nations" but apply human rights in ways that are "fundamentally different" from the UN.[8] The authority of regional organizations was not taken for granted, but had to be asserted.

This strategy of establishing regional authority over human rights first appeared in Latin America, where it developed out of leaders' responses to international pressure in three distinct stages. In the first stage, the government of Chile, led by dictator Augusto Pinochet, began pushing to establish regional authority over human rights in response to the intense international campaign mounted against it.

---

[3] UN Commission on Human Rights 1968a: Para. 26.
[4] UN Commission on Human Rights 1968a: Para. 29.
[5] UN Commission on Human Rights 1968a: Para. 30.
[6] UN Commission on Human Rights 1968a: Para. 28.
[7] UN General Assembly 1976d: Para. 31.
[8] UN General Assembly 1978b: Para. 14.

Notably, the Chilean government first expressed a preference for dealing with criticism in the United Nations, and the regional approach emerged later, as a strategic response to the unfolding situation. Chile had agreed to visits from both the OAS and the UN, but the visit from the OAS's Inter-American Commission on Human Rights (IACHR) was conducted before the UN sent its own investigative group, and before the Chilean government understood how significant the pressure campaign against them was going to be. They abruptly called off the visit from the UN and attempted to manipulate regional enforcement to dampen international pressure. This was a strategy of regime survival at this point, in which Chilean leaders tried to manufacture less challenging enforcement.

In the second stage, it developed into a collective strategy by leaders in the region to establish regional authority over the situation in Chile. It was at this point that the strategy became more genuinely challenging to state authority. Self-determination became an important factor at this stage, with Latin American governments responding to what they regarded as the biased and politicized targeting of Chile and the stifling of their voices within the UN. Both democracies and authoritarian leaders became willing to break the prohibition against interference by discussing and condemning Chile in the OAS while, at the same time, sharply criticizing UN enforcement.

The final stage occurred once the Carter administration's economic enforcement policies emerged as a challenge to self-determination throughout the region. Economic enforcement – which worked by exploiting states' economic dependence – conflicted with widely held views in the region about self-determination, and Latin American leaders, including democratic leaders, rejected it. However, they faced a US administration that was committed to enforcing human rights using "the full range of its diplomatic tools."[9]

It was at this point that governments throughout Latin America fully changed their approach to interference. They accepted regional authority over themselves, expanded the authority of the regional system, and insisted that others defer to regional enforcement. In attempting to reshape human rights enforcement, they gravitated toward *regional* institutions because of shared frustration at enforcement taking place

---

[9] *FRUS* 2013: Document 29; Presidential Directive NSC-30: Human Rights 1978.

within the UN and shared beliefs that UN enforcement, too, was inconsistent with self-determination.

As I show, Latin American leaders changed their approach toward interference within the Inter-American system as a way of creating forms of human rights enforcement that were more consistent with the principle of self-determination, as this principle had long been understood in the region. This approach was effective because the regional human rights system, once accepted by member states and allowed to function, met the US government and others' expectations regarding what constituted legitimate and effective enforcement of human rights.

I begin this chapter by showing that this change in approach to interference, which unfolded over the course of just a few years, was an abrupt and dramatic shift after many decades of consistently prioritizing non-interference over human rights. Despite a long history of engagement with human rights, by the early 1970s, regional commitment to non-interference strictly limited the kinds of human rights promotion that states were willing to accept. This was true even of institutions that would later become central to human rights enforcement: the Inter-American Commission on Human Rights and the American Convention on Human Rights. Additionally, by the 1970s, the United States' Cold War interference had left Latin American leaders wary of doing anything to soften regional norms or law restricting interference.[10]

4.1 Human Rights and Non-Interference in the Inter-American System

Both human rights and the norm of non-interference have long been central to Latin American foreign relations and Inter-American institutions, and institutions dealing with human rights and non-interference developed alongside and in tension with one another. Through the early 1970s, the tension between them was consistently resolved in favor of non-interference. Leaders in the region, of both democracies and dictatorships, remained hesitant to create institutions that formally sanctioned interference due, in large part, to their

---

[10] Portions of this chapter were published in Beall (2024b).

concerns about interference by the United States.[11] In fact, human rights institutions were often a response to immediate concerns about intervention, aimed at curtailing or preventing intervention.

The earliest efforts at regional collective action and institution-building were directed at gaining and then consolidating Latin American sovereignty. This involved first ending European rule and, after independence, strengthening the state to protect against the threat of reconquest and military intervention.[12] These efforts later shifted to focus on constraining the United States, first because of the US's considerable advantages in size, wealth, and military power and, by the end of the nineteenth century, because of its overtly interventionist foreign policy, derided in Latin America as "Yankee imperialism." International law and institutions were seen as important tools for Latin America given their weakness relative to Europe and the US.

The International Union of American Republics, or Pan-American Union, was created in 1890, becoming the first Inter-American regional organization. Latin American leaders saw it as a tool for eliminating European intervention and codifying sovereign equality between themselves and the US, including by institutionalizing dispute-settlement through arbitration.[13] The US had not yet fully emerged as an interventionist power, but it was already substantially more powerful than any other state in the Western hemisphere, and the US government had begun to project its power in ways that worried the rest of the region, including its annexation of Mexican territory in the 1848 Mexican–American war.[14]

It was just a few years after the formation of the Pan-American Union that the US began to intervene throughout Latin America. Between 1898 and 1933, the US occupied Cuba, the Dominican Republic, Haiti, Panama, and Nicaragua and intervened frequently in Latin America to protect its commercial interests as part of the "Banana Wars."[15] This was part of a shift in US foreign policy. The US government had declared in 1895 that it had "practically sovereign" control over the Western hemisphere and in 1904 that it

---

[11] Cabranes 1967; Dreier 1968; Friedman and Long 2015; Goldman 2009; Long and Friedman 2020; Santa-Cruz 2013.
[12] Ball 1961: 21; Cabranes 1967: 1151; Finnemore 2003; Mace 1988: 404–5; Simon 2017.
[13] Crapol 2000: 119–20; Ridpath 1893.   [14] Corrales and Feinberg 1999: 4–7.
[15] Langley 2001.

4.1 Human Rights and Non-Interference

intended to act as an "international police power" in the region.[16] The latter policy justified US intervention in states if their governments did not uphold domestic order or protect rights within their borders.[17]

As this happened, Latin American governments attempted to constrain the US through their shared regional organization, and creating human rights institutions was one strategy for doing so.[18] From 1902 to 1928, several treaties were adopted that focused on rights of citizens outside of their home countries. These early institutions were aimed, in large part, at limiting intervention by eliminating the "need" for the US or any other country to intervene.[19] These advances overlapped with Latin American efforts, between 1928 and 1948, to codify increasingly strict and detailed treaties on non-interference and to get the US to sign them.[20]

This idea that human rights treaties would limit interference was also a consideration in the drafting and adoption of the American Declaration on the Rights and Duties of Man, the first declaration of its kind in the world.[21] At the 1945 Inter-American Conference on War and Peace, states adopted a resolution calling for the Inter-American Juridicial Committee to draft a Declaration on the Essential Rights of Man, with the resolution specifying that this "would eliminate the misuse of diplomatic protection of citizens abroad, the exercise of which has more than once led to the violation of the principles of non-intervention."[22]

By contrast, leaders showed little interest in human rights institutions that would compromise on the norm of non-interference. When the Juridicial Committee produced its draft declaration the following year, it did so alongside a report envisioning sovereignty-respecting forms of implementation, with an emphasis on "separate adjustment by each state according to its national constitution."[23] In terms of international action, the committee foresaw a regional human rights body that would advise states, including through the "study of

---

[16] Klare 1969: 257. [17] Glanville 2011; Veeser 2002.
[18] Cabranes 1967: 1153; Corrales and Feinberg 1999: 7; Quintara 2024.
[19] Cabranes 1968: 891 n9; Obregón 2009: 95–96; Glanville 2011: 246; Goldman 2009: 858.
[20] Cabranes 1967: 1153; Corrales and Feinberg 1999: 7; Thomas, Jr. 1959: 73.
[21] Cabranes 1968: 891–92; Medina Quiroga 1988: 29; Obregón 2009: 95–96.
[22] Cabranes 1968: 892. [23] Inter-American Juridical Committee 1946: 111.

practical problems involved in the protection of human rights,"[24] though no such body was created at the time.[25] When the American Declaration was adopted in 1948, most states voted against adopting it as a binding treaty, a more sovereignty-challenging option. This included the democratic governments of Argentina, Brazil, Chile, Costa Rica, and Peru.

The Larreta Doctrine was another example where the tension between human rights and non-interference was resolved in favor of non-interference. In 1945, the foreign minister of Uruguay, Eduardo Rodríguez Larreta, proposed a mechanism for "multilateral intervention" in defense of human rights. The proposal was supported by the US, Guatemala, Panama, and Venezuela,[26] but rejected by the region's remaining leaders.[27] The government of Colombia, a democratic country that rejected the Larreta Doctrine, noted in private correspondence with the US their concern that the norm of non-interference had "cost the American peoples a great deal to consecrate," and stressed the importance of considering how policies would affect "smaller and defenseless nations."[28]

When the Pan-American Union was reconstituted into the Organization of American States in 1948, non-interference remained a core principle underlying regional relations. Three full articles of the OAS charter were devoted to non-interference, in language that prohibited actions that were otherwise legal under international law.[29] By contrast, references to human rights in the charter were broad and called on states only to follow, in their own way, a path to achieving these rights. No mechanisms were established to push states toward better human rights practices or to hold them accountable for their commitments.[30]

The final advance toward institutionalizing human rights during this period was the creation of the Inter-American Commission on Human Rights and the American Convention on Human Rights. Today, these are arguably the region's most important human rights institutions. However, at the time they were created, these two institutions did not

---

[24] Inter-American Juridicial Committee 1946: 112–13.
[25] Medina Quiroga 1988: 38.   [26] Cabranes 1967: 1160 n25.
[27] Cabranes 1967: 1160 n25.   [28] FRUS 1969: Document 156.
[29] Cabranes 1967: 1153–54 n12.
[30] Organization of American States 1948: Article 5(j), Article 29; Thomas and Thomas 1974: 323.

represent a move away from the norm of non-interference, and there was no notable change in attitudes or practice toward the norm of non-interference that accompanied their creation.

The impetus for creating these new institutions was a crisis in the Caribbean, in which Rafael Trujillo, the repressive dictator of the Dominican Republic, had repeatedly intervened in nearby Venezuela and Cuba in attempts to overthrow their governments.[31] An emergency Meeting of Consultation of American Foreign Ministers was convened in August 1959 to prevent the crisis from escalating. Latin American leaders increasingly saw a link between Trujillo's violent domestic behavior and his government's aggressive, interventionist foreign policy. Because of this, human rights were prominently discussed at the meeting, and those in attendance struggled with the tension between the norm of non-intervention and human rights, both of which affected inter-state peace. Ultimately, only Cuba and Venezuela argued for compromising on non-interference.[32]

The meeting's Final Act called for the creation of the Inter-American Commission on Human Rights, and the Commission's statute was drafted and adopted by the OAS Council of Ministers in June 1960. The statute did not give the IACHR any authority to interfere in states' domestic affairs. It could not investigate or comment on states' human rights practices,[33] and it was tasked only with "develop[ing] an awareness" of human rights and making "general" recommendations to states.[34] A proposal to give the IACHR more interventionist authority, in this case to rule on complaints from individuals alleging human rights violations, was put to a vote and defeated. As before, democracies were among those withholding support.[35]

It was the commissioners who gave themselves more interventionist authority through an expansive interpretation of the commission's statute. Though the member states had expressly voted against giving the IACHR authority to issue decisions on individual human rights complaints, the commissioners interpreted their mandate as allowing them to receive and use the complaints for their own informational and

---

[31] Atkins and Wilson 1972: 104.
[32] Atkins and Wilson 1972: 105; Organization of American States 1959: 5; Rabe 1996: 62.
[33] Norris 1980: 48–49.   [34] Goldman 2009: 862.
[35] The democracies that withheld support were Brazil, Costa Rica, and Uruguay (Schreiber 2019: 36).

investigative purposes, as well as to conduct in-country visits to investigate human rights and to produce reports on individual countries.[36]

When the commissioners requested that member states affirm this expanded authority in 1962, the request was rejected.[37] It was finally agreed to a few years later, with the decision motivated by their attempts to constrain intervention, this time in response to the United States' 1965 unsanctioned unilateral intervention in the Dominican Republic. The IACHR had been sent into the Dominican Republic on an emergency basis to oversee the return to order and as part of the OAS's larger effort to re-assert authority over the US intervention.[38] Member states affirmed the IACHR's expanded authority during an emergency session, making the decision while the IACHR was already in the Dominican Republic carrying out its work.[39] They also added new limits to the commission's powers, including a requirement that local remedies for human rights violations must be exhausted before the commission could become involved and specifying that the commission's reports would be confidential unless the member states decided to make them public.[40]

Having expanded the commission's authority, there was no change in how states engaged with the it.[41] By 1973, only the Dominican Republic had consented to an on-site investigation of its domestic human rights practices.[42] The commission's requests to conduct in-country visits in other states were rebuffed as improper interference and either ignored outright or met with insufficient cooperation.[43]

The other important regional institution that came out of the 1959 Meeting of Ministers of Foreign Affairs was the American Convention on Human Rights. Leaders were slow to make progress on the convention. It was adopted in 1969 in a process that was mostly ignored by the authoritarian states,[44] and it received little state support, with only 12 out of 23 states signing it.[45] Barbados, Haiti, Jamaica, and Bolivia did not even send representatives to the meeting where it was adopted, though Jamaica and Barbados were both

---

[36] Goldman 2009: 868; Sandifer 1965: 517. [37] Schreiber 2019: 51.
[38] Akehurst 1967: 203–9. [39] Akehurst 1967: 203–9; Schreiber 2019: 51.
[40] Fox 1968: 380–81. [41] Sandifer 1965.
[42] Three states consented to visits to investigate violations occurring in another state or following an inter-state conflict (Organization of American States n.d.).
[43] Norris 1980; Thomas and Thomas 1974: 342. [44] Goldman 2009: 863–65.
[45] Buergenthal 1971: 121.

democracies. By the end of 1976, only Costa Rica and Colombia had ratified the convention.[46] Venezuela, Jamaica, Barbados, Trinidad and Tobago, Uruguay, Ecuador, and Chile all opted *not* to ratify the ACHR despite having democratic governments at some point between 1969 and 1976.

Through the early 1970s, the norm of non-interference remained firmly in place, with states refraining from accepting the authority of the OAS to interfere to enforce human rights. Concerns about interference continued to be stoked by the United States' Cold War policies. As late as 1974, a report by the IACHR on human rights violations in Brazil was completed without cooperation from the Brazilian government and presented to the OAS Council of Ministers, where states silenced the report by tabling it without discussion and refraining from making it public. This was done through a unanimous vote, with what few democracies there were in the region at the time voting against publication.[47] The same thing happened with the IACHR's report on Chile the following year.

4.2 Chile's Turn to Regional Enforcement

In 1975, Augusto Pinochet's government in Chile became the first to argue that regional organizations have special authority over human rights. The attention on human rights violations in Chile was unprecedented, and the Chilean government could not have predicted how consequential, prolonged, and isolating the global human rights campaign against them would be. Their early actions reflected the belief that they could control the international response by strategically engaging with human rights enforcement with the help of their powerful ally, the United States. Chile turned to arguing for regional authority as a strategic response to the unfolding events, expecting wrongly that it would allow them to regain control over the situation.

In the immediate aftermath of the 1973 coup, Chile's military dictatorship agreed to on-site visits from the IACHR, Amnesty International, the International Commission of the Red Cross, and the UN Commission on Human Rights (UNCHR). Amnesty International's visit was conducted in 1973, after which Amnesty released a critical report that the Chilean government dismissed as

---

[46] Costa Rica (1970) and Colombia (1973). [47] Diuguid 1974.

Soviet propaganda.[48] The Executive Director of the IACHR conducted an initial solo visit in 1973, which was followed by a full IACHR visit in 1974. The UNCHR's ad hoc working group on Chile was created in 1974 and its visit scheduled for July 1975.

As is clear from these invitations, the Chilean government showed no particular preference for regional enforcement in their early responses to this international attention, and the outcome of the IACHR's visit did nothing to make a regional strategy seem more appealing. The commission had grown increasingly activist over the previous decade, and it produced a scathing, 175-page report on Chile.[49] The report detailed massive and widespread violations of human rights, including allegations that the right to physical security was "directly and seriously violated by the practice of psychological and physical abuse" and that many of the 5,500 people imprisoned by the new Chilean government had not been charged or brought before a court.[50]

The US was an important ally to Chile under Pinochet and had provided support to the military coup that removed Salvador Allende, a socialist, from power. The two governments were in regular communication about the pressure Chile faced and the difficulties this created for the United States' continued support, particularly given the US Congress's new human rights activism. In May 1975, US Secretary of State, Henry Kissinger, and a group of Chilean diplomats met in Washington D.C., where they discussed the human rights issue. Kissinger noting the "strong pressures" both faced and their "mutual interest" in "avoid[ing] embarrassment."[51] Over breakfast, the group laid out a strategy for dealing with the IACHR report, which would be presented to states at the OAS General Assembly the following month. Manuel Trucco, Chile's ambassador to the US, stated clearly that his government "prefer[red] to send this matter to the UN,"[52] and the approach they discussed involved curtailing discussion of human rights at the OAS meeting by suggesting the matter be dealt with at the global body. When Kissinger asked Trucco if they would have problems at the UN, Trucco shrugged off the concern, noting that the human rights issue "is already there."[53]

[48] Kelly 2018: 145. [49] Bernardi 2018; Kelly 2018: 144–45; Sandifer 1965.
[50] Inter-American Commission on Human Rights 1974: chapter XVI.
[51] FRUS 2015: Document 188. [52] FRUS 2015: Document 188.
[53] FRUS 2015: Document 188.

4.2 Chile's Turn to Regional Enforcement

This initial preference for dealing with the issue in the UN quickly changed. At the OAS General Assembly the following month, the IACHR presented its report to the member states, and, as the Chilean government wanted, leaders refrained from discussing the report or making it public. Instead, they adopted a short resolution simply thanking the commission for its work.[54] However, this was not the end of the commission's report. The Executive Director of the IACHR handed the silenced report over to the UN working group which, in turn, leaked it to the press, where it garnered substantial attention. The report corroborated the accusations of severe human rights violations being leveled against Chile and undermined the government's attempts to brush off criticisms as Soviet subversion.[55]

Pinochet quickly lost patience with the UN working group. In addition to giving this confidential report to the press, the working group had started to hear testimony from Chilean exiles in advance of the group's visit to Chile, which Pinochet complained was inappropriate and demonstrated the group's bias.[56] On July 4, 1975, two days before the UN working group was scheduled to begin its visit, the Chilean government withdrew the group's invitation. In a private discussion with the US's ambassador, Pinochet justified the decision by arguing that the consequences of the condemnation they anticipated from receiving from the working group "would be worse than those of denying the group entry."[57]

It was at this point, just two months after expressing their preference to "send the matter to the U.N.," that the Chilean government began to deal with international pressure by asserting the OAS's authority over human rights and accepting its authority over themselves, though the latter they did in ways that were intended to undermine the effectiveness of the regional system. While they were unhappy with the IACHR, the regional commission's visit had already taken place, and the damage was done. However, Chilean officials could point to their cooperation with the IACHR to deflect criticisms for not allowing the UN to visit and as evidence that they were positively engaging with human rights criticisms. They also expected that, with the help of the US and other countries they believed would be sympathetic, they could

---

[54] Binder 1975.   [55] Kelly 2018: 145.   [56] FRUS 2015: Document 188.
[57] FRUS 2015: Document 195.

work within the regional system to provide themselves with additional cover.

At the 1975 UN General Assembly, with the IACHR report public and with Chile having canceled the UN visit, Chile's representatives began to assert the authority of the OAS. The previous year, they had made no special appeals to regional authority, merely noting their cooperation with the OAS alongside references to the Red Cross and the International Labor Organization.[58] In 1975, the Chilean representatives began to distinguish between illegitimate interference by the UN and legitimate interference by the OAS and to argue that the UN's response violated Chile's "exercise of its sovereignty and self-determination."[59]

During debates, Chilean representatives asserted that Latin America "placed particular value on the principle of non-intervention," at the same time as it gave "special weight to questions of human rights." Latin America "had established its own machinery in that field and ... would not tolerate intervention in the hemisphere."[60] Chile's representative defended the decision to cancel the UN working group's visit by pointing to the visit from the IACHR.[61] Chile's delegation also submitted a draft resolution aimed at institutionalizing the role of regional organizations in enforcing human rights. The resolution proposed a new, independent mechanism within the UN to investigate allegations of human rights violations, which would both replace the UN's *ad hoc* working group and "allow for appropriate participation of regional organizations." The proposal failed when put to a vote.[62]

Chilean officials grew increasingly frustrated with the targeting and condemnation they were experiencing in the UN. The Chilean government argued that they were being disproportionately singled out for political reasons while similar or worse human rights abuses in other countries were ignored. They also expressed frustration that their

---

[58] Records of debates in the UN General Assembly's Summary Records of the 2015th to 2110th Meetings, 3rd Committee, 29th Session (UN General Assembly 1974b). Reference to Chile's cooperation with the IACHR is Summary Record 2068, Paragraph 72. Records of all of Chile's statements in the General Assembly open debates can be found here: https://ask.un.org/faq/73684.
[59] UN General Assembly 1975b: Para 25.
[60] UN General Assembly 1975d: Para 29.
[61] UN General Assembly 1975b: Para. 46, 1975c: Para. 15, 1975e: Para. 35.
[62] UN General Assembly 1975e: Para. 35–38, 1975a: Para. 2 (Author translation).

domestic circumstances were not being taken into consideration. One confidential report from within the State Department noted the Chilean government's "burning resentment" that what they regarded as real improvements led to more criticism.[63]

As their frustration grew, Chilean officials doubled down on asserting the authority of the OAS. At the 1976 UN General Assembly, Chile argued again that intervention violated their self-determination. They expanded their arguments for deference to the OAS, arguing that the UN working group lacked objectivity and denied them due process. They rejected what they characterized as biased procedures, while noting approvingly the efforts of the OAS and repeatedly emphasizing their positive cooperation within the regional system.[64]

At the 1977 General Assembly, Chile's delegation proposed another resolution recognizing regional authority. The resolution, proposing a new UN mechanism to replace the ad hoc working group, was very similar to the one they proposed in 1975, but with stronger language asserting regional authority. It stated that the proposed mechanism should "recognize the *principal and determining* participation of regional organizations" and "avoid duplication of competence."[65] The Chilean representative made clear during debates that their intent was to institutionalize the UN's deference to regional enforcement, stating that the resolution would ensure that "the rights of regions would thus be recognized."[66]

Through all of this, pressure on the Chilean government continued. Both political pressure and legislation from the US Congress had complicated the White House's efforts to support Pinochet. In November 1975, congressional action led to the suspension of the US military aid to Chile. In the first half of 1976, cuts in economic and security assistance were debated by the US Congress, something that US officials regularly discussed with members of the Chilean government.[67] In 1976, the US voted against a development loan to Chile in the Inter-American Development Bank on human rights grounds.[68] A May 1976 telegram between the Chilean Embassy and

[63] *FRUS* 2013: Document 42, 2015: Document 165, 2018b: Document 193.
[64] UN General Assembly 1976a: Para. 1–25.   [65] UN General Assembly 1977b.
[66] UN General Assembly 1977h: Para. 42–43.
[67] Binder 1975; *FRUS* 2015: Document 217, 218, 220, 223.
[68] Weissbrodt 1977: 259.

Washington stated that the US treasury secretary had made it clear to the Chilean government that "desired economic cooperation depended on what happened with human rights in Chile."[69]

Officials from the United States repeatedly emphasized to the Chilean government that canceling the UN visit had made things difficult for them and that cooperating with a human rights investigation would make things easier.[70] In response, Chilean officials appealed to their positive cooperation with the OAS, suggesting that this should be presented to Congress as evidence that the human rights situation was improving and that they were taking steps to deal with their problems.[71]

This continued threat of losing support created pressure for the Chilean government to engage with human rights enforcement. They did so strategically, accepting the authority of the regional system in ways that attempted to manipulate and undermine actual regional enforcement and to spare them any real scrutiny or criticism. After the critical report released by the IACHR, the Chilean government was unwilling to accept another visit, and in fact, they introduced an unsuccessful proposal in advance of the 1976 OAS General Assembly to restrict the commission's autonomy and subject it to greater state control.

Instead of accepting a visit from the IACHR, Chile decided that one way to relieve pressure would be to hold the 1976 OAS General Assembly in Santiago, an idea they put forward after canceling the visit from the UN working group.[72] In place of another visit from the IACHR, the Chilean government arranged an alternative on-site visit by the Secretary General of the OAS, Alejandro Orfila, which was carried out while the meeting of the OAS General Assembly was being held. Orfila released a statement that he had witnessed no evidence of torture. These attempts at manipulation were transparent and failed to dampen international pressure, and they led to Orfila being widely criticized.[73]

What differentiates the strategy of establishing regional authority, as I develop in this book, from the kind of authoritarian survival strategy employed by Chile is whether or not states actually accept challenging

---

[69] *FRUS* 2015: Document 219. [70] *FRUS* 2015: Document 201, 221, 223, 236.
[71] *FRUS* 2015: Document 236. [72] Binder 1975.
[73] de Onis 1976a, 1976c. See also "El secretario general de la OEA habla de los derechos humanos en Chile" 1976.

authority within their regional organizations. For the Chilean government, this remained a strategy of regime survival. However, Chile was not alone in growing frustrated with UN enforcement. Other Latin American leaders, including democratic leaders that prominently supported human rights, saw enforcement in the UN as dysfunctional and biased in its approach to human rights in Chile and, soon the region as a whole.[74] In 1976, a Colombian delegate argued that the UN working group and resolutions were not recognizing improvements being made by the Chilean government.[75] Costa Rica, a democracy and important proponent of human rights, became one of the harshest critics of UN action on Chile. At the 1977 UN General Assembly, a Costa Rican delegate referred to the UN working group as an "unending nightmare," suggesting that "no country would subject itself to the kind of ordeal experienced by Chile."[76]

This strategy quickly evolved to challenge state authority – and to compromise on the norm of non-interference – once other Latin American leaders became involved in 1976. Latin American leaders attempted to claw back authority over the situation in Chile, accepting the authority of the OAS to deal with human rights there in ways that contrasted starkly with how they had dealt with human rights previously, while also asserting that the region should be allowed to handle the situation. After the IACHR's report on Chile was effectively silenced at the 1975 OAS General Assembly,[77] the 1976 meeting was dominated by discussion and condemnation of human rights violations in Chile. The OAS member states released the IACHR's report on Chile and called for the Chilean government to allow the IACHR back in the country. They also adopted the first ever human rights resolution, targeting Chile, which was supported by every state except for Chile and Brazil.[78] These actions may seem minimal by current standards, but at the time, they were a significant break from their practice of non-interference.

As with the OAS, the UN General Assembly went very differently in 1976 than it had the previous year. In 1975, having gone along with Chile's request to have the human rights issue dealt with in the UN

---

[74] This was primarily leaders from Spanish-speaking Latin America. The English-speaking Caribbean was more involved with the Non-Aligned Movement, and acted with the NAM in pressuring Chile throughout this time.
[75] UN General Assembly 1976f: Para. 4.
[76] UN General Assembly 1977j: Para. 6.   [77] Kelly 2018: 147.
[78] de Onis 1976a, 1976b.

rather than the OAS, only one other Latin American representative echoed Chile's arguments that the OAS was the proper authority to deal with human rights in Latin America. In 1976, Latin American representatives began to widely assert regional authority over the situation in Chile. One delegate suggested that, where there were institutions with overlapping authority in the area of human rights, there "existed an institution whose competence to deal with regional matters was not subject to any doubt, namely, the Organization of American States."[79]

Latin American delegates criticized others for failing to recognize efforts being made within the OAS to address human rights in Chile, pointing to the actions that had been taken at the OAS General Assembly several months earlier.[80] They complained about the lack of respect for the OAS's legitimate voice over human rights issues within the region. One representative complained that the UN working group on Chile "had not solicited the views" of the OAS Secretary General.[81] Others complained that the UN group's report had "made no mention" of the OAS's involvement or its resolution on Chile.[82]

That year, a group of Latin American delegations introduced a UN resolution criticizing Chile's human rights abuses and recognizing the OAS's contributions toward dealing with the situation, countering what the delegates argued was a biased resolution on Chile introduced by non-aligned states. The Latin American resolution was initiated by a group of authoritarian states, but it was also co-sponsored by Costa Rica, who spoke in support of the resolution's "genuine concern over the situation of human rights in Chile" and its "necessary objectivity." The resolution was killed without even being put to a vote, and the other "biased" resolution was adopted, further fueling the sense that Latin America was being shut out of UN human rights enforcement.[83]

4.3 A Region-Wide Effort to Establish Regional Authority

These first steps toward establishing regional authority over human rights in Chile laid the groundwork for leaders to apply this strategy

---

[79] UN General Assembly 1976b: Para. 24–27.
[80] UN General Assembly 1977i: Para. 35, 45.
[81] UN General Assembly 1976d: Para. 20.
[82] UN General Assembly 1976c: Para. 19. See also UN General Assembly 1976d: Para. 7.
[83] UN General Assembly 1976e: Para. 5, 1976f: Para. 65–82.

4.3 A Regional Effort to Establish Regional Authority

more broadly once the US began to impose human rights enforcement throughout the entire region. In response, Latin American leaders quickly expanded their efforts from establishing regional authority over the situation in Chile to establishing authority over human rights generally. This involved accepting the OAS's authority over themselves and pushing the US government to work within the regional system.

The kinds of pressure facing Chile had started to slowly spread to other Latin American countries,[84] though up until 1976 it was limited by conflicts between the Republican White House and Democrats in Congress, with congressional efforts aimed at forcing the hand of a reluctant executive branch. Neither President Gerald Ford nor Secretary of State Henry Kissinger was interested in pursuing a foreign policy that emphasized human rights. Kissinger made it clear that he did not view human rights as "appropriate for discussion in a foreign policy context"[85] and, as discussed above, worked with Chile to formulate strategies for dealing with the human rights pressure.

However, when Jimmy Carter, a Democrat who campaigned on a platform of promoting human rights, became president in 1977, human rights became an important element of US foreign policy and a consideration in economic relations with all of Latin America. As discussed in Chapter 3, Carter announced at the UN General Assembly in 1977 his position that membership in the UN meant acceptance of international involvement in human rights. In late May, First Lady Roslyn Carter embarked on a tour of the region, during which she communicated the new human rights policy.[86] At the OAS General Assembly in June 1977, US Secretary of State Cyrus Vance discussed the US government's intention to link human rights with aid and trade with the region,[87] and they broached the issue of human rights at an Inter-American Development Bank meeting that same month.[88]

The effect of these policies was to impose human rights enforcement on Latin America. All states that traded with or received assistance from the US – all of them, apart from Cuba – were effectively made subject to these policies, while there were no avenues for meaningfully consenting to the policies, influencing them, or imposing

---

[84] *FRUS* 2015: Document 348.   [85] *FRUS* 2015: Document 188.
[86] Hovey 1977.   [87] DeYoung 1977.
[88] "Kidnapping Mars IDB Meeting" 1977.

accountability. The US government controlled economic support and preferential trade, while Latin American states lacked means to participate in decision-making, which increasingly took place in IFIs and through domestic contestation within the US. These policies were widely regarded by Latin American leaders as counter to the principle of self-determination.

Self-determination was an important regional value, and these policies clashed with ideas that had been developing in the region for decades, ideas which held that exploitation of their economic dependence was one of the primary means through which their self-determination was undermined.[89] In their relations with the US, a form of enforcement that was completely in the hands of the US government was undesirable given the unpredictability of US foreign policy, its tendency to undermine Latin American democracies and support authoritarian governments, and traditional Latin American interests in curtailing US influence.[90]

In the preceding years, Latin America had made important contributions to institutionalizing the idea that interference and economic coercion violated the right to self-determination, and they had played an active role in ensuring that the right to self-determination, including its economic dimension, was included in the UN human rights covenants.[91] Latin American leaders had long argued that non-interference was a necessary corollary to self-determination.[92] These ideas were institutionalized in the non-interference clauses of the OAS Charter. The charter's expansive language had, in turn, served as the basis for the 1965 UN Declaration on the Inadmissibility of Intervention in the Domestic Affairs of States, which institutionalized a link between self-determination and non-interference.[93]

These ideas were not limited to governments. During the 1960s, the idea that economic exploitation undermined self-determination was developed by a number of Latin American intellectuals.[94] Helio Jaguaribe, one influential Brazilian scholar and exiled critic of the Brazilian dictatorship, detailed an "inter-imperial" international system characterized by "decreasing capacity for self-determination."[95] This

---

[89] Jaguaribe 1979; Lerner 1980; Sunkel 1969; Tickner 2014.
[90] Tickner 2014: 74.
[91] Humphrey 1983: 412; UN General Assembly 1965b: Para. 127–28.
[92] Fenn 1963; Tourinho 2015: 87.   [93] Chapter 2.   [94] Tickner 2014.
[95] Jaguaribe 1979: 91.

4.3 A Regional Effort to Establish Regional Authority

scholarship developed the concept of "autonomy," or state capacity for self-determined action, and identified Latin America's economic dependence as a constraint on their autonomy.[96]

This understanding of self-determination was linked directly to human rights. American imperialism and economic exploitation had long been seen as a threat to individual rights and self-rule, including by advocates for women's rights and economic and social rights.[97] An explicit link was made between US imperialism and the rise of right-wing dictatorships in the region, with anti-imperial activists viewing US imperialism as the cause of human rights violations in these countries. This viewpoint had motivated the second Russell Tribunals, in which civil society actors put the US government on trial for violations of international law and the right to self-determination in Latin America.[98] Armando Uribe, a former diplomat for Allende's government who criticized Pinochet's government while in exile, wrote *The Black Book of American Intervention* shortly after the coup. In it, he characterized the anti-Pinochet resistance as "the Chilean people's resistance to fascism and imperialism" and "their historical will to be a sovereign nation."[99]

Another proponent of this perspective was Fabiola Letelier, a prominent Chilean human rights activist and an important opponent of Pinochet's government. Her brother, Orlando, was a fierce critic of Pinochet who was murdered by the Chilean government in a high-profile assassination in Washington DC. Letelier characterized Latin American relations with the US as one of economic dependence and articulated a "need for economic independence in order to achieve liberty, justice, and sovereignty."[100]

As human rights took on greater global prominence, the importance that Latin American leaders placed on self-determination was not diminished. In 1976, the representative of Colombia made clear during UN debates that their government supported "the principle of self-determination ... just as adamantly as it supported respect for human rights."[101] Many critics of Pinochet, and of other dictatorships, supported cutting off support to violent governments as a means of severing imperialist control. However, this did not translate into

---

[96] Jaguaribe 1979; Lerner 1980; Sunkel 1969; Tickner 2014.
[97] Dussel 1981: 106–13, 127–239; Marino 2019; Sanders 1970.
[98] Tulli 2021.   [99] Uribe 1975: iv.   [100] Letelier 1986.
[101] UN General Assembly 1976f: Para. 7.

support for a wider system of enforcement that relied on imperialist powers and Western-dominated institutions to manipulate the behavior of leaders of developing countries.

Carlos Andrés Pérez, the president of Venezuela and an important partner of Jimmy Carter in promoting human rights in the region, made clear that these economic enforcement policies were inconsistent with self-determination.[102] In the lead-up to the 1977 meeting of the OAS General Assembly, Andrés Pérez had communicated to the US State Department that he was "anxious to cooperate with [the US] in all areas and to take a strong stand on human rights."[103] After the US government announced at the meeting its intentions to broadly apply human rights conditions, Andrés Pérez again expressed support for the US stance toward human rights but criticized these particular policies as counter to regional norms of "self-determination, nonintervention [sic], and mutual respect."[104] He specified that human rights enforcement should happen through "supranational organizations at regional and world levels."[105]

The president of Colombia, Alfonso López Michelsen, also noted that he "generally supported [the US's] human rights policy" but that the US should not act as the "world's moral policeman" and should conduct its human rights policy through international organizations.[106] In another meeting, he stated that it would be "inadvisable for the US to act as a 'protector' of human rights," as this was "the collective obligation of the OAS and UN." He then proposed creating a new human rights commissioner within the OAS, though this initiative was never pursued.[107]

Carter rejected the idea that these new policies represented illegitimate or inappropriate interference, though he and officials in his administration regularly expressed concern with provoking accusations of imperialism and intervention.[108] Confronted with the reality of these policies and unable to stop the US from employing them, leaders in Latin America instead attempted to encourage the US to channel its human rights policy through international organizations rather than use economic pressure.

As both Andrés Pérez and López Michelsen's above comments indicate, both regional and global enforcement could be consistent with

---

[102] Franczak 2018.   [103] *FRUS* 2018b: Document 4.
[104] Andrés Pérez 1977.   [105] Andrés Pérez 1977.
[106] *FRUS* 2018b: Document 14.   [107] *FRUS* 2018b: Document 240.
[108] *FRUS* 2013: Document 13, 29, 190; Hovey 1977.

4.3 A Regional Effort to Establish Regional Authority

self-determination, in theory. However, in practice, UN enforcement was heavily biased against Latin America. This bias persisted in subsequent years, with country-specific working groups and UN resolutions created almost exclusively for Latin America.[109] Latin American governments quickly soured on the United Nations and were angered by their inability to meaningfully shape or influence the enforcement that was taking place. By 1977, a report prepared by the CIA suggested that governments in Latin America, including Chile, "would probably prefer dealing with the OAS than with the UN" and the "radical Third World countries."[110] This frustration came to a boil during the 1979 meeting of the UNCHR, where a US State Department memorandum described Latin American representatives as "traumatized" by the targeting of the region, including efforts to add Uruguay, Paraguay, Nicaragua, and Guatemala to the public agenda. According to the memo, the ambassador of Colombia "openly expressed his disgust" with other countries "for protecting their own regions ... all while pretending to take an objective stand" against Latin America.[111]

Because of this, Latin American leaders adopted the strategy of establishing the OAS as an authority over human rights, both accepting and asserting the OAS's authority over that of the UN. For democracies and states concerned with protecting human rights in the region, they objected as a matter of principle to both US economic pressure and to disproportionate targeting within the UN, while they saw the regional system as offering both the possibility for real, effective action on human rights and, for some, an opportunity for leadership within the regional system. For leaders that were being targeted by these policies, or who were concerned that they would be targeted, the regional system offered them a less biased way to avoid economic sanctions.

4.3.1 Accepting the Authority of the OAS

The year 1977 represented a watershed in the willingness of OAS member states to accept and facilitate the work of the regional organization's human rights institutions. As explored in detail at the start of this chapter, the architecture of the regional human rights system was

---

[109] Brysk 1993: 270–71; Limon and Power 2014: 8–9; Weinstein 1976: 821–22.
[110] *FRUS* 2018b: Document 16.   [111] *FRUS* 2013: Document 184.

in place before the 1970s, but states had not accepted its authority, nor had they allowed it to carry out its work. Through the early 1970s, the IACHR was highly constrained by states in carrying out its functions.[112] By 1973, only the Dominican Republic had consented to an on-site investigation of its own domestic human rights record. The commission's requests for in-country visits were rejected, ignored, or met with foot-dragging. The commission's reports on Brazil and Chile had been silenced by states in 1974 and 1975, respectively. Nearly all states, including democracies, had refrained from ratifying the ACHR.

In 1976, growing frustrated with the treatment of Chile in the UN and in the face of mounting US pressure, Latin American leaders started to change their approach toward the norm of non-interference, discussing and condemning human rights violations in Chile, and calling for the Chilean government to continue to cooperate with the IACHR. They released the IACHR's follow-up report on Chile and adopted a resolution on a member state's human rights for the first time.

In 1977, with the region widely subject to economic enforcement policies, this response broadened significantly. An important part of this shift was that governments in the region began to cooperate to address human rights violations within the OAS and to facilitate the IACHR's work. This included authoritarian governments and those that were themselves guilty of serious human rights violations. At the 1977 OAS General Assembly meeting, human rights remained at the top of the agenda, with criticisms widened to focus on other countries besides Chile. Multiple human rights-related resolutions were passed, including one calling out violations in other states and urging Uruguay and Paraguay to allow on-site investigations by the IACHR.[113] They adopted a resolution increasing the IACHR's budget and encouraging states to consent to on-site visits,[114] and the decision was made to move the following year's meeting from Uruguay to the US, in light of human rights abuses in Uruguay.[115]

These dramatic changes in how states utilized the OAS were remarked upon by a representative of the US delegation to the 1978 OAS General Assembly, who asked, "who would have thought

---

[112] Bernardi 2018; Farer 1997: 510; Forsythe 1991; Sandifer 1965.
[113] Norris 1980: 80, fn115.   [114] "Rights Issue Dominates OAS Parley" 1977.
[115] Vogelgesang 1978: 824.

4.3 A Regional Effort to Establish Regional Authority

even two years ago that the General Assembly of this listless organization would endorse overwhelmingly the reports of the [human rights] commission and register the concern of the member governments about the violations reported?"[116] Notably, significant democratization did not begin until the 1980s, and these actions were taken by an OAS whose membership still consisted primarily of authoritarian governments.

This year was a turning point in another sense, with member states now willing to accept the authority of the OAS over themselves by individually accepting and engaging with regional enforcement. As discussed above, prior to this time, the Commission's requests to carry out in-country visits had been rejected, ignored, or had received insufficient cooperation from states.[117] In 1974, Chile made its ill-fated decision to accept a visit, and no additional visits were carried in the next two years. In 1977, states began to consent to in-country visits, and ten were carried out by the Commission over the next five years.[118]

One of the most remarkable and dramatic shifts was the decision by governments throughout the region to ratify the American Convention on Human Rights. As of 1976, only two states, Colombia and Costa Rica, had ratified the American Convention. In 1977 and 1978 alone, eleven new states ratified the treaty. Ratifying the ACHR did more than just recognize a long list of legally binding human rights obligations, though in a region with a strong legal culture, being bound by legal obligations was itself a meaningful change. However, ratification also meant accepting expanded enforcement authority.

Important pieces of this included accepting the authority of the Inter-American Court on Human Rights, along with legal requirements to cooperate with the IACHR. Ratifying the ACHR also expanded the authority of the Inter-American Commission, giving it the power to request the court to "take provisional measures ... to prevent irreparable injury to persons" and strengthening the requirements for states to provide information to the IACHR.[119] It gave the IACHR the authority to publicize country reports without first getting approval from member states, increasing the Commission's autonomy.[120] The IACHR's authority was augmented again in 1979, when a new statute was adopted to govern the commission's activities in states that had

---

[116] Hovey 1977.   [117] Norris 1980; Thomas and Thomas 1974: 342.
[118] Organization of American States n.d.
[119] Inter-American Commission on Human Rights 1980: chapter 1.
[120] Organization of American States 1969: Article 51(3).

ratified the ACHR, which had just come into effect.[121] Several years later, states began to accept the extended jurisdiction of the Inter-American Court to receive complaints from the IACHR, providing a pathway for individuals to access the court.

This new willingness to accept and engage with regional enforcement contrasted with reluctance to delegate authority to the UN. Both new democracies, those with the strongest incentives to ratify human rights treaties, and non-democracies, those most likely to be challenged by enforcement, became willing to accept human rights enforcement, but they did so disproportionately within the OAS. Of the eleven states that ratified the ACHR in 1977 and 1978, eight were non-democracies.[122] At the same time, non-democracies overwhelmingly refrained from ratifying the First Optional Protocol to the International Convention on Civil and Political Rights (ICCPR), the UN treaty with similar content and enforcement authority.[123]

As states democratized, they disproportionately ratified regional treaties and accepted regional enforcement, often ratifying the Optional Protocol to the ICCPR only after democratization was complete and sometimes waiting many years before ratifying the UN treaty.[124] In Paraguay, the government ratified the ACHR in 1989, immediately after dictator Alfredo Stroessner was deposed but years before elections in 1993 completed their democratic transition. The government ratified the ICCPR in 1992 and accepted the extended jurisdiction of the Inter-American Court of Human Rights in 1993. Finally, in 1995, Paraguay ratified the First Optional Protocol to the ICCPR. Honduras began its democratic transition in 1977 with the approval of a new electoral law. The military government ratified the ACHR that same year. In 1981, the government accepted the expanded jurisdiction of the Inter-American Court months before competitive elections completed the transition to democracy. The government did not ratify the ICCPR or its First Optional Protocol until 1997 and 2005, respectively.

---

[121] Organization of American States 1979.
[122] Ecuador, Haiti, Honduras, El Salvador, Grenada, Guatemala, Panama, and Peru.
[123] Both establish an individual complaints system through which a group of human rights experts make non-binding decisions, while the ICCPR alone creates a self-reporting mechanism.
[124] Beall 2024b: 11.

4.3 A Regional Effort to Establish Regional Authority

Latin American states also overwhelmingly voted against UN General Assembly resolutions on human rights. In 1979, seventeen out of twenty-eight members of the OAS (61 percent), and six of its twelve democratic members, withheld support for the UN resolution against Chile. This was part of a broad pattern of voting on such resolutions. Among those that voted yes, some nevertheless criticized the resolution.[125]

Importantly, leaders do not seem to have believed that regional enforcement would be unchallenging. The IACHR's reports on Brazil and Chile showed the Commission to be a critical and highly independent human rights body, and the Chilean government's frustration with the Commission was discussed at length earlier in this chapter. Argentina considered leaving the OAS due to human rights criticism, and Southern Cone dictatorships mounted unsuccessful attempts to "reform" the IACHR by subjecting it to greater state control.[126] Anastasio Somoza, the dictator of Nicaragua, privately noted to the US his government's hesitation to open themselves up for "attack" in the Inter-American Court by ratifying the ACHR.[127] It was in spite of these fears that states gravitated toward regional enforcement.

4.3.2 Asserting the Authority of the OAS

In addition to accepting regional authority, Latin American leaders began to widely assert the authority of the OAS over human rights. As discussed at the beginning of this chapter, by the mid-1970s, it was not at all taken for granted that regional organizations possessed special authority or legitimacy when it came to human rights or human rights enforcement. The idea of universality worked against thinking of regions as authorities over this issue area, and the authority of regional organizations had to be asserted.

As discussed earlier in this chapter, these assertions of regional authority began with Chile in 1975 and expanded dramatically in 1976. By 1977, debates in the UN General Assembly's Third Committee were full of arguments made by Latin American representatives that, as one Nicaraguan delegate asserted, "Latin Americans were very well aware of their own history and idiosyncrasies and were the only ones entitled and able to solve Latin

---

[125] Beall 2024b: 9.   [126] *FRUS* 2018b: 109.   [127] *FRUS* 2016: 78.

American problems."¹²⁸ The Dominican Republic, Paraguay, and Uruguay each criticized the UN resolution on Chile for "ignor[ing]" or "disregard[ing]" the OAS's role in resolving the situation in Chile.¹²⁹ The representative of Peru criticized the UN resolution on Chile for "totally ignor[ing] the role which the relevant and authoritative regional organization, the Organization of American States, should play."¹³⁰

Governments that were subjected to scrutiny responded by aggressively asserting regional authority over human rights. When the government of Guatemala came under pressure, it defended itself, as Chile had done, by framing regional enforcement as legitimate and extra-regional enforcement as inappropriate interference. At the UN General Assembly, their delegate asserted that the "Guatemalan people ... rejects any kind of interference in its domestic affairs," and that "Precisely for that reason, ... we have extended an invitation – already accepted – to the Inter-American Commission on Human Rights ... to visit Guatemala."¹³¹ The president of El Salvador responded to attacks on his government's human rights practices by arguing that the "international system ... is structured from the regional to the global level" and that "it has been the constant practice of [the UN] not to deal with situations which have been dealt with in regional organizations."¹³²

Democracies also asserted regional authority, with Venezuela the most vocal. During UN debates in 1977, the representative of Venezuela pointed to the fact that the OAS was dealing with the situation in Chile and stated that they hoped the item would be removed from the UN's agenda in recognition of this.¹³³ Venezuela's representatives eventually became much more forceful in these assertions, arguing in General Assembly debates that "the problems of Latin America should be solved by Latin Americans, without foreign interference and without direct or indirect interference or extra-hemispheric intervention."¹³⁴

Western governments, most importantly the US, were ultimately amenable to accepting the OAS's authority over human rights. Their

---

[128] UN General Assembly 1977i: Para. 45.
[129] UN General Assembly 1977j: Para. 2, 14, 1977i: Para. 35.
[130] UN General Assembly 1977j: Para. 13.
[131] UN General Assembly 1980b: Para. 302–3.
[132] UN General Assembly 1981: Para. 25.
[133] UN General Assembly 1977j: Para. 50.
[134] UN General Assembly 1980a: Para. 235.

beliefs about legitimacy had changed significantly, and they were no longer willing to defer to the norm of non-interference where human rights were concerned.[135] At the same time, the US continued to be concerned about their relations with Latin America being perceived as "Yankee imperialism" and a continuation of "big stick" policies and eliciting backlash. Under both Ford and Carter, individuals in the administration expressed a preference for operating within the regional system as a way of avoiding this.[136]

Internal documents from the Carter administration show concern about backlash and perceptions of "human rights imperialism."[137] Carter was eager to work through the OAS to "multilateralize" his administration's efforts in order to avoid such accusations.[138] A paper produced by his National Security Council highlighted the need for US human rights policy to "avoid smothering regional efforts with a Big Brother embrace" and "let Latin American states take the lead."[139] Officials in Carter's administration expressed a belief that Latin American governments would prefer the OAS to the UN, along with the view that the OAS system, and the IACHR specifically, was quite effective.[140] A 1977 strategy document stressed that they should "take advantage of the significant potential" of the OAS.[141] Officials within the Carter administration offered positive assessments of the IACHR and the assertiveness of individual commissioners, an assessment that was echoed by other Western leaders.[142] At the UN General Assembly in 1979, Western delegates spoke positively of the Inter-American human rights system, which one singled out as an example of an "effectively operating regional human rights system."[143]

The Inter-American system met shared standards as to what constituted appropriate and effective enforcement, and Carter and European governments had both the incentive and the opportunity to accept the authority of the OAS over human rights. The US was ultimately willing to channel its efforts through the regional system, pressuring Latin American states to accept regional authority and working to enhance

---

[135] Chapter 3.
[136] For Carter, see *FRUS* 2013: Document 13, 105, and 207. For Ford, see *FRUS* 2015: Document 238.
[137] *FRUS* 2013: Document 190, 193.   [138] *FRUS* 2013: Document 105.
[139] *FRUS* 2013: Document 205.   [140] *FRUS* 2013: Document 16.
[141] *FRUS* 2013: Document 29.   [142] *FRUS* 2013: Document 16; Hovey 1977.
[143] UN General Assembly 1979b: Para. 14.

the commission's capacity. A US official framed the decision they were offering to Latin American governments as a choice between either economic pressure or cooperation with the OAS, explaining that, "you call our criticism interference in your internal affairs, but if you won't cooperate with the [OAS] Human Rights Commission we have no choice but to go the government-to-government route."[144]

4.4 From Emergence to Consolidation of Regional Authority

Over the course of just a few years, efforts to establish regional authority transformed from one state's authoritarian survival strategy into a region-wide effort at accepting and expanding regional human rights enforcement. Changing perceptions of regional authority were further consolidated by the election in 1982 of Peruvian diplomat Javier Pérez de Cuéllar as Secretary General of the UN. De Cuéllar's position was that the UN should, where possible, play the role of supporting and cooperating with regional organizations, an attitude which he claimed reflected his background as a Latin American.[145]

By 1989, the extent to which a regional approach had taken hold within the UN Commission on Human Rights was the subject of criticism from the International Service for Human Rights, an international NGO that monitored and reported on the commission's activities. In reports from 1989 and 1990, the organization's director expressed his displeasure that "regionalization" had taken over the Commission.[146] He suggested that the strategy had been first employed by Latin American countries, with other regions emulating their approach.[147]

The regionalization of human rights was not an inevitable response to the pressures faced by Latin American leaders. The region had strong institutions in place at the time that they began to encounter these pressures, and there was a long history of engagement with human rights and with using the regional system to limit the imposition of authority by more powerful states and increase their ability to participate in both regional and global decision-making. At the same time, prior to these events, there was no clearly established idea that

---

[144] Hovey 1977.
[145] "De Cuellar Urges Non-Interference in Latin America" 1983; de Soto 2018: 126–28; Gauhar and de Cuellar 1984: 20–21; Hills and Shaw 1990: 92.
[146] Zoller 1989: 211–12.   [147] Zoller 1990: 142–43.

regions have special authority over human rights. Many Latin American supporters of human rights continued to believe in the promise of global institutions, and the Chilean government's initial inclination was to deal with human rights within the UN.

Instead, the fact that regional institutions were there, both suitable and available; the history of using the OAS to safeguard their self-determination; and the perceived shortcomings of UN enforcement led leaders toward establishing the OAS as the appropriate authority for dealing with human rights. In other words, this strategy emerged not because leaders saw the regional system as particularly effective, knowledgeable, or well-suited to the task. Rather, it was a mutually satisfactory response for a range of different actors with different interests in the enforcement of human rights in the region. It resulted in authoritarian states and democracies cooperating to resist the imposition of human rights enforcement. As I discuss in the next chapter, when African leaders began to encounter similar kinds of imposed enforcement from European governments, they had been observing Latin American governments for several years, and they had a clear model for responding to these pressures.

5 | From Non-Interference to African Enforcement

For several years after the emergence of the international campaign against Chile, non-*apartheid* African states were spared the kinds of pressures faced by Latin America. This changed in 1977, when the brutality of Idi Amin's government in Uganda became the subject of international attention and outrage. Amin had been in power since 1971, and his abuses had been well-known for years, but it was Amnesty International's reports on Uganda in 1977, released in the context of new global interest in human rights, that sparked international attention to the situation and brought about economic pressures on the region.

African leaders first responded by appealing to the norm of non-interference, but when these appeals were unsuccessful, they moved to establish their own regional organization, the Organization of African Unity, as an authority over human rights. Like in Latin America, these institutional developments, and the decision to accept interference, were a response to the imposition of human rights enforcement. They represented an effort by both supporters and violators of human rights to create an alternative authority to enforce human rights once simply rejecting interference became ineffective.

This strategy was in some ways a less obvious approach for Africa, as the OAU had no existing human rights institutions for monitoring and policing human rights in member states. In fact, early on, the initiative to create regional institutions was rivaled by several other proposals for creating or expanding institutions for enforcing human rights. In 1977, the Gambia proposed a human rights commission within the Commonwealth of Nations, an international organization consisting of the United Kingdom and its former colonies.[1] Another proposal from Senegal called for a mechanism to discuss human rights violations within the joint parliamentary bodies of the Lomé system

---

[1] Kirby 2021; Ouguergouz 2003: 32.

that they shared with European states. Yet another occurred in the context of the Franco-African Summit. Following an Amnesty International report on the massacre of schoolchildren in the Central African Empire, African leaders formed an *ad hoc* commission of independent jurists to investigate what had happened.[2]

There was also significant African support for expanding the UN's human rights institutions. A proposal calling for states to permanently give their consent to visits by the Commission on Human Rights was made by Senegal in 1977.[3] That same year, Nigeria put forward a resolution giving the UN Economic and Social Commission's regional economic commissions the authority to promote and protect human rights.[4] Finally, a 1977 resolution to set up a UN High Commissioner for Human Rights, an independent post with a wide range of enforcement functions, was co-sponsored by Senegal, the Gambia, Lesotho, and Botswana.[5]

Ultimately, it was only the regional approach that received enough support from African governments to materialize at this time. In 1979, African leaders unanimously approved a resolution calling for the drafting of a regional charter and the creation of a regional commission, and the African Charter on Human and Peoples' Rights, establishing an African Commission, was formally adopted and opened to ratification in 1981.

Appraisals of the African human rights system have been far more mixed than for the Latin American system, with both the African Charter and African Commission criticized for their shortcomings. These criticisms certainly have merit. Yet, these institutions represented a genuine departure from the norm of non-interference, and they were regarded as such at the time they were adopted. They included a commission that was independent from state control, with authority to "resort to any appropriate method of investigation," receive and act on complaints of violations by individuals, and apply not only the African charter, but all relevant international human rights law.[6] As I detail here, this was authority that leaders in the region regarded as challenging and that many strongly opposed.

[2] "Africa Commission Says Bokassa Had Role in Massacre of Children" 1979; "Bokassa's Accomplices" 1979.
[3] UN General Assembly 1977c.   [4] UN General Assembly 1977g, 1977k.
[5] UN General Assembly 1977a.
[6] Organization of African Unity 1981: Articles 45(2), 46, and 60.

These regional institutions came about at the initiative of a small number of individuals within Africa who, in the context of changing Western attention to human rights, wanted to see real improvements in human rights in the region and wanted these to come through an African-owned regional system. These included Edem Kodjo, the newly appointed Secretary General of the OAU; Keba M'Baye, a prominent legal scholar and then the president of an important international human rights NGO and Senegal's representative to the UN Commission on Human Rights; and Léopold Senghor and William Tolbert, the presidents of Liberia and Senegal, respectively, who were active supporters of international human rights protections. The institutions were accepted by leaders that were abusing human rights amid the credible threat of economic sanctions by Western governments.

5.1 Self-Determination, Human Rights, and Non-Interference in Africa

When African leaders created regional institutions aimed at regulating their own domestic behavior, it represented a significant reorientation of regional cooperation, which had long been aimed at securing state sovereignty and minimizing interference, particularly by Western states. An example of this cooperation was Pan-Africanism, a transnational movement aimed at dismantling international and domestic racial domination, including by bringing an end to colonialism in Africa and the Caribbean.[7] The struggle against racism within countries like the United States was conceptualized as linked to the struggle against colonial domination of non-White peoples throughout the world, a link made by WEB Du Bois's concept of the global color line.[8]

In the first half of the twentieth century, Pan-African Congresses – international gatherings of Pan-Africanists – were the center of the movement's anti-colonial organizing. Leaders and activists in Africa and the Caribbean responded to the self-determination clause of the 1941 Atlantic Charter, and their own contributions to the Allies' victory in WWII, by demanding that Western governments recognize self-determination in colonized territories.[9] Decolonization in Africa

---

[7] Henderson 2018.   [8] Du Bois 1961: 23.
[9] Adi 2018; Eckert 2012; Esedebe 1994; Ibhawoh 2018: 130–33; Kufuor 2010: 1–2; Lauren 1983.

5.1 Human Rights and Non-Interference

commenced in the late 1950s and progressed rapidly. In 1960 alone, seventeen African countries gained their independence, and in the 1950s and 1960s, a total of twenty-nine African states became independent.

Following decolonization, African leaders prioritized non-interference as a way of responding to continued threats to their political independence. Regional collective action focused on both completing decolonization and resisting neo-colonialism, and when the OAU was formed in 1963, these were among the main goals laid out in the organization's charter.[10] One of the OAU's first official acts was to create a Liberation Committee to provide material and financial support to liberation movements.[11] Through their joint action, African delegates pushed the UN to accept liberation movements as the representatives of their states.[12]

As for independent African states, collective action focused on consolidating their post-independence sovereignty.[13] Independence leaders expressed concerns that their individual weakness and vulnerability limited their *de facto* independence and left them vulnerable to both overt intervention and informal control, a dynamic they termed neo-colonialism.[14] Throughout this time, leaders used the OAU to call out violations of the norm of non-interference and to insist on respect for sovereignty and territorial integrity.[15]

In these first years, regional human rights priorities focused on increasing respect for African sovereignty and state-building. These included apartheid, decolonization, racial discrimination, and the right to development, each of which focused on violations of human rights in African states that were committed by those outside of the continent or by racist minority governments.[16] By contrast, there was almost no focus on human rights violations by OAU members against their own people.

By contrast, almost nothing was done to develop human rights institutions to address their own domestic behaviors. In 1958, an

---

[10] Duursma 2020; Gutteridge 1983: 24–25; Organization of African Unity 1963: Article II(c) and (d); Umozurike 1979.
[11] Murray 2004: 10.   [12] Amate 1986: 29–30   [13] Gutteridge 1983: 24–25
[14] Getachew 2019: 98–104
[15] Gutteridge 1983: 24–25. Examples include condemnation of intervention by Israel in 1973, France in Djibouti and Comoros in 1976, and Israel in Uganda in 1976.
[16] Amate 1986: 29–30; Beall 2022; Binaisa 1977: 58–59; Klotz 1995; Murray 2004: 10.

African human rights committee was proposed during a meeting of the All-African Peoples' Conference. The committee would provide "an example to imperial nations who abuse and ignore the extension of ... rights to Africans."[17] However, there is no mention of the committee in documentation from the next meeting in 1960.[18] In 1962, Nnamdi Azikiwe, the first leader of independent Nigeria, proposed an African Convention on Human Rights in 1962, the year after a meeting of civil society actors met in in Nigeria and adopted the Law of Lagos, a human rights charter,[19] but he did not pursue this proposal within the OAU.

When the OAU Charter was adopted in 1963, it contained few references to human rights, and the references it did include were broad and came without enforcement mechanisms. There is a reference in the charter's preamble to that fact that the signatories are "[p]ersuaded that the Charter of the United Nations and the Universal Declaration of Human Rights ... provide a solid foundation for peaceful and positive cooperation among States." The organization's purposes include "promot[ing] international cooperation, having due regard to the Charter of the United Nations and the Universal Declaration of Human Rights."[20]

In practice, African leaders adhered closely to the norm of non-interference. This, plus a focus on apartheid and human rights violations perpetrated by actors outside of Africa, meant that major human rights violations committed by members of the OAU were largely ignored. This included mass killings that occurred during the Biafran separatist conflict in Nigeria from 1967 to 1970; ethnic violence resulting in the death of over 150,000 Hutu in Burundi in 1972 and 1973; frequent mass expulsions of migrants; and the actions of the brutal and violent governments of Uganda, Equatorial Guinea, and the Central African Empire (now Republic) throughout the 1970s.[21]

Though there were only a small number of democracies in Africa at this time, those democracies that did exist were ambivalent about compromising on the norm of non-interference. During the Biafran civil conflict in Nigeria, which attracted a great deal of international attention and was labeled by many a genocide, Tanzania, Gabon, Cote

---

[17] All-African Peoples' Conference 1958: Conference Resolutions on Imperialism and Colonialism, Para. 7 and 9.
[18] All-African Peoples' Conference 1960.
[19] "Nnamdi Azikiwe, 'The Future of Pan-Africanism'" 2009.
[20] OAU Charter 1963: Preamble, 1(e).   [21] Weinstein 1976: 17–18.

d'Ivoire, and Zambia were the only states to publicly object to the actions of the Nigerian government, supporting the self-determination claims of the Biafran separatists.[22] By contrast, Senegal, Mauritius, the Gambia, Botswana, and Somalia, all then democracies, maintained their silence publicly. The Biafran situation also demonstrated the overwhelming emphasis on non-interference within the OAU. The international attention on Nigeria provoked concerns of Western intervention, leading to the establishment of an OAU ad hoc group of heads of state to mediate.[23] However, the group never wavered from the goal of preserving Nigerian sovereignty.[24]

African leaders also abided by the norm of non-interference throughout the entirety of Idi Amin's violent rule in Uganda. One of the very few exceptions to this occurred in the lead-up to the 1975 annual meeting of the OAU's Assembly of Heads of State and Government. The meeting was scheduled to be held in Uganda, in spite of what was by then common knowledge of the massive violations of human rights being committed there. The governments of Tanzania, Zambia, Botswana, and Mozambique opposed holding the meeting there and, with the exception of Mozambique, boycotted the meeting. Leaders of other democracies, including Senegal, the Gambia, and Mauritius, chose to attend the meeting.[25]

As late as 1977, a group of Western European delegations introduced a draft resolution targeting Uganda in the UN General Assembly. They withdrew it after African leaders asserted that the matter should be left to the OAU, where no action was taken.[26] That same year, the prime minister of Mauritius, a democracy, asserted at the UN General Assembly that, while the "denial of human rights is still widespread, ... [r]ather than criticizing others, it would be better that we each put our own house in order."[27]

5.2 Economic Conditions Subvert the "Spirit of Lomé"

It took several years for the attention on human rights in Latin America to spread to Africa. In 1977, officials in Jimmy Carter's administration noted "a certain myopia" from the United States Congress with respect

---

[22] Muyangwa and Vogt 2000: 6. [23] Krishna Ramphul 1983: 381–82.
[24] Krishna Ramphul 1983: 381–82. [25] Kannyo 1981: 16.
[26] UN General Assembly 1977f, 1979c: Para. 33.
[27] UN General Assembly 1977e: Para. 43.

to human rights violations in Africa.[28] The governments of the Netherlands and the United Kingdom had taken some early steps toward acting on events in Uganda, but their actions had not otherwise extended beyond major, attention-grabbing abuses. The tight coalition among non-aligned and Soviet states in the UN also allowed African leaders to quiet efforts to criticize human rights violations against OAU members, even while they helped mount campaigns against Chile, Israel, and South Africa.[29] Transnational advocacy networks first focused concerted attention on Africa with Amnesty International's 1977 reports on Uganda. These reports, alongside Amin's targeting of Americans living in Uganda, drew international attention to Idi Amin's wider abuses and elicited a strong reaction in the West.[30]

Under Jimmy Carter, the United States was the most prominent and influential Western government to promote human rights in its foreign policy in the 1970s. In 1977, Carter's administration began to target Uganda, followed quickly by several other African countries. In 1978 and 1979, economic sanctions were leveled against Uganda, the Central African Empire, Mozambique, Angola, Zambia, Ethiopia, Guinea, and Tanzania.[31]

The promotion of human rights by a superpower cast a long shadow, but the US was not ultimately the most important source of pressure for Africa. Because of patterns of dependency and economic exchange established during the colonial era, most of Africa's economic relations, including development assistance and trade, were with Europe. Beginning in 1975, a large proportion of these economic relations were conducted through the Lomé Convention (Lomé), an association agreement governing the European Economic Community's (EEC) preferential trade and development aid for their former colonies, known collectively as the African, Caribbean, and Pacific (ACP) states.[32] African states made up the largest proportion of ACP states by far, representing 47 out of 56 ACP states in 1978.

Following the 1977 reports on Uganda, European leaders came under considerable pressure to suspend Lomé assistance to

---

[28] *FRUS* 2013: Document 627.
[29] Tolley 1984; Van Boven 1977; Weinstein 1976.
[30] Fierro 2003: 45; Gertzel 1980: 464; Moravcsik 1995: 166; Oberdorfer 1977.
[31] *FRUS* 2013: Document 42, 53, 104, 105; Fredman 1979; Rubner 2011: 187, 196.
[32] Arts 2000, Elgström 2000; Garnick and Twitchett 1979.

5.2 Economic Conditions Subvert the "Spirit of Lomé"

Uganda.[33] They responded in June 1977 with the "Uganda Guidelines," a policy document stating that the EEC would "take steps ... under the Lomé Convention to ensure that any assistance ... does not in any way have as its effect a reinforcement or prolongation of the denial of basic human rights."[34] Aid to Uganda was substantially reduced, and the aid that continued was redirected to humanitarian causes.[35] The same guidelines were applied to Equatorial Guinea in 1978 and to the Central African Empire in January and April 1979.[36]

The Lomé Convention was designed to be renegotiated every five years, and the first round of renegotiations was scheduled to start in 1978. At a meeting between European and ACP ministers in June 1977, the European ministers announced their intention to alter Lomé to institutionalize the Uganda Guidelines, allowing for cooperation to be suspended with countries that violated human rights. When renegotiations began in July 1978, adding human rights language was part of the mandate of European negotiators.[37]

The use of economic conditions as a method for enforcing human rights directly conflicted with ideas that were widely held in Africa about the self-determination of independent states; these were expressed as matters of economic self-determination, economic independence, and neo-colonialism. These concepts all focused on how exploitation of economic dependence undermined a state's political independence, allowing outside actors to impose policies onto African states. Putting these conditions in Lomé would impose them broadly on all Lomé recipients, including those that had relatively good records of human rights and that viewed themselves as human rights advocates, while establishing European governments as their enforcer. Because European governments controlled the resources allocated by Lomé, they wielded disproportionate control over decision-making over how these policies were implemented, even though formal institutional rules gave ACP states equal voice in decision-making.

African leaders and non-state actors within Africa had been important advocates for the idea that self-determination was undermined through exploitation of their economic dependence. Ghanaian leader Kwame Nkrumah was among the most prominent to articulate this as

---

[33] Fierro 2003: 53; Garnick and Twitchett 1979: 543.   [34] King 1997: 55.
[35] Fierro 2003: 45; Moravcsik 1995: 166.   [36] Arts 2000: 324–25, 423.
[37] Arts 2000: 168; Garnick and Twitchett 1979; Smits 1980; Young-Anawaty 1980.

a problem of neo-colonialism. Nkrumah argued that state weakness and pre-independence forms of economic control allowed external actors to undermine the ability of African states to chart their own independent domestic and foreign policies.[38] This was an important motivation for pan-African solidarity, which its supporters, including Nkrumah, argued would allow them to resist the undermining of their sovereign authority.[39]

As human rights became an important international issue in the 1970s, self-determination as it applied to international rules continued to be important to African leaders, including those that also supported human rights. Liberian president William Tolbert was both a critic of neocolonialism and an important supporter of human rights, articulating both positions in a private conversation with Jimmy Carter in 1979. A memorandum of conversation between the two notes that Tolbert emphasized to Carter that "Africans should have the same standards for human rights as they expect from the rest of the world." At the same time, Tolbert stated that "if economic dependency and underdevelopment continue, Africans will not be free."[40]

Many non-state actors also advanced this understanding of self-determination and its relation to economic pressure by Western governments. In his influential book, *How Europe Underdeveloped Africa,* prominent pan-African activist Walter Rodney wrote that "economic independence does not mean isolation," but it does "require a capacity to exercise choice."[41] The Universal Declaration of the Rights of Peoples, adopted in Algeria in 1976 by a gathering of anti-imperial civil society actors, defined the right to self-determination as including both the right of peoples to a democratic government that respects human rights *and* to "determine its political status freely and without foreign interference."[42] Nigerian legal scholar Oji Umozurike, who later served as the chair of the African Commission on Human and Peoples' Rights, developed similar ideas. In 1970, Umozurike wrote of economic self-determination that a state "reserves the right to organize its economic future" and that, "without this right

---

[38] Nkrumah 1963, 1965.
[39] Getachew 2019; Nkrumah 1965; "Nnamdi Azikiwe, 'The Future of Pan-Africanism'" 2009.
[40] FRUS 2018c: Document 49.   [41] Rodney 1972: 31.
[42] Universal Declaration on the Rights of Peoples 1976: Preamble, II(5), (7).

observed, what appears to be sovereignty on the surface becomes ... 'a ghost of a hollow sovereignty.'"⁴³

An inability to meaningfully participate in international policymaking – or in the design and enforcement of rules to which they were subject – was also singled out as undermining self-determination. Many pan-African activists and leaders saw this as a bridge between the denial of the right to self-determination that had occurred under colonialism and its denial in independent states.⁴⁴ For example, Tunisian anti-colonial philosopher Albert Memmi had singled out for criticism denial of participation in their own affairs, explaining how colonialism had meant the "usurp[ation of] any free role in either war or peace, every decision contributing to his destiny and that of the world, and all cultural and social responsibility."⁴⁵

For leaders that proposed decolonization through the transformation of the French empire into a French federation, most prominently Léopold Senghor of Senegal and Aimé Césaire of Martinique, institutional guarantees of equal representation and participation were among the central features distinguishing self-determination from the continuation of colonial relations.⁴⁶ The importance of participation was also referenced in the 1973 African Declaration on Co-operation, Development and Economic Independence, in which African heads of state identified "ensur[ing] effective and equitable African representation in international organizations" as an important component of economic independence.⁴⁷ The importance of playing an active role in the world and in decisions that affected them was also pointed to by Rodney, who discussed the difference between independent Africa being a maker versus an object of history.⁴⁸

These ideas persisted alongside growing interest within Africa in the enforcement of human rights. One example of this occurred during a February 1979 symposium organized by OAU Secretary General Edem Kodjo and hosted in Liberia by Tolbert. The symposium was attended mostly by development experts and OAU and UN officials, and its final report called for the creation of a human rights department in the OAU Secretariat.⁴⁹ It also included a "refus[al]" for Africa "to become integrated into a world of vassals" and declared an intention for

---

⁴³ Umozurike 1970, 80.   ⁴⁴ Getachew 2019: 23.
⁴⁵ Memmi quoted in Rodney 1972: 272.   ⁴⁶ Wilder 2015.
⁴⁷ OAU Assembly of Heads of State and Government 1973: A.6.
⁴⁸ Rodney 1972.   ⁴⁹ OAU Secretariat 1979: 19.

Africans to "take over the management of all [their] own affairs and not merely participate to the extent dictated by others."[50] As I discuss below, Kodjo himself played an important role in the creation of African human rights institutions. He later suggested that creation of the system was motivated by "the twin objectives of liberation vis-à-vis the rest of the world and the internal democratization of African societies."[51]

Growing interest in human rights existed alongside opposition to the use of economic pressure by Western governments to enforce human rights. The addition of language to Lomé that would allow European governments to use economic conditions to enforce human rights was consistently rejected by the ACP group. Though some African leaders had privately expressed limited support for cutting aid in cases of especially egregious governments like Amin's, their support did not carry over to being made subject to these rules themselves via their broad institutionalization in Lomé.[52] In fact, the addition of these conditions to Lomé was especially objectionable because of what the convention was meant to represent – a transformation of relations between the two groups of states in the aftermath of decolonization through the codification of equality and partnership, referred to as the "spirit of Lomé."[53]

The suspension clause quickly emerged as one of the biggest points of contention during renegotiations of Lomé.[54] One European official involved in the negotiations noted in 1978 that "when others outside Africa took this question [of human rights] up, the automatic African reaction was to close ranks."[55] Throughout the negotiating period, ACP states regularly met amongst themselves to discuss and update their positions, and they emerged from each of these meetings with a unanimous position that the introduction of human rights into the convention was inappropriate.[56] After one meeting, an ACP spokesperson asserted that "our concern for human rights is no less than

---

[50] OAU Secretariat 1979: 28.   [51] Kodjo 1990: 273–74.
[52] King 1997: 56; *FRUS* 2013: Document 42.
[53] Elgström 2000; Oyewumi 1991.
[54] Garnick and Twitchett 1979; Smits 1980: 53 n37, 55 n37; Young-Anawaty 1980.
[55] Quoted in Ferrari 2015: 228.
[56] Arts 2000: 168; European Commission 1978a: III, 1978b: II–III; Stormorken 1984: 17.

yours," but that "any eventual agreement between us must be based on strict respect for equality between partners."[57]

Leaders that supported human rights were among those that objected to a suspension clause. Following the removal of Idi Amin in April 1979, the new government of Uganda was extremely critical of the failure of the OAU and the UN to respond to the previous government's abuses, calling for greater international action by both.[58] Yet, when asked about the inclusion of human rights provisions in the Lomé Convention less than a year after Amin was removed from power, a Ugandan ambassador stated that ACP states were "very clear" that human rights should not be a part of Lomé and expressed concerns that "[o]nce you put it in the Convention it is very easy, maybe by accident, to try to make use of it."[59]

The only record of an African or ACP official offering support for adding human rights to the Lomé Convention during the negotiations came from Senegal, a country that is widely acknowledged to have been an important advocate for and supporter of international human rights during this time. However, what the Senegalese official actually proposed was a mechanism to discuss and condemn human rights violations, not to rescind aid. André Guillabert, the Senegalese representative who introduced the proposal, stated that a "reference to human rights would be a powerful weapon for the ACP States in showing that Europeans did not respect the rights of the individual," a reference to Europe's mistreatment of migrants from ACP countries and support for apartheid governments. The proposal received some initial support before it was dropped in favor of excluding human rights from Lomé.[60]

5.3 The Emergence of African Enforcement

By May 1979, nearly two years after adopting the Uganda Guidelines and a year into the renegotiations of Lomé, European negotiators were still pushing for a reference to human rights in Lomé that would allow the treaty to be suspended.[61] European resolve to add a human rights

---

[57] European Commission 1978b: II.
[58] Kannyo 1981: 18; Ouguergouz 2003: 38; UN General Assembly 1979c: Para. 32.
[59] European Commission 1980a: 24–25.   [60] Stormorken 1984: 17.
[61] Smits 1980: 53 n37.

clause had only increased after Amnesty International released another bombshell report on another African country. The report, released in April 1979, detailed a massacre of over one hundred schoolchildren in the Central African Empire in response to student demonstrations over school uniforms. It alleged that the Central African Empire's leader, Jean-Bédel Bokassa, was personally involved in the killings.

The report triggered outrage throughout the West. This was particularly consequential for the French government, which had opposed human rights conditions but was deeply embarrassed by the report because of the French president's personal relationship with Bokassa and France's funding of his government. Both Lomé assistance and French bilateral aid were quickly cut off.[62]

Simply rejecting a suspension clause as interference in Africa's domestic affairs had not brought an end to efforts to add the provision to Lomé or to the actual use of suspensions, and human rights were becoming an increasingly common consideration in Western states' economic relations with the developing world outside of the Lomé system.[63] The decision to establish the OAU as an authority over human rights enforcement – to create and assert the authority of African human rights institutions – occurred in the context of this new status quo.

5.3.1 Accepting Regional Authority

For African governments, accepting regional authority over themselves occurred in two stages. In the first stage, African leaders adopted a resolution calling for the creation of a regional human rights system, formally dropping their rhetorical opposition to the use of interference in states' human rights practices and setting the process of creating regional institutions into motion. The second stage consisted of approving and bringing into existence these regional human rights institutions. Both stages happened at the initiative of human rights supporters, with those that opposed regional human rights institutions resisting before ultimately accepting them in the face of the new reality of Western human rights pressure.

---

[62] "Papa Bok is a Millstone to France" 1979; "Vive la France?" 1979; Welch 1981: 406–8.
[63] Eckel 2019: 190–242; Lorenzini et al. 2022; Umozurike 1983: 904.

5.3 The Emergence of African Enforcement

This process was initiated by Edem Kodjo, the above-mentioned Secretary General of the OAU, and Keba M'Baye, a Senegalese jurist who was then the president of the International Commission of Jurists and Senegal's representative on the UN Commission on Human Rights. In the late 1970s, both Kodjo and M'Baye separately organized regional conferences through their respective organizations to discuss the creation of regional human rights institutions and then lobbied African heads of state to make this happen.[64] Both separately approached Léopold Senghor, the president of Senegal and a strong supporter of human rights, about taking the lead within the OAU on this initiative, emphasizing to Senghor the value of creating African-owned and -led human rights institutions.[65] It was Senghor who then introduced the resolution calling for an African regional human rights system at the July 1979 meeting of the OAU Assembly of Heads of State and Government.

This initiative fit well with Senghor's own political philosophy and his ideas about self-determination and assimilation. According to Senghor, what Africa needed was not to reject non-African influences or authority or to remain unintegrated in the non-African world, but to integrate and assimilate on their terms, in ways that gave Africa an equal voice and enabled them to contribute what was valuable from African culture.[66] Senghor utilized this distinction, and this understanding of choice and agency, in talking about regional human rights institutions. Presiding over the drafting of the African charter in 1979, he asserted that, in developing its regional institutions, Africa should "assimilate but not be assimilated."[67]

Several other African leaders offered support for the initiative during this meeting. William Tolbert, the president of Liberia and host of that year's meeting, opened the meeting by calling for an end to the practice of deferring to the norm of non-interference where human rights were concerned.[68] The governments of Nigeria, Mauritius, Uganda (post-Idi Amin), and the Gambia also argued in support of the resolution.[69]

Senghor bypassed the usual procedures for introducing resolutions, according to which the resolution should have been introduced into an

[64] Rubner 2011: 250–52; Tolley 1989: 578–79.
[65] Rubner 2011: 252, 254; Tolley 1989: 578–79.
[66] Senghor 1963; Wilder 2015. [67] Jallow 2007: 30.
[68] Dash 1979; Rubner 2011: 256.
[69] Dash 1979; Jallow 2007: 24; Ouguergouz 2003: 38–39; Rubner 2011: 248–62.

earlier meeting of the OAU Council of Ministers for approval prior to the meeting of the heads of state and then placed on the meeting's official agenda. Instead, he introduced the resolution at the end of the Assembly of Heads of State and Government without placing it on the agenda in advance, thus avoiding opportunities for the resolution to quietly be killed.[70] In a significant break from their previous stance on non-interference, African leaders unanimously adopted the resolution calling for a human rights charter and a treaty body to implement the charter.[71]

The resolution passed because of the essential actions of human rights supporters within the region, and the way the resolution was introduced and passed suggest this was not an effort to undermine the global human rights regime. At the same time, these supporters of human rights were not alone in approving the resolution. In gaining unanimous acceptance, the resolution was approved by dictators, leaders that were accused of violating human rights, and those that viewed human rights as Western Cold War propaganda; together, this made up the majority of African states at the time. The leaders of Equatorial Guinea and the Central African Empire, accused of horrific and widespread human rights abuses, were still in power and were among those offering their support.[72]

The adoption of the human rights resolution also clashed with the continued, significant support for the norm of non-interference at the meeting. Several months earlier, Julius Nyerere, the leader of Tanzania and an outspoken critic of Idi Amin, had taken advantage of a border dispute to invade Uganda and overthrow Amin. Much of the meeting was spent condemning Nyerere for violating the norm of non-interference.[73] At another point during the meeting, Amin's successor gave an address criticizing the other heads of state for failing to take action to stop Amin's abuses and for continuing to do so in Equatorial Guinea and the Central African Empire. The remarks were stricken from the meeting's record.[74] In other words, the proceedings of this meeting suggest that attitudes toward human rights and the norm of non-interference were unsettled, and that there was still significant

---

[70] Rubner 2011: 257.   [71] Ouguergouz 2003: 39.
[72] Rubner 2011: 261; Umozurike 1983: 902–3.
[73] Dash 1979; Kannyo 1981: 16–18; Ouguergouz 2003: 38–39; Rubner 2011: 265.
[74] Dash 1979; Kannyo 1981: 18; Ouguergouz 2003: 38–39.

5.3 The Emergence of African Enforcement

opposition to even openly condemning human rights violations. The resolution to create regional human rights institutions was adopted despite this and likely reflects the expectation on the part of some that the resolution would not be followed through on.

Just three months after African leaders adopted the resolution calling for African human rights institutions, in October 1979, the final negotiation session for the Lomé Convention was concluded. Discussion of adding human rights provisions to Lomé was dropped, and the new agreement was signed. The EEC Development Commissioner pointed to the OAU resolution as justification for leaving human rights out, saying that the resolution was "exactly what we wanted to say and show to our peoples."[75] However, European pressure did not go away. In November 1979, just one month later, the European Community adopted a policy statement announcing their intention to generalize the Uganda Guidelines and employ sanctions in cases of human rights violations.[76] Shortly after, in 1980, the EEC suspended Lomé assistance to Liberia following a violent coup.[77]

With this in the background, African leaders proceeded with the second stage of accepting regional authority: bringing regional institutions into existence. An initial draft of the charter, which established an African human rights commission, was produced months after the OAU resolution calling for it. M'Baye, as head of the committee of experts tasked with drafting the charter, produced the first draft, and an amended version was completed by the expert committee in December 1979. The draft was then sent to states to begin the process of approval and adoption.[78]

The process of bringing these institutions into existence was marked throughout by resistance, and with leaders expressing concern about interference. With the charter drafted and turned over to the states, a period of foot-dragging ensued on the part of governments that continued to oppose regional human rights institutions. The first of three steps in the process of state adoption was approval by a special meeting of governmental ministers, which was scheduled for March 1980 in Addis Ababa. The Ethiopian government, the meeting's host, was among the socialist governments that saw human rights as Cold War

---

[75] Young-Anawaty 1980: 92–93 n127. [76] Arts 2000: 174–75.
[77] Arts 2000: 423.
[78] Jallow 2007: 25–31; Ouguergouz 2003: 40–43; Rubner 2011: 276, 279–82, 286.

propaganda, and they refused to approve visas for a number of delegations. Other state representatives simply did not show up, and the meeting failed to reach a quorum.[79]

The meeting was rescheduled and relocated to the Gambia, a choice meant to assist in the adoption of the charter, given the Gambian government's support for regional human rights institutions. However, this second meeting was also unsuccessful.[80] After prolonged debate, the ministers approved only eleven articles of the charter, despite barely altering the articles from the original draft.[81] Yet *another* meeting was scheduled for January 1981, again in the Gambia. Prior to this meeting, OAU Secretary General Kodjo intervened in the process. At his request, the Gambian president introduced a resolution at the June 1980 meeting of the OAU Council of Ministers "urg[ing]" the group of governmental ministers involved in the drafting process "to deploy every effort to complete the ... Draft Charter and to ensure that the final draft is submitted to the Eighteenth Assembly of Heads of State and Government."[82] The resolution had the intended effect, and the charter was finally approved.[83]

The charter moved more smoothly through the remaining stages of state approval, though not without controversy. The OAU Council of Ministers was the second round of government approval. The ministers did not actually approve the charter, instead expressing concerns about it and nature of the authority of the commission that it established. These concerns included the fact that the charter "did not make it clear that the Commission does not have the authority to interfere with the internal affairs of the OAU member States" or that the "sole right of interpretation [of the Charter] should be invested entirely with the Assembly of Heads of State and Government."[84] One delegate wanted the enforcement mechanisms of the commission to be part of an optional protocol rather than an integral part of the treaty.[85] They nevertheless passed along the charter, along with their concerns, to the

---

[79] Jallow 2007: 35; Rubner 2011: 287.
[80] Jallow 2007: 35–36, 38–42; Ouguergouz 2003: 44–45; Rubner 2011: 288–90.
[81] Jallow 2007: 42; Welch 1981: 420.
[82] Jallow 2007: 43; M'Baye 1992: 158; OAU Council of Ministers 1980.
[83] Jallow 2007: 45–47.
[84] Quoted in Gittleman 1981: 669 n10. See also Jallow 2007: 50; Ouguergouz 2003: 47 n182.
[85] Ouguergouz 2003: 46 n178.

5.3 The Emergence of African Enforcement

Assembly of Heads of State and Government, who adopted it unanimously and without amendment.[86]

The design of the African human rights system itself suggests real tension between the pressure to create regional institutions that could interfere in states' domestic affairs, on the one hand, and the continued reluctance to delegate too much authority, on the other. One important piece of authority was a system for private individuals to submit complaints that their human rights had been violated and to have those complaints adjudicated by the commission. The charter gives the African Commission the power to receive what it terms "other communications."[87] Though it does not specify what these "other" communications might consist of, M'Baye's first draft specified individual communications, and the language was changed to refer to "other communications" during the drafting process.[88] This provision was immediately interpreted by the commissioners as allowing them to receive communications from individuals, as well as NGOs. The strange wording of this provision makes sense as an artifact of the reluctant acceptance of interference.

This tension, and the willingness of leaders to delegate more enforcement authority than they would have preferred, is also evident in the level of independence given to the African Commission. According to the African Charter, commissioners should have competence in the area of human rights and should serve in their personal capacity, not as state representatives. At the same time, there are important limits to this independence. The initial drafters added language to the charter expressly prohibiting government officials from serving as commissioners, but this prohibition was removed by state representatives during the approval process. Additionally, the commission's work is subject to approval and publication by the OAU's intergovernmental bodies.[89] At the same time, the base level of independence that the commission was granted has made it possible for commissioners to expand their own powers considerably.[90]

Finally, the African Charter bears the marks of this tension. It contains all basic civil, political, and physical integrity rights, though

---

[86] Jallow 2007: 49–55; Ouguergouz 2003: 47–48, 47 n182; Rubner 2011: 294.
[87] Organization of African Unity 1981: Article 55–56.
[88] Compare [Mbaye] Draft African Charter on Human and Peoples' Rights (1979) and [Dakar Draft] African Charter on Human and Peoples' Rights (1979).
[89] Kannyo 1981: 18.   [90] Heyns 2004: 688–98; Viljoen 2007: 325–26, 346–49.

with "clawback clauses" subordinating many rights to domestic law. Yet, there are no such clauses for physical integrity rights, such as the right to life and prohibition against torture, which appear without qualification.[91] This is notable because in the late 1970s and early 1980s, physical integrity rights were the main focus of international advocacy and Western pressure.[92] In other words, where African states faced the most pressure, they gave themselves the least space for national discretion.

In the years after the African Charter was adopted, individual African leaders began to themselves accept the authority of the OAU, often in response to external pressure or in efforts to improve relations with the West. In 1982, Guinea ratified the charter as part of Sekou Touré's attempts at rapprochement with the West, which also included liberalization of the economy and a trip to the United States and France in search of economic support.[93] Liberia ratified the treaty in 1982, two years after the violent overthrow of the previous government for which Lomé assistance was cut off. This happened while the repressive government of Samuel Doe was attempting to improve relations with Western states. In 1983, Nigeria ratified the African charter in response to Western criticism of its decision to expel Ghanaian immigrants.[94] In 1986, Omar Bongo of Gabon, a long-time dictator and close client state of France, ratified the charter as his government was seeking a loan from the IMF, following increased pressure on France from human rights activists.[95]

A brief discussion of the case of Burundi illustrates how some African leaders went from rejecting interference to strategically accepting regional authority in response to Western economic pressure. Burundi ratified the African Charter in 1989 in response to Western pressure over an outbreak of ethnic violence that had taken place the previous year. Western governments had threatened to cut off Burundi's economic assistance and called on Burundi to accept an independent investigatory commission, with both the European Commission and the UN offering to furnish the commission.

---

[91] For example, see Organization of African Unity 1981: Article 4.
[92] FRUS 2013: Documents 1, 54; Scoble and Wiseberg 1981; Smits 1980: 51 n25.
[93] Blackburn 1984; Pomonti 1982; Rondos 1983: 9.
[94] "Nigerian Minister's Criticism of Western and Ghanaian Media" 1983.
[95] "Gabon Nears Accord With IMF." 1986; Reed 1987; "Return to Gabon of Member of 'Government-in-Exile.'" 1985.

5.3 The Emergence of African Enforcement

In response, Burundi first re-asserted the norm of non-interference, with the country's foreign minister stating that Burundi is "an independent state which has the situation under control. There is no place for such a commission."[96] However, within several months, the government of Burundi accepted a visit from a small OAU team, met to discuss the violence with the heads of state of the sub-regional organization the Economic Community of the States of the Great Lake, sent a representative to a meeting of the recently formed African Commission on Human and Peoples' Rights to discuss the situation, and, finally, ratified the African Charter on Human and Peoples' Rights. Burundi waited an additional two years to ratify the ICCPR, and never ratified the First Optional Protocol to the ICCPR, in spite of undergoing significant political liberalization in 1992 and 1993 and becoming a full democracy in 2005.

By 1986, the charter had come into effect after being ratified by 32 states, the majority of which were authoritarian governments with poor human rights records.[97] As in Latin America, this new willingness on the part of African leaders to ratify regional treaties, and in doing so, to accept human rights enforcement contrasted with their ongoing reluctance to ratify global treaties. In 1986 when the African Charter came into effect, 32 members of the OAU had ratified the African Charter compared to only 20 that had ratified the ICCPR and a mere 9 that had ratified the First Optional Protocol to the ICCPR. This gap in accepting regional versus global enforcement only widened as African leaders created and accepted new regional institutions, including regional and sub-regional human rights courts.

5.3.2 Asserting Regional Authority

At the same time as they began to create and accept regional human rights institutions, African leaders also began to assert the authority of regional organizations over human rights, both in the UN and within the Lomé system. An important move toward asserting regional authority within the UN came in 1977, when the Nigerian delegation introduced a resolution to the UN General Assembly which called for

---

[96] "Commission on Killings Ruled Out by Burundi" 1988.
[97] Of the 30 states that ratified the treaty by 1986, 22 had a Polity score of −7 or lower the year of ratification.

states to consider creating "regional arrangements for the promotion and protection of human rights" in regions without such an arrangement. The resolution was introduced in December 1977, amid growing international attention to Uganda and after the announcement by European states, six months earlier, that they intended to add human rights conditions to the Lomé Convention.

Nigeria's resolution asserted that regions were uniquely well-suited to deal with human rights within their own geographic area, with the text urging states to "devis[e] local arrangements concerning human rights which would reflect the characteristics of the regions themselves."[98] It stressed "the importance of encouraging regional cooperation for the promotion and protection of human rights" and requested that the UN Secretary General provide support to regions to assist them in setting up their own commissions. The following year, as part of the same initiative, Nigeria revived an earlier project of organizing UN seminars to support regions in setting up human rights commissions, calling for a seminar to be organized in Africa.

Leaders also asserted regional authority within the Lomé system and in the context of their relations with the European Community. Following the signing of the Lomé Convention in 1979, the president of the ACP Council of Ministers spoke on behalf of the entire ACP group in emphasizing the legitimacy of the African initiative to create regional human rights institutions. The diplomat stated that "as a group, our concern for human rights is no less than yours ... Those of us who are members of the Organization of African Unity have reaffirmed that intention at the level of heads of State in the now famous resolution in Monrovia in July 1979 ... Thus we too are militants for human rights."[99] In future negotiations over Lomé, they put forward the argument that, because they already had a regional human rights system, adding human rights to Lomé was unnecessary and would duplicate what was already being done regionally.[100]

The adoption of a regional system coincided with a shift in rhetoric. African leaders went from arguing against interference to arguing that Africa be given space to handle its own human rights issues. In January 1983, the Nigerian government came under scrutiny for its mass expulsion of Ghanaian citizens residing in Nigeria – one of the first major

---

[98] UN General Assembly 1977k: Para. 85.
[99] Young-Anawaty 1980: 93–94 n129.   [100] Gueye 1996: 25.

human rights-related incidents in Africa to make international headlines after the adoption of African Charter in 1981. In addition to the expulsion, there were reports from the Western media of torture and murder of immigrants in Nigeria.[101] The ACP-EEC Joint Parliament, a body of European and ACP parliamentarians set up to oversee implementation of the Lomé Convention, was scheduled to meet the month after the expulsions began. In advance of the meeting, the European Parliament requested that they add the situation to the meeting's agenda.

Rather than object to the interest from the European Parliament as inappropriate interference, a report on the meeting drawn up by the European Parliament notes that ACP states "express[ed] understanding" of the European Parliament's concern. An ACP spokesperson, a representative of Uganda, asserted that they "wanted the matter to be settled by the Africans themselves," and asked the European Parliament to "trust the OAU, ECOWAS and the countries directly concerned to find a humanitarian and fair solution."[102] The African Charter and Commission had not yet come into force, but in February 1983, the sub-regional organization ECOWAS sent a fact-finding delegation to Ghana, and Nigeria's president signed into law a bill on the ratification and enforcement of the African Charter.[103] This was a significant departure from the region's response to the many mass expulsions that had taken place in the preceding two decades, each of which had been treated as a matter of states' domestic affairs.[104] Nigeria did not ratify the ICCPR for another decade, and has yet to ratify the First Optional Protocol.

These efforts at establishing regional authority were effective because they appealed to European concerns about legitimate relations with their former colonies. With decolonization so recent, and with the Lomé system having been created for the express purpose of establishing equality and partnership between Europe and formerly colonized states, European governments were sensitive to criticisms that adding human rights to Lomé was inappropriate.[105] For example, in discussing Lomé in 1976, Development Commissioner Claude Cheysson had made clear that "we are resolved not to meddle in any way in internal

---

[101] "Nigerian Minister's Criticism of Western and Ghanaian Media" 1983.
[102] European Parliament 1983b.
[103] "ECOWAS Delegation in Ghana: Aid for Deportees" 1983; "Nigeria's Ratification of African Charter on Human Rights" 1983.
[104] Umozurike 1979.   [105] Beall 2024a.

matters."[106] Some were also concerned about how the pursuit of human rights within Lomé would affect their Cold War strategies.[107]

As a result, European leaders were open to accepting and deferring to an African regional system, and the new regional institutions proved to be relatively effective at blunting economic pressure from European governments and staving off the addition of a suspension clause to the Lomé Convention. As noted above, after the renegotiated Lomé Convention was signed without human rights language, the EEC Commissioner pointed to the decision by African heads of state to create a human rights charter in justifying the omission.[108] From the US side, Jimmy Carter similarly expressed interest in supporting African regional initiatives.[109]

An important reason for the effectiveness of this strategy was that the African human rights institutions were regarded, at the time, as a positive step toward dealing with human rights within the region. The government of the Netherlands, one of the European states pushing most assertively for human rights conditions to be added to Lomé, responded to Nigeria's 1977 resolution on regional human rights commissions by suggesting that "governments would be less reluctant to explain their actions to others in the same region than to a world organization," while at the same time cautioning against the risk of "regional organs which had no real and effective powers yet claimed precedence over the United Nations."[110] The UK, the other member of the European Commission that was pushing for human rights conditions, noted in response to the OAU's 1979 resolution that "the proposal to establish a regional human rights system for Africa was particularly encouraging."[111] One European observer noted that "ACP countries are willing to admit now, particularly since ... the OAU's adoption of a human rights charter" that international attention to their own human rights was sometimes warranted.[112] The president of the European Parliament observed that human rights can "now ... be discussed among Africans and with Africans."[113] A prominent scholar of Africa noted that the "decision to adopt a

---

[106] European Communities 1976: 7.
[107] Fierro 2003: 49–50; Pflüger 1989: 707.
[108] Quoted in Young-Anawaty 1980: 92–93 n127.
[109] *FRUS* 2013: Document 105.   [110] UN General Assembly 1978b: Para. 14.
[111] UN General Assembly 1979d: Para. 13.   [112] European Commission 1983.
[113] European Commission 1980b: 9.

human rights document will legitimize the consideration of human rights by Africans and by outsiders."[114] Even where outside observers remained skeptical, the fact that African institutions had been set up created incentives to channel pressure toward pushing for governments to engage with the regional system and supporting the institution's work.

As noted above, this did not stop European governments from deciding internally that they would suspend aid to enforce human rights. Throughout the 1980s, they continued to demonstrate an interest in human rights, including by pushing again in 1983 to add human rights language to the next iteration of the Lomé Convention.[115] In 1986, the European Community Foreign Ministers issued a formal policy statement designating human rights an "important element" in the "development of their relations with non-member States as well as in the administration of aid."[116] The European Parliament continued to press for human rights to be a consideration in economic relations.[117]

Yet, in practice, apart from severing Lomé cooperation with Liberia in 1980, during the 1980s, European states refrained from outright suspensions of existing aid or development projects. Instead, they sometimes delayed or chose not to approve new projects in countries where there were serious human rights concerns.[118] For example, in 1987, the EC decided to withhold approval of a $52 million project for Burkina Faso.[119] They would also employ behind-the-scenes pressure during trade negotiations to push for greater observance of human rights.[120] This was in addition to the nearly constant pressure on African countries from the European Parliament.[121]

It is perhaps not surprising that African leaders asserted the norm of regional solutions to regional problems with respect to human rights enforcement.[122] This norm may be best associated with its use by African governments in calling for "African solutions," something which they have done since the creation of the OAU. What changed is that these assertions were now coupled with a rhetorical shift toward the norm of non-interference. African leaders began to deploy this

---

[114] Weinstein 1980: 132.   [115] Hill 1985.   [116] Arts 2000: 119–20.
[117] Arts 2000: 251; Boumans and Norbart 1989: 137; Kemps 1984.
[118] Kamminga 1989: 33.   [119] Marantis 1994: 7 n30.
[120] European Parliament 1993: 4.
[121] Arts 2000: 251; Boumans and Norbart 1989: 137; Kemps 1984.
[122] Apuuli 2012; Duursma 2020.

norm not to argue against interference, but to argue that any interference should be led by Africa. The adoption of African human rights institutions marked an important shift away from across-the-board objections to interference and toward a conception of African solutions to African problems that was tolerant of interference, as long as it came from within or was led by Africa.

5.4 Post-Cold War Marginalization and Deepening Regional Cooperation

In the years after the Cold War ended, Africa became increasingly marginalized in global politics. Western governments became less responsive to the voices and preferences of African governments, even as democratization resulted in more governments that were themselves representative of and responsive to their citizens.[123] Importantly, marginalization did not mean a complete lack of interest in Africa or an end to international interference. It meant that interference in the region increasingly ignored the input and preferences of African governments, as the concerns Western states had about protecting relations with African governments evaporated.

At this time, Africa became increasingly subject to economic conditions, despite the continued objections of African leaders. Both European governments and the US began to widely pursue aid conditionality aimed at promoting human rights in Africa, in addition to other liberal norms like democracy and good governance.[124] This was the case with Lomé. In the 1980s, European states had refrained from suspending Lomé outright, with the one exception being Liberia in 1980. By contrast, in 1990, Lomé cooperation was suspended on three occasions, to Liberia, Sudan, and Somalia. In 1991, there were an additional five instances of suspension, followed by four in 1992, three in 1993, and another four in 1994.[125]

African states again objected to these measures, even as the African continent democratized.[126] In 1990, Nelson Mandela visited Kenya,

---

[123] Muyangwa and Vogt 2000: 1.
[124] Adebajo and Landsberg 2001: 4; Bekker 2007: 159; Crawford 1996; Marantis 1994; Murray 2004: 25, 43–44.
[125] Numbers are taken from compilations of uses of negative conditionality by Arts (2000: 423–26) and Hazelzet (2005: 4–5).
[126] Beall 2024a.

5.4 Post-Cold War Marginalization Deepens Cooperation

whose leader was facing pressure from Western governments to conduct multi-party elections. During the visit, Mandela challenged this Western pressure, asking "What right have the whites anywhere to teach us about democracy, when they executed those who asked for democracy during the time of colonial rule?"[127] In 1990, the OAU passed a resolution expressing concern at the "increasing tendency to impose conditionalities of a political nature for assistance to Africa."[128] In an address in 1994, the President of the ACP Council expressed concern that "punitive measures" for addressing human rights problems can be "dysfunctional."[129] In 1995, the President of Namibia, a country with a fairly positive record of human rights and democratic governance, was asked about human rights conditions on aid, to which he replied: "We do not want to be subjected to this kind of thing by foreigners ... for them to impose their foreign policy because of aid is deplorable."[130]

These protests had little effect. In August 1991, the Vice President of the ACP-EEC Joint Assembly, a representative of the ACP, stated simply that "it is a fact" that aid was being linked to political conditions.[131] Similarly, in 1993 an ACP trade official noted that donor governments "have decided" to condition aid on human rights.[132] A news report on Lomé renegotiations in 1993 suggested that adding a suspension clause would simply be "rubberstamp[ing]" the policy.[133]

As this unfolded, African states deepened their engagement with the regional human rights system. Between 1989 and 1992, 15 states ratified the African Charter. Members became much more willing to cooperate with the African Commission and to allow it to conduct on-site investigations, including under the Special Rapporteur system and the commission's promotional mandate, as well as fact-finding missions in response to individual complaints of human rights violations.[134]

African leaders also began to act on cases of human rights violations in their intergovernmental bodies. In 1991, for the first time, member states issued decisions and resolutions on internal human rights violations.[135] That year, they began to publicly release the African

---

[127] Alcindor 2003.
[128] OAU Assembly of Heads of State and Government 1990.
[129] European Commission 1994: II. [130] European Commission 1995: 35.
[131] European Commission 1991: 53. [132] European Commission 1993: 70.
[133] McKenzie 1993. [134] Viljoen 2007: 344–48.
[135] OAU Assembly of Heads of State and Government 1993; OAU Council of Ministers 1991, 1992, 1994a, 1994b.

Commission's annual reports. At the time, these reports did not contain any controversial content, but in 1994, the Commission began to include its findings on individual human rights violations in the annual report that it submitted to the OAU, and African governments continued to release the reports to the public.[136] A treaty establishing the African Court on Human and Peoples' Rights was adopted in 1998 and came into effect in 2004. In the late 1990s, leaders institutionalized the responsibility to protect in the reconstituted African Union.[137]

Significant subregional institutionalization of human rights also emerged at this time, with states revising the statutes of their subregional organizations to include human rights in their mandates. The Southern African Development Community did so in 1992; ECOWAS, the Common Market for Eastern and Southern Africa, and the Economic Community of Central African States in 1993; and the Central African Economic and Monetary Community and the West African Economic and Monetary Union in 1994.

Post-Cold War developments in Africa highlight the two sides of self-determination, as well as the different consequences of its absence. On the one hand, African political actors have often been unable to domestically affirm or meaningfully participate in the design and implementation of human rights enforcement being carried out in Africa. On the other hand, they have struggled to influence global decision-making and elicit action in cases where they *do* want global support.[138] The Rwandan genocide was a painful illustration of the second of these two dynamics. African leaders and the OAU Secretary General pleaded with the UN Security Council to take action, pushing to expand the size of the UN peacekeeping mission and offering African troops at a time when Western states were attempting to shrink the mission or remove it altogether.[139] This was immediately followed by a similar failure to fulfill requests for a UN peacekeeping force in response to the 1994 genocide in neighboring Burundi.[140]

Scholars have characterized post-Cold War changes in African regional governance as a shift in regional norms from "non-interference

---

[136] Mutua 2000: 19–20; Odinkalu and Christensen 1998: 277.
[137] African Union 2000: 4(h).   [138] Beall 2022.
[139] International Panel of Eminent Personalities 2000: 15.11, 15.13, 15.88, 15.89–91; Muyangwa and Vogt 2000: 11–12.
[140] Murray 2004: 11–12.

to non-indifference" following post-Cold War liberalization and in the aftermath of the Rwandan genocide.[141] Of course, these developments played an important role in accelerating efforts by African states to pursue regional cooperation to address human rights. However, as this chapter highlights, the genocide occurred amid changes that were already underway, accelerating and deepening these changes rather than initiating a reorientation toward the norm of non-interference. By the time the genocide began, there was no question for African leaders as to whether intervention was an appropriate response. The question was whether the rest of the world could be counted on to respond to their calls to do something, and the unambiguous answer from Rwanda was that they could not. Increased regional cooperation was, in part, a recognition of this reality.

---

[141] For just three of many examples, see Apuuli (2012), Kioko (2003: 819), and Williams (2007).

6 | Short-Circuiting Regional Institutions in the Middle East

Where the 1970s and 1980s marked a period of dramatic change in the use of regional organizations and attitudes toward the norm of non-interference in Latin America and Africa, the Middle East followed a very different trajectory. There was, in fact, a flurry of human rights activity within the Middle Eastern regional organization, the League of Arab States, in the late 1960s and early 1970s. In September 1968, Middle Eastern leaders held the first Arab Conference on Human Rights, at which they formed the Permanent Arab Committee on Human Rights. This was an intergovernmental human rights body that was mandated to promote human rights, bring about Arab self-rule in Palestine, and encourage ratification of human rights instruments by Arab League member states. In 1968, Arab leaders called for a human rights charter to be drafted, and in 1970, the Council of the Arab League established a Committee of Experts that they tasked with drafting a regional human rights declaration, which was completed and sent to states in 1971.

The timing of these initiatives was fortuitous. They took place right as transnational advocacy networks were about to reshape beliefs about human rights and sovereignty and right as Western governments were about to assume the role of global enforcers of human rights. Yet, these initiatives did not get caught up in the wave of changes sweeping the world. Instead, they came to a sudden halt. The proposal for a human rights charter and declaration petered out, and the Arab Permanent Committee on Human Rights focused its attention almost exclusively on Palestinian independence in the coming decades, rather than on the human rights practices of the organization's member states. In the late 1970s and early 1980s, a new series of reforms was proposed within the Arab League, aimed at making human rights a formal part of the organization's mandate, but these too were unsuccessful. It wasn't until 1994 that a regional human rights charter was adopted. The charter, however, was roundly criticized by non-governmental organizations, and only one state even signed it.¹

As global norms around sovereignty and human rights transformed in the 1970s and 1980s, in the Middle East, leaders remained firmly committed to the norm of non-interference. In the Arab League, no institutions with any conceivably interventionist authority were created until the early 2000s. Even these lacked basic powers associated with effective and legitimate enforcement of human rights.

A common explanation for the unwillingness of Middle Eastern governments to delegate meaningful authority to enforce human rights is that there is a lack of coherence or overlap between human rights and regional norms. The Middle East has often been portrayed as particularly unreceptive to human rights. Since the end of the Cold War, it has frequently been at the center of debates over cultural relativism.² The individualism of human rights, it has been argued, clashes with Islam's emphasis on duties of the individual to their community, while the secular nature of human rights conflicts with the divine nature of religious belief.³ This picture is, of course, contested, with many pointing out its reliance on a non-existent internal unity for both Islam and the Middle East, while underestimating the degree of overlap and compatibility between human rights and Islam.⁴

In fact, the apparent clash between religious belief and human rights was not nearly as pronounced in the early years of institutionalizing human rights.⁵ For example, while Saudi Arabian representative Jamil Baroody objected to the provision on the freedom of religion in the Universal Declaration on Human Rights, he did so because he believed it had been drafted in a way that unfairly targeted religion. While specifying that all people have the freedom of thought, conscience, and religion, the provision singled out only the right to change one's religion.⁶ Of the Middle Eastern states that were independent in 1948, only Baroody withheld support for adopting the declaration.

Another common explanation is the persistence of authoritarianism in the Middle East, with authoritarian governments using sovereignty norms to protect themselves at the expense of human rights. Yet, major

---

¹ Rishmawi 2005.   ² Bielefeldt 1995; Chase and Hamzawy 2008.
³ Halliday 1995.
⁴ An-Na'im 2006; Chase and Hamzawy 2008; Halliday 1995; Waltz 2004.
⁵ Morsink 1999: 24–25; Waltz 2004: 819–22.
⁶ Morsink 1999: 25–26; Waltz 2004: 815.

moves toward the regional institutionalization of human rights in both Latin America and Africa occurred at especially low moments for democracy in these two regions, and they happened with the active involvement of authoritarian governments. There were also moves toward political liberalization in several Arab League member states in the late 1980s and early 1990s that failed to produce more successful institutionalization of human rights. At these moments, and more generally, pressure from the West has aimed to ensure that governments in the Middle East are friendly to Western interests. As Amaney Jamal has demonstrated, this has often run counter to and had the effect of undermining domestic liberalizing forces.[7]

I show in this chapter that an important reason for the lack of reorientation toward human rights and sovereignty in the Middle East is the absence of the kind of concerted economic pressure experienced by governments in Latin America and Africa on governments' human rights practices. From the beginning of the Cold War, the Middle East was viewed as a region of high geostrategic importance for both the US and Western Europe. At the very moment that human rights were becoming a prominent global issue that Western governments were incorporating into their economic relations with the Global South, the Middle East became more central to the economic and strategic interests of Western governments and less vulnerable to Western economic pressure. Because of this, human rights were simply not prioritized in Western relations with the Middle East.

This ambivalence on the part of Western states toward political liberalization in the Middle East is an important reason why regional human rights institutions fall far short of those in Latin America and Africa. Western governments have consistently prioritized stability and the maintenance of friendly relations in the Middle East, even while utilizing the language of freedom and human rights. As a result, there has been no reason for the members of the Arab League to move to give up the protection offered by the norm of non-interference. This, combined with the cynical use of human rights rhetoric by Western governments, has made it hard to shake the associations that have formed between human rights and Western pressure. It has made human rights advocates within the region vulnerable to charges that they are puppets of the West.

---

[7] Jamal 2012.

6.1 Pan-Arabism and the Consolidation of Non-Interference

Regional cooperation in the Middle East shares many traits with cooperation in other regions of the Global South, having arisen in response to many of the same kinds of pressure and pursued similar goals.[8] Chief among these goals was resistance to external control and domination. Early regional cooperation was aimed at gaining independence and, upon doing so, ensuring respect for their sovereignty.[9]

These projects manifested as Pan-Arabism, which emerged at a time when much of the Middle East was under Ottoman rule and gained traction during World War I, with a rising Arab national consciousness responding to a weakening Ottoman empire.[10] An important moment in the rise of Pan-Arabism was the 1916 Arab Revolt, which aimed to free Arab states from Ottoman rule and to establish a single, unified Arab state.[11]

Western leaders supported Arab nationalism because of its potential to internally undermine the Ottomans during World War I. They promised to recognize the independence of Arab states once the war was over. However, in secret, the British and French governments made a deal to carve up the Ottoman Empire's Middle Eastern colonies as part of the Sykes–Picot Agreement. Once the war ended, rather than independence, Middle Eastern colonies were placed under the control of France and Great Britain through the mandate system of the League of Nations. This added the territories of what are now Iraq, Syria, Jordon, Lebanon, Palestine, and Israel to the European powers' other colonies in the wider Middle East, which included the Gulf peninsula and Northern Africa.[12]

During the inter-war years Arab nationalism continued to grow, having now evolved to push for an end to Western imperialism. Many political leaders within this region conceived of Pan-Arab unity as the answer to the problem of external domination, now by the

---

[8] This section is heavily indebted to the work of Michael Barnett for the discussion of the development of regional order in the Middle East, the clash between sovereignty norms and Pan-Arabism, and how these were eventually resolved in favor of state sovereignty and non-interference.
[9] Barnett 1995b: 480; Barnett and Solingen 2007: 193; Khadduri 1946a: 756–57; King 1978: 108–9.
[10] Barnett 1993: 280.   [11] Almakky 2015: 103; Karsh and Karsh 1997: 267.
[12] Almakky 2015: 103–5; Barnett 1993: 281; Khadduri 1946b: 90; Al-Sayyid 1997: 27; Wright 1968: 5.

West.[13] In 1931, the World Islamic Congress was convened in Jerusalem, gathering together supporters of Pan-Arabism, including a number of nationalist leaders. As a result of the congress, they adopted the Pan-Arab Covenant which asserted the indivisibility of the "Arab Nation," the shared aim of "total independence," and the rejection of imperialism "in all its forms."[14] Pan-Arabism came to form an important part of Middle Eastern independence movements in the 1930s and 1940s, and during World War II, Arab nationalism and agitation for independence continued to grow.[15]

In the years leading up to their independence in the 1940s, some leaders favored creating a united Arab state and others favored inter-governmental cooperation among independent states.[16] Intergovernmentalism prevailed, and the Alexandria Protocols, adopted in 1944, and the Charter of the League of Arab States, adopted in 1945, affirmed the idea of Arab unity for the sake of "protect[ing]" or "safeguarding" their individual independence and sovereignty,[17] while affirming their existence as independent, sovereign states rather than a single Pan-Arab state.[18] They declared the importance of *eventual* political unification.[19]

The Arab League formally institutionalized individual sovereign statehood, but inter-state politics in the region continued to be characterized by clashes between conflicting ideals of Pan-Arabism, on the one hand, and state nationalism and territorial sovereignty, on the other.[20] This clash caused a great deal of intra-regional conflict and intervention between 1945 and 1967, with some leaders rejecting the legitimacy of the existence of separate sovereign states.[21]

Though there were disagreements over the appropriate regional order, leaders were generally united on the use of regional cooperation to limit interference from outside of the region. One important form regional collective action took was the coordination of efforts to remove European colonizing powers from the region.[22] At the time

---

[13] Barnett 1993: 281; Rubin 1991: 585–86.   [14] Porath 1986.
[15] Barnett 1993: 281, 284, 1995b: 493; Porath 1986.
[16] Barnett 1993, 1995b; Barnett and Solingen 2007.
[17] Alexandria Protocol 1944: Article 1; League of Arab States 1945: Article II.
[18] Barnett and Solingen 2007: 188–90; MacDonald 1965: 33–38.
[19] Barnett and Solingen 2007: 190, 193; Khadduri 1946b: 96–97.
[20] Barnett 1993: 284; Barnett 1995b: 495; Barnett and Solingen 2007: 189.
[21] Barnett 1993, 1995b.   [22] Boutros-Ghali 1979; MacDonald 1965: 94–96.

that the Arab League was formed in 1945, only seven out of what would eventually be twenty-two member states were independent. Within the Arab League, states advocated for the independence of majority-Arab territories that were still colonized.[23] They provided practical, financial, and military assistance to liberation movements, acted in the United Nations as spokespeople for these movements, and organized common positions on decolonization that they then advocated for at the UN.[24] Throughout this time, Palestinian independence was one of the main issues on which Arab states cooperated.[25]

Equally important was removing unwanted Western involvement and European troops from independent states.[26] Western activity in the Middle East was perceived by many as Western meddling and imperialism, and it was met with strong opposition. This activity included the creation of Israel by the British government in 1948, which turned it into a homeland for Europe's Jewish population in the aftermath of the Holocaust;[27] attempts by the US and Britain to create a NATO-type alliance with states in the region, resulting in the Baghdad Pact in 1955 that Iraq faced significant backlash for joining;[28] the Israeli–British–French invasion of Egypt in 1956 in response to Gamal Nasser's nationalization of the Suez Canal;[29] and the emergence of the US as the primary backer of Israel.[30] Some Arab leaders expressed the belief that the United States had secretly provided support to Israel during the 1967 Six-Day War, in which Egypt was defeated by Israel and which was regarded as a devastating and humiliating loss.[31] Even the government of Saudi Arabia, one of the earliest and most consistent allies of the West in the region, felt compelled by Arab nationalist sentiment to limit Western presence within its borders. This led the Saudi government to terminate a base agreement with the US in 1961.[32]

---

[23] MacDonald 1965: 64; Pogany 1986: 369; Salman 1986: 138.
[24] MacDonald 1965: 94–98; Salman 1986: 139.
[25] King 1978; MacDonald 1965: 82–94.
[26] MacDonald 1965: 64; Pogany 1986: 369; Salman 1986: 138.
[27] Barnett 1995b: 494; King 1978: 108–10.
[28] Barnett and Solingen 2007: 201–6; Podeh 1993.
[29] Podeh 1993: 92, 1996: 163.
[30] Khalidi 2009: 24; MacDonald 1965: 89; Newsom 1981: 301.
[31] Newsom 1981: 302–3, 307.   [32] Khalidi 2009: 15–16.

Socialist, non-aligned states were the loudest voices in objecting to what they characterized as Western imperialism.[33] Of these leaders, Egypt's Gamal Nasser was the most important. Though Egypt is part of both Africa and the Middle East and is a member of both the Arab League and the Organization of African Unity, Nasser gave his attention to the project of Arab unity and was one of the leaders of the movement in the 1950s and 1960s. While Nasser was in power, Egypt was the most influential member of the Arab League,[34] and bringing an end to Western imperialism was central to Nasser's Pan-Arab aims.[35] The Syrian Ba'athists and leaders in Algeria were also important critics of Western interference in the form of spheres of influence and outside domination.[36]

The norm of non-interference as it pertained to inter-state relations within the region took longer to consolidate. A regional order based on Pan-Arabism was permissive of interference, since it denied the legitimacy of states' independent existence.[37] However, the 1967 war represented a turning point for Pan-Arabism in the region.[38] In between the 1967 Six-Day War and the 1973 Yom Kippur War, when Arab states were again defeated by Israel, the idea that Arab lands should be united into a single territory became much less prominent. Arab nationalism continued to be an important political symbol, and Arab identity continued to bear importance for Arab leaders and citizens. However, strict sovereignty norms, including non-interference among Arab states, were consolidated at this time as a core, underlying principle of their regional order.[39] In other words, in the years right before the human rights breakthrough in the 1970s, the norm of non-interference became firmly consolidated.

Moves toward regionalizing human rights during this same time were limited. The mandate of the Arab League, as laid out in its charter as adopted in 1945, did not include human rights.[40] The first activities within the Arab League aimed at institutionalizing human rights occurred in the late 1960s, following the decision within the UN to hold a World Conference on Human Rights. The decision, adopted in 1966, prompted the members of the Arab League to organize their

---

[33] Barnett and Solingen 2007: 201–2; Nasser 1954; Özsu 2015.
[34] King 1978: 108, 110; Podeh 1993: 91; Rubin 1991: 536.
[35] James 2005; Podeh 1996. [36] Özsu 2015; Peretz 1965: 37.
[37] Barnett 1993, 1995b. [38] Barnett 1995b: 488–90; Khalidi 2009: 23–24.
[39] Barnett 1995b: 488–90. [40] League of Arab States 1945.

6.1 Pan-Arabism and Non-Interference

own participation in the conference, also to be held in 1968, and formed an *ad hoc* committee to develop a program for the Year of Human Rights.[41] In 1967, the Council of the Arab League created a second committee to organize the League's participation in the international conference and the Year of Human Rights.[42]

In 1967 and 1968, when the UN Commission on Human Rights began to debate an initiative for the creation of regional human rights commissions within the UN,[43] the Secretary General of the Arab League sent a communication stating that any regional human rights body should be housed within a regional organization.[44] Subsequent to this communication, at the 1968 Arab Conference on Human Rights, leaders created the Arab Permanent Committee on Human Rights and communicated this to the UN.[45]

The Arab Permanent Committee was not given any enforcement powers that would allow it to interfere in members' domestic affairs. It was tasked with promoting human rights, including through education and awareness raising, drafting human rights treaties, providing recommendations on human rights, and formulating common Arab positions on human rights.[46] The committee was also an intergovernmental body whose members were state representatives rather than human rights experts.[47] In practice, the Committee's activities focused almost exclusively on Palestine.[48]

In addition to a human rights commission, there were some moves toward creating regional human rights law. At the same 1968 conference, states instructed the newly formed Arab Permanent Committee to draft an Arab charter on human rights, though no such charter was produced.[49] A second attempt was made in May 1970, when the Arab

---

[41] Al-Midani 2002: 103.   [42] Al-Midani 2002: 103.
[43] Ouguergouz 2003: 27; Umozurike 1983: 903–4; UN Commission on Human Rights 1968a: 3. See Chapter 5.
[44] UN Commission on Human Rights 1968b.
[45] Sahraoui 2004: 346; UN Commission on Human Rights 1968b.
[46] An-Na'im 2001: 712; "Arab Permanent Committee on Human Rights" n.d.; Rishmawi 2008: D.8.
[47] Rishmawi 2008: C.3.
[48] An-Na'im 2001: 713; Pogany 1986: 371; Rishmawi 2008; Sahraoui 2004: 347.
[49] Al-Midani 2002: 106–7. There is some inconsistency in the reporting on when this happened. Rishmawi (2008: 2.17. Allam (2014: 41) writes that states gave this instruction to the Permanent Committee in 1969, while An-Na'im (2001: 712–13) marks September 1970 as the first time that a recommendation for drafting a regional human rights charter or declaration was made.

Permanent Committee recommended that the Arab League Council establish a committee of experts to prepare a human rights declaration. In response, in September 1970, the Council formed the committee of experts,[50] and in July 1971, the committee adopted a draft Declaration on the Rights of Citizens of Arab States and Countries. This draft was submitted to states for comment. Fewer than half of member states responded, and the responses that were received offered mixed reactions.[51] The declaration was not adopted.

Little else happened internally with respect to human rights during this time. There was no attention from Arab League member states to internal human rights practices of members. The Arab Permanent Committee on Human Rights proved to be so inconsequential that, during discussions of reforming the organization in the early 1980s, some state representatives suggested creating a human rights commission and had to be reminded that one already existed.[52]

6.2 A Different Kind of Interdependence Limits Economic Pressure

In the previous chapters, I detailed the economic enforcement of human rights faced by leaders in Latin America and Africa beginning in the 1970s and how this enforcement triggered efforts in these regions to accept interference within their regional organizations. These pressures did not arise in the Middle East. For both the United States and Western Europe, enforcing human rights in the Middle East was far more costly and difficult, becoming even more so in the 1970s. Western states had their own dependence on Arab League members, and because of this, enforcing human rights risked undermining Western governments' strategic and economic interests. Western governments also had fewer clear levers with which to enforce human rights, and even when leverage existed, as was the case with arms sales, Western governments chose not to make use of them.[53]

The Middle East has long been strategically and economically important to the West because of the presence of oil in the region and its location vis-à-vis Europe and the Soviet Union.[54] Early in the

---

[50] Al-Midani 2002: 106–7; Sahraoui 2004: 343.
[51] An-Na'im 2001: 713; Al-Midani 2002: 106–7.   [52] Chaabane 1982: 515–16.
[53] Blanton 2000.   [54] Khalidi 2009: 9.

6.2 A Different Kind of Interdependence

Cold War, Western states sought out more intensive security cooperation with states in the region. Examples of this include the NATO-like Baghdad Pact, the 1957 Eisenhower Doctrine, in which the US announced its support for any Middle Eastern government targeted by "overt armed aggression from any nation controlled by international communism," and the US alliance with Saudi Arabia that, by the 1950s, had taken on great importance for the US.[55]

From the 1950s to the 1970s, states in the Middle East had developed complicated entanglements with the West and the Soviet Union, and the high level of interest of the superpowers in the Middle East resulted in what has been termed the "Arab Cold War."[56] Socialist-leaning, anti-American, and non-aligned governments – including those of Egypt, Syria, and Iraq – developed ties with the Soviet Union. More conservative states – including Jordan, Tunisia, Morocco, Saudi Arabia, other Gulf states – collaborated with the US.[57] This connected the internal fighting within the region with larger Cold War hostilities between the US and the Soviet Union, with Egypt and Saudi Arabia representing the axis of the two camps. Historian Rashid Khalidi notes that this "provided opportunities for Middle Eastern 'clients' to extract support from their superpower patrons, which the latter sometimes were obliged to extend against the better judgement of key policymakers."[58]

In the 1970s, as human rights were entering into the foreign policies of Western states, global events deepened the strategic importance of the Middle East to Western governments, while simultaneously decreasing Middle Eastern economic dependence on the West. For both the United States and Western Europe, human rights had to compete with other important regional priorities, including maintaining access to oil and resolving the Arab–Israeli conflict. In 1973, after the defeat of Arab states in the Yom Kippur War, oil-producing Arab states initiated an oil boycott against Western states that they viewed as supporting Israel. They also halted much of their oil production. This resulted in an "oil shock," quadrupling oil prices and creating major oil shortages.[59] In part because of the effects of the Arab–Israeli conflict on access to oil and in part because of the perceived importance

---

[55] Barnett and Solingen 2007: 203–6; Khalidi 2009: 11–18; Podeh 1993: 92.
[56] Kerr 1965.   [57] Kerr 1965; Khalidi 2009: 18–21.   [58] Khalidi 2009: 18.
[59] Bicchi 2002: 4; Corbett 2013; Nonneman 2006: 59–60, 63.

of stability within the Middle East for the security of Western states, achieving peace in the Middle East became a priority for Western governments. Finally, beginning in the late 1960s and early 1970s, Western states became increasingly concerned with terrorism within the region.[60]

The pull of these competing priorities, and the effect it had on human rights policies and enforcement, was no less acute for the champion of human rights, Jimmy Carter, who made achieving peace in the Middle East one of his administration's main goals. In a 1978 memo by Anthony Lake, the Director of Policy Planning within the State Department, Lake noted that "we have not put primary emphasis on human rights considerations, in view of our other pressing interests, when deciding on arms sales or determining our approach to the area generally,"[61] and "our desire to move Arabs and Israelis toward a peace settlement and the importance of Mideast oil have kept arms sales high."[62] As one former US Ambassador to Libya wrote in 1981, "with no region in the world does a single issue so dominate the relationship ... as does the dispute with Israel in the Arab world."[63]

Far from using economic pressure to enforce human rights, the US government supported friendly authoritarian regimes.[64] This was evident in relations with Saudi Arabia. In 1979, Secretary of State Cyrus Vance requested Carter's approval for a $120 million sale to Saudi Arabia of air munitions, laser-guided bombs, and cluster bombs. In a memo to Carter, Vance provided an overview of the proposed sale, before noting without elaboration that the sale was "consistent with [Carter's] human rights policy and related legislation."[65] This was despite reports from the State Department of substantial human rights problems in Saudi Arabia[66] and what they characterized as the Saudi government's "lack of understanding of human rights."[67] Carter approved the sale.[68]

For European governments and the European Economic Community (EEC), the Middle East was also treated as far more politically and strategically important than other parts of the Global

---

[60] Bicchi 2002. [61] *FRUS* 2013: Document 105.
[62] *FRUS* 2013: Document 105. [63] Newsom 1981: 301.
[64] Baxter and Akbarzadeh 2012; Hamid 2011; Jamal 2012; Khalidi 2009: 18; Wang and Wang 2008.
[65] *FRUS* 2018a: Document 199. [66] *FRUS* 2018a: Document 143.
[67] *FRUS* 2018a: Document 154. [68] *FRUS* 2018a: Document 200.

South.[69] This difference is especially pronounced when comparing Western Europe's relations with the Middle East to those with African, Caribbean, and Pacific states. In the late 1960s and early 1970s, the EEC attempted to bring together its many bilateral treaties and relationships with Northern African, Middle Eastern, and Southern and Eastern European states into a single coherent policy with what they dubbed the "Mediterranean Group."[70] The "Global Mediterranean Policy," according to the EEC Development Commissioner, was intended to be equivalent to their Lomé relations with the African, Caribbean, and Pacific states, though the plan never came to fruition.[71]

In 1974, the European Community and the Arab League initiated the Euro-Arab Dialogue with the goal of increasing political cooperation. The issues to be made part of the dialogue were quickly narrowed down to just economic development, which was seen as the only topic that was not too sensitive. Little happened with the dialogue, and the Arab states abandoned it in 1979.[72] There is no evidence that European governments tried at any point to introduce human rights into discussions for either of these initiatives, whereas human rights came to dominate discussions over Lomé in 1977.

The nature of interdependence between the Middle East and the West was quite different – far more symmetric – than with either Latin America or Africa. Both the US and Western Europe were heavily dependent on Middle Eastern oil, and the rising prices and resulting oil shortages put a great deal of domestic pressure on politicians in the West.[73] The problem of oil access was exacerbated further by the Iranian revolution in 1979, which removed from power a reliably friendly government in the Middle East and an important source of US oil, and resulted in another global increase in oil prices.[74]

The wealth of many Middle Eastern countries also increased by an incredible amount in the 1960s and 1970s.[75] The starkest example was Saudi Arabia, whose GDP, by one estimate, increased by 1,000 percent

---

[69] Tsoukalis 1977: 426.   [70] Albinyana and Fernández 2018; Tsoukalis 1977.
[71] This relationship is discussed in detail in Chapter 6.
[72] Albinyana and Fernández 2018; de la Serre 1980.
[73] Albinyana and Fernández 2018; Bicchi 2002: 4; Corbett 2013; Nonneman 2006: 59–60, 63.
[74] Jones 2012; Sneh 2008: 171, 178.   [75] Alnasrawi 1987; Owen 1981.

between 1970 and 1977.[76] Anthony Lake noted that the lack of human rights attention toward the region was exacerbated by the fact that "Few of them are recipients of economic assistance."[77] Though there were a number of Middle Eastern states that were, in fact, quite weak, unimportant, and dependent on external support, these states tended to develop dependence on other wealthy states within the region.[78] As noted above, where Middle Eastern governments were dependent on the West – on Western arms, in particular – the strategic importance of the region kept Western leaders from exploiting this dependence for human rights purposes.

6.3 Regional Authority Remains an Authoritarian Survival Strategy

Leaders in the Middle East did not face a credible threat that human rights would affect their relations with the West and had no reason to believe that economic pressure was forthcoming. In the absence of such pressure, members of the Arab League refrained from making any significant changes in their stance on the norm of non-interference in the 1970s or 1980s. This continued to be the case after the Cold War. Though governments in the Middle East did begin to encounter new human rights pressures following the end of the Cold War and the onset of the Global War on Terror, these continued to be balanced out by the strategic importance of the Middle East.

This pressure did lead, finally, to institutionalization of human rights, as leaders began to belatedly engage with them through the creation of institutions that looked much more like the kinds of legally binding and interventionist mechanisms that have come to be expected of good human rights enforcement. However, as Shadi Hamid notes, Western governments' interest in human rights in the Middle East continued to be limited by their preference for stability. As a consequence, regional institutions were aimed at deflecting outside attention and pressure, with leaders "dutifully [creating] the appearance of reform, rather than its substance."[79]

---

[76] Owen 1981.   [77] *FRUS* 2013: Document 105.
[78] Alnasrawi 1987: 362–63.
[79] Hamid 2011: 20. See also van Hüllen (2015), who argues that the Arab League's human rights mechanisms were a way for leaders in the region to get the West to "leave [them] alone."

6.3.1 Reversing Course after the Human Rights Breakthrough

There had been notable movement toward regional institutionalization of human rights in the Arab League in the late 1960s and early 1970s. The timing of these developments had occurred just as human rights were about to emerge as an important global issue and as transnational human rights advocacy networks were forming. Yet, rather than bringing about additional regional institutionalization of human rights, interest within the region in institutionalizing human rights mostly died out at this time, with initiatives to create a human rights declaration and a human rights charter dropped.[80]

Beginning in 1979, there had been a minor resurgence in interest in human rights institutions within the region, but these also failed. At the Arab League summit in November 1979, the members officially called for the League's charter to be amended and for a human rights charter to be drafted.[81] These initiatives were part of larger moves to reform the Arab League after Egypt's peace agreement with Israel rattled the region.

By 1982, the amended charter had been drafted and circulated. The draft included, among other changes, the addition of human rights to the organization's objectives, which were amended to include "work[ing] toward ensuring that Arab States guarantee to man in the Arab world his security and all his rights and to enable him to practice his fundamental freedoms."[82] The draft also tasked the Council of Arab Foreign Ministers with "protect[ing] human rights and freedoms" and "support[ing] the Arab Commission on Human Rights."[83] At the meeting at which the amended charter was discussed, some states also floated the suggestion to create a regional human rights commission and were reminded that a commission already existed.[84] The amended charter was never adopted.

There were other moves toward creating a regional human rights charter. The Arab Permanent Committee completed a new draft of a charter in 1982, which they sent to member states. It was considered by the Council of the League in 1983. However, the decision was made to

[80] Saksena 1982: 9.
[81] Al-Ajaji 1990: 35; Chaabane 1982: 510–11; Al-Midani 2002: 107; Pogany 1986: 372.
[82] Al-Ajaji 1990: 36; Chaabane 1982: 515–16; Pogany 1986: 372.
[83] Al-Ajaji 1990: 36.   [84] Chaabane 1982: 515–16.

hold off on adopting a charter. The reason given was that another international organization with overlapping membership, the Organization of Islamic Cooperation, was in the process of adopting the Islamic Declaration on Human Rights and Duties.[85]

There were also no efforts to collectively address human rights violations committed within the region. In 1979, Amnesty International released country reports detailing human rights violations in Syria, Iraq, Sudan, Egypt, Libya, and Tunisia, but these did not receive any attention from the Arab League. The Arab Permanent Committee on Human Rights remained focused on the status of Arab refugees in non-Arab League member countries, the problems of racial discrimination against Arab immigrants residing outside of the region, and the rights of Palestinians, both in terms of the collective right to self-determination and violations of individual rights by the Israeli government.[86]

Although they did not accept regional authority over human rights at this time, some rhetoric nevertheless emerged asserting regional authority in a similar manner as seen from Latin American and African officials but without any corresponding changes in regional institutions or norms. In debates in 1977 over the possibility of creating a UN High Commissioner for Human Rights, the representative of Saudi Arabia suggested that "co-ordination between national committees ... and the regional committees which already existed would be of more benefit to the cause of human rights than any United Nations High Commissioner for Human Rights."[87] Similarly, in response to a 1978 proposal to institutionalize the practice of creating working groups to study human rights violations, the same representative pushed back by asserting that "[w]e have regional

---

[85] Allam 2014: 41; An-Na'im 2001: 713; Sahraoui 2004: 343. There is an unusual amount of confusion regarding which years this second initiative occurred. Contrary to the three cited sources that state that the charter was drafted in 1982 and sent to states in 1983, Al-Midani (2002: 107), Rishmawi (2008: 2.b), and the International Commission of Jurists (1996: 57) all state that the charter was drafted in 1985 and sent to states in 1986. One possible explanation for the discrepancy is that, as per An-Na'im (2001: 713–14) and Sahraoui (2004: 343), in 1986, a charter was drawn up on the initiative of a group of experts from Arab countries in a project that was unaffiliated with state governments or the Arab League. In any case, the outcome of the process was the same in each of these accounts.

[86] Al-Ajaji 1990: 117.   [87] UN General Assembly 1977l: Para. 40.

commissions of human rights" that are "dealing with violations of human rights as seriously as we can" and criticizing the proposal as a "ploy to interfere in states' internal affairs."[88]

6.3.2 The Cold War's End Brings Late, Limited Pressure on Human Rights

Following the end of the Cold War, Western interest in promoting human rights expanded dramatically. The United States' new status as the sole superpower created new opportunities to pursue human rights in ways that had been limited by Cold War politics, and Western governments became more assertive with their use of coercive means for enforcing human rights, including the use of economic conditions and humanitarian intervention.

One effect of this shift was that human rights increasingly came to be used as a justification for US foreign policy in the Middle East. A significant example was the 1991 invasion of Iraq, which the US government justified in large part by recourse to the language of human rights, emphasizing Saddam Hussein's brutality.[89] Policy aims, however, continued to be deeply shaped by US security interests. This problem was lamented by Aryeh Neier, the co-founder of Human Rights Watch and, at the time, the president of the international NGO the Open Society Institute. Neier wrote in 1996 of a "new double standard" in the enforcement of human rights in which "geopolitically or economically significant" states were frequently spared extensive human rights pressures.[90] Neier outlined a situation in which, "[t]ime and again," human rights organizations have noted the "disjunction between what is said in [the State Department human rights] country reports and US policies toward those countries."[91] This was by no means a new double standard, though it did manifest differently after the Cold War ended.

Human rights remained a lower priority for the United States compared to terrorism and the Arab-Palestinian peace process. Because the latter was such a high priority, in eliciting assistance in the peace process, the US would sometimes opt to ignore human rights concerns

---

[88] UN General Assembly 1978a: Para. 220–23.
[89] Dietrich 2006: 274; Labonski and Parker 1991: 155–56.   [90] Neier 1996.
[91] Neier 1996: 99.

for states that they had previously labeled as supporters of terrorism. This was the case when the US government sought out the help of Syrian president Hafez al-Assad, at which point they quieted human rights criticisms of the Syrian government.[92]

Political liberalization within the region remained a lower priority than US security. When, in the late 1980s and early 1990s, liberalization in a number of member states of the Arab League led to the growing power of Islamist political groups, Western governments retreated from their pro-democracy positions. The most notorious example occurred in Algeria, following the democratic elections of the Islamic Salvation Front, which the Algerian military annulled. Western governments did not become involved to urge or pressure the military to reinstate the democratic results, and US Secretary of State James Baker later said that it was the US's decision not to "live with" the election "because we felt that the radical fundamentalists' views were so averse to what we believe in and what we support, and to what we understood the national interests of the United States to be."[93]

Western Europe also continued to downplay human rights in their relations with the Middle East, though there was eventually more of a concerted effort to integrate human rights into their relations. Nevertheless, European policy within the European Community (beginning in 1992, the European Union) and the bilateral relations of many European governments remained focused on regional stability.[94] This was viewed as especially important given the proximity of Europe to the Middle East and, as a result, its exposure to refugee and migrant flows and to terrorism. European states were also concerned that the Middle East peace process would be affected by instability.[95]

By 1990, language on human rights had been incorporated into institutions governing relations between the European Community and Latin America; East and Central Europe; and the African, Caribbean, and Pacific group of states. However, it was not made a part of the European Community's "Renovated Mediterranean Policy," adopted in December 1990. Aid to the region was not only given without consideration of human rights, but there was also much

---

[92] Neier 1996: 96.   [93] Hamid 2011: 25.   [94] Pace 2009.
[95] de Perini 2020: 446; Pace 2009: 41.

more of it. Over the course of the 1990s, EU aid to the Middle East came to exceed aid to Latin America, Asia, and the ACP states.[96]

This lack of emphasis on human rights by European governments clashed with the European Parliament's interest in human rights. In 1992, the European Parliament exercised their power of assent, which allows the parliament to veto association agreements between the European Union and non-member states, to block the adoption of new aid packages for Morocco and Syria on human rights grounds. These actions were strongly opposed by European governments.[97]

Western European leaders remained divided over making human rights a core part of their relations with the Middle East as they expanded the scope of their relations with the region. The 1995 Barcelona Process, aimed at strengthening relations between the two regions and increasing the stability of the Mediterranean region, did include language on human rights and democracy in its establishing Barcelona Declaration, though this was a non-binding document and no mechanisms aimed at enforcing or promoting human rights were established.[98] European governments separately moved to ensure that political reform did not cause short-term instability in the region and preferred to press "discreetly" for domestic political change.[99]

Though human rights did make their way into Western relations with the Middle East in the 1990s, any pressure applied by Western governments was limited, and it was consistently tempered by the Middle East's strategic importance.[100] This produced half-hearted advances toward the creation of regional human mechanisms within the Arab League.

The 1990s was, in fact, a time of declining relevance of the Arab League. In the 1980s, governments had boycotted meetings and increasingly shifted their regional interactions to subregional organizations. During the 1990s, only two Arab League summits were held, and a 1995 celebration of the 50th anniversary of the organization was attended by a single head of state – the host of the country holding it.[101] In spite of this, the process of adopting an Arab Charter on

---

[96] Youngs 2002: 40, 49. [97] Youngs 2002: 40, 49.
[98] Final Declaration of the Barcelona Euro-Mediterranean Ministerial Conference 1995.
[99] Youngs 2002: 42–43. [100] Ottaway and Carothers 2004: 4.
[101] Barnett and Solingen 2007: 209; Dakhlallah 2012: 406; Maksoud 1995: 589.

Human Rights within the Arab League was revived in 1992 by the Arab Permanent Committees on Human Rights and the League's Permanent Legal Committee, which approved a new draft in 1993.[102] The Arab Council adopted the charter in September 1994.[103] According to one account of the meeting, a delegate from Egypt expressly described the charter as a shield against outside pressures.[104]

The charter sat dormant after its adoption, receiving no ratifications and only one signature, from the government of Iraq.[105] Nothing about the circumstances surrounding its adoption indicates any real intention to compromise on the norm of non-interference. On top of states' unwillingness to so much as sign the charter, its adoption occurred alongside the emergence of arguments for cultural relativism by Arab League member states and growing assertions that human rights were a form of Western imperialism.[106]

The mechanisms that were created fell far short of basic external expectations of effectiveness and legitimacy. In terms of content, the 1994 Arab Charter on Human Rights included most of the same rights as other existing human rights treaties.[107] Its shortcoming were in its permissiveness toward derogating from human rights commitments. All human rights treaties allow states to deviate from or suspend some of their obligations under some circumstances, but most do not allow states to derogate under any circumstances from core rights like the right to life and the prohibition against torture.

By contrast, the 1994 Arab Charter permitted derogation from all rights. It also allowed for derogation under an extremely wide range of circumstances, including "where prescribed by law and considered necessary to protect national and economic security, or public order, or public health, or morals, or the rights and freedoms of others" as well as "in times of public emergencies."[108] In other words, torture could be permissible where it was required for upholding public health or morals.

The 1994 charter also fell short of expectations when it came to enforcement. The charter created a new Arab Human Rights Committee, distinct from the intergovernmental Arab Permanent

---

[102] An-Na'im 2001: 714.　[103] International Commission of Jurists 1996: 57.
[104] An-Na'im 2001: 715.　[105] Sahraoui 2004: 339.
[106] Halliday 1995: 152.　[107] Al-Midani et al. 2006: 148.
[108] League of Arab States 1994: Article 4(A) and 4(B).

6.3 Regional Authority and Authoritarian Survival 165

Committee on Human Rights that was established in 1968. This new committee would be made up of human rights experts working in their individual capacity. However, the only power it was given was to receive and comment on reports by states. The Committee could also issue inquiries to states in response to their reports.[109] Finally, the Committee could hold meetings in member states, which, notably, was the basis for the authority of the Organization of American States to carry out in-country visits. The crucial shortcoming of the committee was that it could receive neither individual nor state communications of human rights violations, and it had no investigatory powers beyond examining reports provided by the states. In any case, the Committee was never set up.

6.3.3 The Global War on Terror and the Acceptance of Regional Institutions

It was only after the onset of the Global War on Terror that the leaders of the Arab League finally set up new regional human rights institutions. For both the US and Western Europe, the patterns of subsuming human rights to other considerations in the immediate post-Cold War years were no less pronounced following the September 11 terrorist attacks, though relations between Middle East and the West, and the US in particular, were greatly altered by the 2003 invasion of Iraq.

During the War on Terror, human rights provided an important rhetorical justification for US intervention in the Middle East.[110] In 2002, US Secretary of Defense Donald Rumsfeld asserted that "the War on Terrorism is a war for human rights."[111] Similarly, in a November 2003 speech to the National Endowment on Democracy, George W. Bush announced his administration's "forward strategy for freedom in the Middle East," noting that "Sixty years of Western nations excusing and accommodating the lack of freedom in the Middle East did nothing to make us safe – because in the long run, stability cannot be purchased at the expense of liberty."[112] For leaders in the Middle East, the threat of US military intervention, justified with rhetoric on freedom, was very real.

[109] League of Arab States 1994: Article 41(1)–(3).
[110] Dalacoura 2005; Ottaway and Carothers 2004: 2–3.
[111] Quoted in Brown 2004: 460.
[112] Quoted in Hamid 2011: 23. See also Dalacoura 2005: 964.

Despite their rhetoric, both the US and Europe continued to prioritize regional stability, national security concerns, and the existence of friendly, secular governments.[113] Success in the War on Terror required the cooperation of friendly governments, and this was prioritized over human rights.[114] The US would accept crackdowns on internal opposition groups where doing so was justified as counterterrorism.[115] As in the post-Cold War period, interest in political liberalization in any form was limited by an unwillingness to accept Islamic political movements, many of which were very popular domestically.[116] Where governments pursued human rights in their relations with the Middle East, contemporary commentary noted that the concern for stability led to a preference for "gradualism"[117] in reforms and "evolution rather than revolution."[118]

The next move to create regional human rights institutions occurred in this context. In January 2001, the Arab Permanent Committee on Human Rights issued a recommendation for the 1994 human rights charter to be revised.[119] In decisions adopted in March 2001 and September 2002, the Arab League Council accepted the recommendation, though without actually initiating the revision.[120] It was only during a Council meeting on March 24, 2003, a meeting which took place five days after the start of the US invasion of Iraq, that states actually adopted a resolution and set into motion the creation of a new regional human rights charter.[121]

The charter was drafted by the Arab Permanent Committee on Human Rights in June and October that year. In a notable departure from previous drafting efforts, modifications of the draft were made based on recommendations from an expert group that was set up by the UN Office of the High Commissioner on Human Rights.[122] The charter was formally adopted in May 2004. As drafted, it established a new regional human rights commission named the "Expert Human

---

[113] Baxter and Akbarzadeh 2012; Carothers 2003; Chase and Hamzawy 2008: 9; Esposito and Piscatori 1991; Hamid 2011; Jamal 2012; Wang and Wang 2008.
[114] Ottaway and Carothers 2004: 4.   [115] Dietrich 2006: 289.
[116] Brand 1998: xiii–xiv; Hamid 2011: 21–23.
[117] Hamid 2011: 20. See also Ottaway and Carothers (2004: 3).
[118] Brumberg 2003: 3.   [119] Rishmawi 2008: 2.18; Sahraoui 2004: 339–40 n4.
[120] Rishmawi 2005: 362; Sahraoui 2004: 339–40 n4.
[121] Rishmawi 2005: 363 n7; Zerrougui 2008: 8–9.
[122] Rishmawi 2005: 363; Sahraoui 2004: 340–41; Zerrougui 2008.

Rights Committee."[123] Unlike the previous charter, the 2004 charter was ratified and, in 2008, came into effect. This represented a significant change, with members of the Arab League dropping their rhetorical opposition to interventionist human rights enforcement.

The 2004 charter was regarded as an improvement over the 1994 charter. Unlike the earlier version, it excludes many rights from derogation.[124] The authority given to the Expert Human Rights Committee was also an improvement on the committee created by the 1994 charter. Like the earlier committee, the members of the Expert Committee are to be persons with competence in human rights working in their individual capacity. They receive reports from states on their progress implementing the charter. Unlike the earlier committee, the Expert Committee is authorized to consider the state reports in public, and to prepare public comments on state reporting which should be "disseminate[d] widely."[125] At the same time, the committee cannot receive complaints of human rights violations, even from member states, or carry out investigations in countries where human rights violations are alleged to be taking place.

The final piece of the Arab League's human rights system is the Arab Court on Human Rights. The court was proposed by king of Bahrain in 2012, in the midst of his efforts to resist being forced out of power during the Arab Spring protests, and it was adopted by states in 2014.[126] Unlike the Expert Committee, the court can receive human rights complaints from states, and the statute also allows states to make a declaration in which they allow "one or more NGOs" to be accredited by governments to submit complaints.[127]

On paper, the Arab Court of Human Rights has the most extensive, interventionist power. It can receive and make findings on complaints of human rights violations and issue legally binding decisions on the basis of their findings. However, the court's primary competence allows only complaints by states. The separate declaration to allow the court to receive complaints from accredited NGOs allows states to pick and choose which NGOs can do so. Both conditions seriously

---

[123] League of Arab States 2004.
[124] League of Arab States 2004: Article 4; Rishmawi 2005: 364; Zerrougui 2008.
[125] League of Arab States 2004: Article 48.
[126] An-Na'im 2001: 714; International Commission of Jurists 2015; Rishmawi 2005: 362.
[127] League of Arab States 2014: Article 19.

limit access to the court.[128] To date, only Saudi Arabia has ratified the protocol establishing the court.

6.4 International Actors and the Undermining of Regional Human Rights

The initial breakthrough of human rights in the 1970s and 1980s did not bring any credible threats of Western human rights enforcement in the Middle East. After the Cold War, and even after the start of the War on Terror, the threat of intervention by the US was rhetorically tied to human rights. However, in reality, Western states continued to prioritize terrorism, stability, access to oil, and Middle Eastern peace. Throughout this time, the imposition of human rights enforcement was limited by relations between the Middle East and Western states which became far more symmetric in the 1970s compared to other regions in the Global South, a difference which has only become more pronounced in subsequent decades.

In the absence of costly pressures to engage differently with human rights, regional institutions appeared much later and have been designed in ways that are far less challenging to governments than those in Latin American and Africa. Rather than accepting real, challenging authority, the creation of regional institutions remained a strategy of authoritarian regime survival in which governments hide behind weak regional institutions. An important reason for this is that, at the moment Middle Eastern leaders were on the verge of creating more challenging mechanisms, they became suddenly, acutely aware that human rights could be a real threat. Regional human rights initiatives within the Arab League that had emerged in the late 1960s thus came to a halt in the early 1970s when confronted with the human rights movement of the 1970s.

The fact that the members of the League of Arab States have remained more uniformly authoritarian than other regions must form part of an understanding of the development of human rights mechanisms within the Middle East. Yet, in line with other research that examines how international actors can undermine domestic liberalization, the narrative presented in this chapter suggests that the persistence of authoritarianism in the region, rather than simply a cause of

---

[128] International Commission of Jurists 2015.

ineffectual human rights institutions, may be an outcome of external forces that both undermine domestic liberalizing forces and encourage the idea that human rights are a Western concept being foisted upon other parts of the world as a cover for political or ideological motives. This dynamic has made human rights promotion difficult for actors within the region, who must contend with charges that they are puppets of the West.[129] High levels of authoritarianism and an absence of effective human rights institutions may thus be related to one another and to international factors in a more complicated way than is often recognized.

[129] Chase and Hamzawy 2008: 12–13; Dwyer 1991.

7 Regional Authority and Self-Determination in International Politics

What can a study of the origins and design of regional human rights institutions, one that occurred primarily in the 1970s and 1980s, contribute to international relations theory more broadly? What can it tell us about international politics today? Though this book is primarily a historical study, a fuller understanding of the reasons that leaders in the Global South have empowered their regional organizations and a recognition of the importance of self-determination has wider implications, including for contemporary politics. To the extent that self-determination was not fully realized with decolonization, it will likely continue to be an important motivation for states and their citizens, as well as a goal of their international relations.

Self-determination, as it relates to the international system and relations between states, continues to be an important and under-explored goal of states in the international system. After receding in the immediate post-Cold War years, explicit demands for self-determination have re-emerged and now form an important part of attempts to reshape the international order and reform international institutions. In 2001, the UN General Assembly adopted a resolution calling for the creation of a "democratic and equitable international order." A key element of this order is "[t]he right of all peoples to self-determination, by virtue of which they can freely determine their political status and freely pursue their economic, social and cultural development." The resolution also calls for the "promotion ... of transparent, democratic, just and accountable international institutions ... through the implementation of the principles of full and equal participation in their respective decision-making mechanisms."[1]

This resolution has become an annual item on the General Assembly's agenda, and voting on these resolutions has fallen across North–South lines. In 2001, when the resolution first appeared, all

[1] UN General Assembly 2001: 3(a), 3(g).

OECD countries voted no, while all but ten states from the Global South voted yes.[2] As before, democratic states in the Global South continue to support calls for greater respect for self-determination.

An important point developed in this book is that self-determination is not the same as sovereign independence. The self-determination of sovereign states can be undermined in ways that are sometimes obvious and sometimes more subtle. Recognizing this highlights ways that the agency of weaker states can be quietly undermined, along with ways of responding to these challenges. This has included using regional organizations to increase voice and influence. Weaker states are not without power, though they often have different strategies available for exercising influence and navigating their relations with more powerful actors. Recognizing the limitations that these states operate under is a core part of understanding their agency, including how they respond and adapt to structures that limit their freedom of movement but make available other possibilities for action.[3]

Where self-determination is a distinct goal of governments, certain behaviors and outcomes at the international level cannot be fully explained without accounting for it. The importance of self-determination for political actors helps to account for why states that had only recently achieved self-rule in the form of sovereign independence would turn around and give up pieces of that independence by creating institutions to enforce human rights. It bears emphasizing how close the changes in human rights enforcement in the 1970s, and the subsequent move to create regional human rights mechanisms, were to the end of decolonization. Decolonization peaked in the 1960s, but it had a long tail, extending well into the 1970s, with the independence of Portuguese colonies in Africa, parts of the Gulf peninsula, and the last of the small, Caribbean and Pacific island states. In other words, these regions had only just consolidated their independence when many made the decision to turn around and surrender some of this newly won sovereign authority.

---

[2] In 2023, all European and OECD countries voted against the resolution while, from the Global South, only the Marshall Islands, Micronesia, and Palau voted no. Armenia, Chile, Costa Rica, Mexico, Peru, and Uruguay abstained (UN General Assembly 2023: 16).

[3] For a discussion of the international structures, especially of hierarchy, that weak states operate within, see Adler-Nissen and Zarakol (2021) and Bially Mattern and Zarakol (2016).

In both Latin America and Africa, regions where this change toward regional enforcement happened, certain dynamics of institution-creation and the behaviors of individual leaders confound the expectations of existing explanations as to why states would delegate this kind of authority. There is extensive evidence that leaders that genuinely supported human rights also criticized and pushed back against the imposition of what they regarded as inappropriate, one-sided, and biased enforcement. In both Africa and Latin America, the onset of economic pressure aligned with the timing of the decision to compromise on non-interference and with changes in the behavior of individual governments. Prior to these pressures, democracies with relatively good records of respecting human rights had often expressed ambivalence toward compromising on non-interference due to the protection that this norm offered. This was exemplified by the Colombian government reminding the US of the importance of considering how policies to intervene to enforce human rights would affect "smaller and defenseless nations."[4] Similarly, the representative of democratic Mauritius cautioned that "it would be better that we each put our own house in order" rather than attend to human rights violations in other states.[5] This is not to say that these governments had uniformly prioritized the norm of non-interference over human rights. Yet, they were also far from as wholeheartedly in support of international human rights enforcement as existing theories might expect, and they showed considerable concern about the long-term implications of compromising on the norm of non-interference.

After they began to face economic enforcement, leaders that supported human rights and those that stood to be the most challenged by human rights enforcement suddenly accepted regional enforcement. In fact, one counterintuitive behavior highlighted in this book is that leaders of democracies that most strongly supported human rights and dictatorships that were targeted for their human rights violations responded to these new pressures by cooperating with one another to establish their regional organizations as authorities over human rights.

In Latin America, governments with a range of different interests in and attitudes toward international human rights enforcement began to collectively condemn human rights violations within the region and cooperate with enforcement, doing so even while they criticized

---

[4] *FRUS* 1969: Document 156.   [5] UN General Assembly 1977e: Para. 43.

enforcement coming from outside of the region. This was in spite of the fact that in 1976, when they first moved to discuss and condemn human rights violations in Chile, fewer than 40 percent of states in the OAS were democratic. In Africa, human rights advocates initiated the process of creating regional human rights mechanisms, and they were responsible for shepherding the process along. Yet, these mechanisms were adopted unanimously by a membership that had very few democracies and included governments that were skeptical of human rights and worried about how human rights enforcement would affect them. We can observe significant differences in the effectiveness of these two regional systems and in the amount of authority states gave them. Nevertheless, both required real, significant compromises, and both represented turning points in accepting regional interference.

By contrast, in the Middle East, this remained an authoritarian survival strategy. Throughout this time, there was an absence of sustained pressure or credible threats of economic sanctions from Western governments on human rights in the Middle East. This made it easy for the governments of the Arab League to maintain their strict stance on non-interference, both with respect to other states in the region and external actors. In fact, the consolidation of a sovereignty-respecting regional system occurred at nearly the same time as human rights pressures were leading other regions to adopt a strategy permitting regional enforcement of human rights.

Finally, my argument and evidence complicate understandings that regional enforcement is intrinsically more legitimate or more compatible with regional norms, and that this is why governments have tended to prefer it to global enforcement. States did systematically prefer to ratify regional human rights treaties and disproportionately engaged with regional enforcement over other kinds of enforcement. Leaders also argued that regions were uniquely well-suited to dealing with their own human rights problems. At the same time, they did not reject outside enforcement outright. Both before and after these shifts, leaders that supported human rights engaged with and expressed enthusiasm toward many different forms of enforcement, where it allowed for equitable participation. The version of human rights institutionalized within regional organizations also had many features associated with global or "Western" versions of human rights. Ultimately, it was the fact that regional organizations were designed to offer their member states more voice and were more accountable to them that created a preference for regional institutions.

7.1 Broader Implications for Order, Regions, and Norms

In the rest of this concluding chapter, I explore the implications of my argument for international relations theory and for thinking about contemporary international politics. I focus on the importance of self-determination in understanding challenges to the liberal international order from states in the Global South, the continued expansion of regionalism, and the shape of international norms.

7.1.1 Delegation, Agency, and International Order

One of the main ideas put forward in this book is that much of the existing theorizing on international cooperation, delegation, and political order has failed to accurately capture the agency of weak states, in general, and states in the Global South, in particular. These theories do not factor in the full range of reasons that weak or dependent states might make decisions to delegate authority or comply with the demands of more powerful states. Instead, this research has equated participation in cooperative arrangements, along with an absence of open contestation or resistance, as a sign that weak states view these arrangements as beneficial and legitimate.

This fails to recognize the extent to which leaders of weak states make foreign policy decisions in the shadow of power relations. They act with the knowledge that overt contestation and resistance can elicit discipline and retaliation and in the expectation that such contestation has a low chance of success. Because of this, decisions to delegate authority, align policies with more powerful states, and participate in international institutions and political orders are often the product of rational anticipation of discipline or retaliation. The concept of self-determination captures the distinction between types of decision-making and gradations of voluntariness, as well as the different limits on the capacity of weaker states to influence global governance.

This matters if political actors value self-determination and object to it being undermined, and if these things shape understandings of their political environment. In 2019, the US Ambassador to Jamaica publicly expressed concern about Jamaica's deepening cooperation with the Chinese government, admonishing the Jamaican people to be wary of Chinese aid and loans. An editorial in Jamaica's leading newspaper, the *Jamaican Gleaner*, responded by stating that the ambassador "should be given a message about where Jamaica's foreign policy is formulated, which oughn't be Foggy Bottom."[6] In the case of a state like Jamaica, in which democratic norms are deeply institutionalized, increased interest in cooperating with illiberal governments may not be driven by a desire to engage in undemocratic practices. Instead, such governments may be attracted to cooperation with and no-strings-attached aid from these countries because it reflects their beliefs about the inappropriateness of powerful actors using others' dependence to dictate their domestic and foreign policies and their resentment at the forms of control that have been exercised over them.

More broadly, long-simmering unhappiness with the limits on self-determination within the liberal international order may help to explain the interest of democracies in the Global South in cooperating with illiberal powers in recent years. China's influence throughout the Global South must be seen, in part, through the lens of its expansive approach to non-interference, which has traditionally been more compatible with self-determination. Similarly, the alternative international order China and others have championed is attractive to those that support an international order that enables equitable participation.[7]

Within an international environment where weaker states face what Stephen Krasner has characterized as "external pressures that they cannot influence through unilateral action,"[8] regionalism has been one way that weak states have exercised agency and attempted to compensate for their vulnerability to these pressures. As I showed in this book, delegation to and cooperation within regional organizations can be a way for weak states to mitigate the effects of inequality, manage the involvement of powerful actors in their affairs, and reshape international political orders to their benefit. Regionalism can be a way to push back against external pressures in ways that do not read to powerful states as resistance. In doing so, states employing this approach can increase their ability to participate in their own governance and resist what they regard as illegitimate imposition or domination.

---

[6] MacDonald 2019.   [7] Goldstein 2020.   [8] Krasner 1985: 4.

In fact, one reason for the surge in regionalism following the end of the Cold War may have been the closing of space for outright contestation at the height of American hegemony. This was a time when positive relations with the West, and especially the US, took on heightened importance for states in the Global South, and when liberal norms, as defined in the West, were presented to the rest of the world as a *fait accompli*, with compliance increasingly a precondition for access to economic benefits. The expansion of regionalism can be seen as a way to retain control over global governance in this context.

Seen in this way, cooperation in the post-Cold War years may have been the result of power disparities so large that they looked like consensus, with weak states cooperating because they lacked other options. As the international system has become increasingly multipolar and states in the Global South emerge as powerful actors in their own right, it has re-opened space for more overt contestation. At the same time, the strategies discussed in this book were developed specifically to manage relations with Western governments, based on those governments' beliefs about international institutions and commitment to liberal values. It is yet to be seen how they will work in relations with rising powers from outside of the West.

7.1.2 The Successful Construction of Regional Authority

The ideas that regions are, by their nature, effective and legitimate sites for governance and that regions are entitled to special recognition and representation in international decision-making run counter to the now-well accepted academic understanding of regions as themselves unnatural and socially constructed.[9] The regionalization of human rights makes the unnaturalness of norms that privilege regional solutions and participation especially apparent, as regionalism sits in tension with a fundamental tenet of human rights: their universality. By focusing on human rights, I have demonstrated that the idea that regional organizations are especially effective and uniquely legitimate is, in part, the product of the active cultivation of this idea by smaller and weaker states. These states benefit from international norms that

---

[9] Adler et al. 2006; Dirlik 1992; Hemmer and Katzenstein 2002; Hettne 2005; Hettne and Söderbaum 2000; Hurrell 1995; Waever 1993.

7.1 Broader Implications for Order, Regions, and Norms

enhance their opportunities for participation, influence, and voice over global governance.

Norms of regional solutions and regional participation have been strategically constructed throughout modern history. During the negotiations over the UN Charter, it was Latin American and Arab states that pushed for recognition of regional organizations (or "arrangements"), attempted to establish these organizations as autonomous rather than subordinate to the UN, and argued for regional representation on the UN Security Council.[10] The acceptance of regions as a central link in the democratic legitimacy of global governance has manifested in a number of developments over the past few decades. These include efforts to increase formal coordination between regional organizations and the UN and the growing tendency for the UN Security Council to consult with and formally recognize the role of "relevant regional organizations" in their debates and resolutions.[11] This has reconfigured the logic of collective legitimation, with regional organizations becoming an important source of legitimation for global action.[12]

This provides another way of explaining the growth of regionalism since the end of the Cold War. As global governance has spread into more issue areas, many of which touch on sensitive aspects of states' domestic politics, the scope and authority of regional governance has likewise grown.[13] The Caribbean Community, a regional organization first created to facilitate economic exchange between Caribbean states, sent election observers to Haitian elections in 1990. In 1994, it contributed peacekeeping troops as part of the US operation to return the ousted president of Haiti, Jean-Bertrand Aristide, to power.[14] In 2012, the Lake Chad Basin Commission, a small regional organization created for the narrow purpose of coordinating sustainable use of its eponymous natural resource, created the Multinational Joint Task Force to fight terrorism in the region.[15] After years of backlash against

---

[10] MacDonald 1965: 4–11, 19.
[11] Barnett 1995a; Bellamy and Williams 2011; Hettne and Söderbaum 2006.
[12] Barnett 1995a: 428; Claude 1966.
[13] Acharya and Johnston 2007; Barnett 1995a; Börzel and Risse 2016; Börzel and van Hüllen 2015; Buzan and Waever 2003; Fawcett 2004; Fawcett and Hurrell 1995; Fawcett and Seranno 2005; Katzenstein 2005; Kelly 2007; Milner and Mansfield 1997; Hettne 2000; Hettne et al. 1999; Söderbaum 2016; Söderbaum and Shaw 2003.
[14] Smith 2005: 183. [15] Baffour Frimpong 2020.

the perceived targeting of Africa by the International Criminal Court, in 2014, African leaders expanded the jurisdiction of the African Court of Human and Peoples' Rights to include international criminal law. These developments can be understood as attempts to establish regional organizations as authorities over issue areas in which leaders experience or anticipate pressure from more powerful states.

There are many factors that have led to the parallel expansion of regional and global governance, including learning, emulation, mimicry, and localization.[16] This book suggests that the expansion of regional organizations throughout the Global South and arguments in favor of norms privileging regional organizations are, in part, strategic efforts of weaker states that benefit from carving out space for regional policymaking and representation. As global governance has expanded, establishing regional authority is a way for states to retain, via regional organizations, influence over global policy and, by extension, their own governance. In this process, weaker states have taught powerful actors to listen and defer to regions.

The success of actors in the Global South in establishing regional authority has, in turn, encouraged the construction of new regions. With the idea of regional authority consolidated, there are incentives for new regions to be "recovered" by their members and cooperative efforts to be framed as "regional." One example is the Indian Ocean Rim region, which consists of African and Asian states that border the Indian Ocean. The charter of the Indian Ocean Rim Association for Regional Cooperation, adopted in 1997, frames the organization not as creating a new region, but as engaging in a project of "recovery of history," encouraging cooperation within a region that was already there.[17] The Organization of the Black Sea Economic Cooperation, formed in 1992, has been seen as a transparent attempt at constructing a Black Sea region and cultivating a sense of "regionness."[18]

The successful construction of regional authority can also help account for another phenomenon that has received growing scholarly attention: the expansion of what are referred to as authoritarian regional organizations. Whereas international organizations have historically been tools of democratic states, in recent years, authoritarian

---

[16] Börzel and Risse 2016; Börzel and van Hüllen 2015; van Hüllen 2015; McNamara 2002; Meyer and Rowen 1977; Meyer et al. 1997; Risse 2016.
[17] Indian Ocean Rim Association 2014: Preamble.
[18] Ciută 2008; Waever 1993.

7.1 Broader Implications for Order, Regions, and Norms

leaders have developed and utilized these organizations for coordinating and legitimizing repression and aiding authoritarian survival.[19]

One prominent example is the Shanghai Cooperation Organisation (SCO), which was created in 2001 by China, Russia, and the countries of Central Asia. In 2009, under the aegis of the SCO, states formed the Regional Anti-Terrorism Structure (RATS) and signed a convention that, among other things, provides a legal basis for agents of member states to enter one another's the territory to pursue a suspect.[20] The SCO's Astana Declaration of 2005 states that members will "not provide asylum for individuals accused or suspected of conducting terrorism, separatist and extremist activity, and [will] extradite such individuals at respective requests on the part of other SCO member states,"[21] allowing for extradition of members of the opposition who have sought asylum in neighboring states. Human rights groups have complained that these and other mechanisms are being used for the purpose of cooperating to suppress domestic dissent.[22] Similarly, members of the Gulf Cooperation Council (GCC) signed a Joint Security agreement in 2012, during the Arab Spring, to aid one another in intelligence sharing, to assist in monitoring one another's political opposition, and to facilitate extradition of political domestic opponents.[23] They did so alongside the adoption of a regional human rights declaration.

One important reason for this development may be that the authoritarian leaders creating and making use of these organizations are following in the footsteps of successful efforts by actors in the Global South to assert the authority of regional organizations. After decades of pushing for powerful actors to accept the right of regional organizations to manage their own affairs, it is perhaps unsurprising that authoritarian leaders would capitalize on this legitimacy.

This raises important questions concerning how to distinguish between, on the one hand, legitimate resistance to outside pressures and genuine contestation of global norms within the framework of regional organizations and, on the other hand, cynical attempts to

---

[19] Cooley 2015; Debre 2021; Ginsburg 2020; Hafner-Burton and Schneider 2019; Libman and Obydenkova 2018; Obydenkova and Libman 2019; Roberts 2017.
[20] UN Office on Drugs and Crime n.d.
[21] Shanghai Cooperation Organisation 2005: Article III.
[22] International Federation for Human Rights 2012.
[23] Carlson and Koremenos 2021.

legitimate repression and hide bad behaviors. It cautions against painting with too broad of a brush in applying the label of "authoritarian regional organization." In drawing attention to regionalism as an authoritarian strategy, it is important to distinguish between organizations that aim to subvert international norms and legitimize repression from those that were created for legitimate self-governance, even where the latter includes authoritarian members. For example, African regional and subregional organizations are sometimes labeled as authoritarian organizations despite historical evidence, including evidence presented in this book, suggesting that they were not created for dubious authoritarian purposes, but rather to support cooperation between weak states, create economies of scale, and consolidate their region's independence.

7.1.3 Human Rights, Participation, and the Shape of Norms

A final implication of this book relates to theories of human rights and international norms, more broadly. Whether or not certain actors are able to meaningfully participate in the formation and elaboration of norms affects the shape that these norms come to take over time, what gets left out of norms, and what is and is not pursued by transnational advocacy networks.[24] As Ayoob notes, "the question of agency – who constructs and codifies human rights – becomes important" as "those who define human rights and decree they have been violated also decide when and where intervention to protect such rights should and must take place."[25] Where weaker states lack the ability to effectively participate, it can lead to the marginalization and exclusion of their priorities and beliefs from norms as they are consolidated and institutionalized at the global level. The exclusion from the process of defining and elaborating on norms may then lead excluded actors to experience the implementation of these norms as an imposition.

Many scholars contest the idea that international norms, and human rights in particular, have been imposed upon weaker or smaller states. It is true that many of the beliefs and values of weaker states have been captured in the content of global norms, often against the interests of

---

[24] Carpenter 2007, 2014.   [25] Ayoob 2002: 81.

7.1 Broader Implications for Order, Regions, and Norms 181

more powerful states.[26] Yet, it is also the case that weaker states face disadvantages in shaping norms.[27] Even when global norms overlap with regional or local perspectives in terms of content, weaker states may still be shut out of the political process of institutional design, elaboration, implementation, and enforcement. These disadvantages can lead to the exclusion of understandings of norms that are especially challenging or unacceptable to powerful actors as they are consolidated at the global level.

In the case of human rights, this has included the marginalization of international responsibility, which requires international wealth redistribution and limits the use of economic pressure as a means of enforcing human rights, and which formed an important part of advocacy for human rights by the Global South in the 1970s and 1980s. This kind of marginalization may have long-term effects on how states perceive and engage with norms. Research on international norms does not account for what happens to those goals, priorities, and aspirations that are excluded from consolidated versions of global norms. The mechanisms that lead to the spread of norms, including socialization, diffusion, and learning, do not remove the material or historical conditions that brought about local perspectives on norms. If local perspectives respond to real, salient problems, then there is good reason to expect that they will persist.

This may help to explain the re-emergence of demands for a model of human rights that holds developed states responsible for violations of human rights in developing states. This re-emergence has included a recent increase in demands from the Global South for former colonial powers to provide reparations to formerly colonized states to compensate for the damages of colonialism, slavery, and native genocide. This has been framed expressly as a human rights movement.[28] The persistence of domestic poverty and under-development, the reality of massive global inequality, and the historical fact that both of these came to be, in part, through centuries of slavery and colonization has kept this way of understanding human rights alive for people in many parts of the world. Its marginalization in spite of its wide salience and appeal

---

[26] Acharya 2013; Finnemore and Jurkovich 2014; Klotz 1995; Lauren 1983; Sikkink 2014.
[27] Abbott and Snidal 1998; Bailey 2008: 304–5; Barkin 2003; de Nevers 2007; Donno 2010; Grovogui 2011: 43–44; Ikenberry and Kupchan 1990.
[28] CARICOM Reparations Commission 2021.

may also explain backlash against international norms, with domestic actors feeling increasingly unrepresented by global norms and the actors and institutions that propagate them.

Bringing this back to discussions of regionalism, one way that weak states have responded to difficulties in meaningfully participating at the global level is through delegating authority to engage with and enforce norms to their own regional organizations. One example of this is the codification of the right to development in the African Charter on Human and Peoples' Rights at a time when more powerful states refused to recognize this right.[29] In this way, norm localization, in terms of infusing the content of norms with local beliefs and values, may not always be the primary aim of creating regional mechanisms. It may instead be the outcome of vesting authority for norm elaboration, implementation, and enforcement in institutions that offer greater possibilities for participation by a wider range of actors.

7.2 The Global South and International Relations Theory

Theories in international relations have tended to disproportionately draw from the strategies, goals, and limitations of states that are, on average, more powerful, more economically developed, more self-reliant, and relatively privileged by the existing rules of the international system by merit of having created many of them. The development of regional human rights institutions in the Global South, the main focus of this book and the main lens through which I explore regional organizations in the Global South, provides a stark example of the ways that the foreign policies of states in the Global South depart in important ways from what theories focusing on the West would expect.

States in the Global South have histories and internal structures that are different from states in the West, and they have tended to occupy radically different positions in the international system. They have faced different constraints on their actions, often operating within subordinate positions in different international hierarchies in ways that structure their decision-making. All of these factors have led them to conduct their international affairs in ways that are quite different from Western governments.

---

[29] Alston 1988; Cornwall and Nyamu-Musembi 2004; Ibhawoh 2011.

The point of drawing attention to these factors is not simply to note the existence of difference nor to highlight the fact that certain perspectives have been overshadowed. Ignoring these differences and contributions has led to theories that provide insufficient explanations for international relations. In the case of regional organizations, it leads to the conclusion that governments in the Global South are using their regional organizations poorly or wrong, that these organizations are under-developed or under-utilized, or that they are being co-opted for nefarious, illiberal purposes. If regional organizations are understood primarily as mechanisms for deepening integration, expanding collaboration toward goals like economic development or democratization, and creating mechanisms to govern their member states, then many regional organizations in the Global South have fallen short of their intended goals.

Framing regional organizations in this way legitimizes forms of pressure aimed at altering the behavior of the members of these regional organizations. It suggests that an appropriate goal of policymakers and scholars is to assist, pressure, and persuade governments in the Global South toward better and more effective use of their regional organizations. It explains difference from Western policies and institutional design as an aberration or deficiency, or as a challenge to liberal norms.

To the extent that improving certain governance outcomes of their member states is one goal of regional organizations in the Global South, it is true that they have often fallen short. However, these internal goals are separate from and often in tension with other, equally important goals, which involve managing their members' place in the international system and their relations with powerful actors. If we understand these regional organizations as mechanisms for reordering the international system, upholding the principle of self-determination, resisting domination by more powerful actors, and transforming how powerful actors understand what constitutes appropriate conduct in their relations with the Global South, we may see them as remarkably effective.

Expanded understandings of global phenomena that draw from the Global South can, in turn, provide insights that apply more generally, offering new ways of thinking about important questions. To what extent can a more expansive understanding of self-determination shed light on resurgent nationalism, backlash against international institutions, and receptiveness to populist appeals throughout the world? What can it illuminate about democratic deficits in international organizations, and how might this give us new ways of thinking about challenges to globalism in the West? What challenges does it highlight with respect to the long-term sustainability of global governance, and what reforms does it call for? What are the implications for Western actors' own self-identification as operating in the international system through cooperation and persuasion rather than coercion? These are important questions, and recognizing the continued importance of self-determination, and different ways that self-determination has been understood and pursued, may lead us to answer them differently.

References

Abbott, Kenneth, and Duncan Snidal. 1998. "Why States Act through Formal International Organizations." *Journal of Conflict Resolution*, 42(1): 3–32.
  2000. "Hard and Soft Law in International Governance." *International Organization*, 54(3): 421–56.
Acharya, Amitav. 1994. "Regional Approaches to Security in the Third World: Lessons and Prospects." In Larry Swatuk and Timothy Shaw, eds. *The South at the End of the Twentieth Century: Rethinking the Political Economy of Foreign Policy in Africa, Asia, the Caribbean and Latin America*. Palgrave Macmillan: 79–94.
  2004. "How Ideas Spread: Whose Norms Matter? Norm Localization and Institutional Change in Asian Regionalism." *International Organization*, 58(2): 239–75.
  2007. "The Emerging Regional Architecture of World Politics." *World Politics*, 59(4): 629–52.
  2009. *Whose Ideas Matter? Agency and Power in Asian Regionalism*. Cornell University Press.
  2011. "Norm Subsidiarity and Regional Orders: Sovereignty, Regionalism, and Rule-Making in the Third World: Norm Subsidiarity and Regional Orders." *International Studies Quarterly*, 55(1): 95–123.
  2013. "The R2P and Norm Diffusion: Towards a framework of norm circulation." *Global Responsibility to Protect*, 5(4): 466–79.
Acharya, Amitav and Alistair Iain Johnston. 2007. *Crafting Cooperation*. Cambridge University Press.
Adebajo, Adekeye and Chris Landsberg. 2001. "The Heirs of Nkrumah: Africa's New Investments." Pugwash Occasional Papers. Pugwash Conferences on Science and World Affairs. Available at: https://pugwashconferences.files.wordpress.com/2018/02/200101_como_opapers_adebajo-lansberg_africa.pdf. Accessed on 28 January 2025.
Adesnik, David and Michael McFaul. 2006. "Engaging Autocratic Allies to Promote Democracy." *Washington Quarterly*, 29(2): 5–26.

Adi, Hakim. 2018. *Pan-Africanism: A History*. London, United Kingdom: Bloomsbury Publishing.

Adler, Emanuel, Federica Bicchi, Beverly Crawford, and Raffaella A. Del Sarto, eds. 2006. *The Convergence of Civilizations: Constructing a Mediterranean Region*. University of Toronto Press.

Adler-Nissen, Rebecca and Ayse Zarakol. 2021. "Struggles for Recognition: The Liberal International Order and the Merger of Its Discontents." *International Organization*, 75(2): 611–34.

"Administration Said to Follow Double Standard on Human Rights." 1982. *Associated Press*, 10 December.

"Africa Commission Says Bokassa Had Role in Massacre of Children." 1979. *New York Times*, 17 August.

African Union. 2000. Constitutive Act of the African Union. Lomé, Togo. 11 July.

Aggarwal, Vinod. 1985. *Liberal Protectionism*. University of California Press.

Al-Ajaji, Mohammed S.M. 1990. "The League of Arab States and the Promotion and Protection of Human Rights." Unpublished Master's thesis, University of British Columbia.

Akehurst, Michael. 1967. "Enforcement Action by Regional Agencies." *British Yearbook of International Law*, 42: 175–229.

Albinyana, Roger and Fátima Fernández. 2018. "From the Euro-Arab Dialogue to a Euro-Arab Summit: Revamping the EU-Arab Partnership." Mediterranean Yearbook. European Institute of the Mediterranean.

Alcindor, Yamiche. 2003. "Daniel arap Moi, Former Kenyan President Who Ruled with Iron Fist, Dies at 95." *Washington Post*. 3 February.

Alesina, Alberto and David Dollar. 2000. "Who Gives Foreign Aid to Whom and Why?" *Journal of Economic Growth*, 5(1): 33–63.

Alexandria Protocol. 1944. Adopted by the Preliminary Committee of the General Arab Conference. 7 October.

All-African Peoples' Conference. 1958. First Session of the All-African Peoples' Conference. Accra, Ghana. 5–13 December.

1960. Second Session of the All-African Peoples' Conference. Tunis, Tunisia, 25–30 January.

Allam, Wael. 2014. "The Arab Charter on Human Rights: Main Features." *Arab Law Quarterly*, 28(1): 40–63.

Almakky, Rawa Ghazy. 2015. "The League of Arab States and the Protection of Human Right: A Legal Analysis." Unpublished PhD dissertation, Brunel University.

Alnasrawi, Abbas. 1987. "The Role of Oil in the Middle East." *Arab Studies Quarterly*, 9(3): 327–36.

Alston, Philip. 1988. "Making Space for New Human Rights: The Case of the Right to Development." *Harvard Human Rights Yearbook*, 1: 3–40.
Alston, Philip and Gerard Quinn. 1987. "The Nature and Scope of States Parties' Obligations under the International Covenant on Economic, Social and Cultural Rights." *Human Rights Quarterly*, 9(2): 157–229.
Amnesty International. 1994. "Indonesia: Power and Impunity: Human Rights under the New World Order." 1 September 1994. Available at: www.refworld.org/reference/countryrep/amnesty/1994/en/91506. Accessed on 21 August 2025.
Amate, C.O.C. 1986. *Inside the OAU: Pan-Africanism in Practice*. London: Macmillan.
An-Na'im, Abdullahi. 2001. "Human Rights in the Arab World: A Regional Perspective." *Human Rights Quarterly*, 23(3): 701–32.
  2006. "Why Should Muslims Abandon Jihad? Human Rights and the Future of International Law." *Third World Quarterly*, 27(5): 785–97.
Andrés Pérez, Carlos. 1977. Interview. "The 'Third World' Has Given Everything and Received Little." *U.S. News*. 25 July.
Anghie, Antony. 2005. *Imperialism, Sovereignty and the Making of International Law*. Cambridge University Press.
  2013. "Whose Utopia? Human Rights, Development, and the Third World." *Qui Parle*, 22(1): 63–80.
  2015. "Legal Aspects of the New International Economic Order." Humanity, 6(1): 145–58.
  2019. "Inequality, Human Rights, and the New International Economic Order." *Humanity*, 10(3): 429–42.
Apuuli, Kasaija Phillip. 2012. "The African Union's Notion of 'African Solutions to African Problems' and the Crises in Côte d'Ivoire (2010–2011) and Libya (2011)." *African Journal on Conflict Resolution* 12(2): 135–60.
"Arab Permanent Committee on Human Rights." n.d. Centre for Women, Peace and Security. London School of Economics. Available at: https://blogs.lse.ac.uk/vaw/regional/arab-league/arab-permanent-committee-on-human-rights/. Accessed on 28 January 2025.
Armstrong, Elisabeth. 2016. "Before Bandung: The Anti-imperialist Women's Movement in Asia and the Women's International Democratic Federation." *Signs*, 41(2): 305–31.
Arts, Karin. 2000. *Integrating Human Rights into Development Cooperation*. The Hague, The Netherlands: Kluwer Law International.
Association of Southeast Asian Nations. 1980. Cooperation Agreement between Member Countries of ASEAN and European Community. 7 March. Available at: https://asean.org/cooperation-agree

ment-between-member-countries-of-asean-and-european-community-kuala-lumpur-7-march-1980/. Accessed on 28 January 2025.
Association of Southeast Asian Nations. 2009. ASEAN Intergovernmental Commission on Human Rights (Terms of Reference).
Atkins, Pope, and Larman Wilson. 1972. *The United States and the Trujillo Regime*. New Brunswick, NJ: Rutgers University Press.
Autesserre, Severine. 2016. "Paternalism and Peacebuilding: Capacity, Knowledge, and Resistance in International Intervention." In Michael Barnett, ed. *Paternalism beyond Borders*. Cambridge University Press: 161–84.
Avant, Deborah, Martha Finnemore, and Susan Sell. 2010. "Who Governs the Globe?" In *Who Governs the Globe?* Cambridge University Press: 1–31.
"Award Ceremony Speech." 1977. Nobel Peace Prize. Available at: www.nobelprize.org/prizes/peace/1977/ceremony-speech/. Accessed on 17 February 2024.
Ayoob, Mohammed. 2002. "Humanitarian Intervention and State Sovereignty." *International Journal of Human Rights*, 6(1): 81–102.
Baffour Frimpong, Osei. 2020. "Climate Change and Violent Extremism in the Lake Chad Basin: Key Issues and Way Forward." Africa Program Occasional Paper. Wilson Center. Available at: www.wilsoncenter.org/sites/default/files/media/uploads/documents/Climate%20Change%20and%20Violent%20Extremism%20in%20the%20Lake%20Chad%20Basin%20Key%20Issues%20and%20Way%20Forward_0.pdf. Accessed on 23 August 2025.
Bailey, Jennifer. 2008. "Arrested Development: The Fight to End Commercial Whaling as a Case of Failed Norm Change." *European Journal of International Relations*, 14(2): 289–318.
Ball, Margaret. 1961. "Issue for the Americas: Non-Intervention v. Human Rights and the Preservation of Democratic Institutions." *International Organization*, 15(1): 21–37.
Bandyopadhyaya, Jayantanuja. 1977. "The Non-aligned Movement and International Relations." *India Quarterly*, 33(2): 137–64.
Barkin, Samuel. 2003. "Realist Constructivism." *International Studies Review*, 5(3): 325–42.
Barnett, Michael. 1993. "Institutions, Roles, and Disorder: The Case of the Arab States System." *International Studies Quarterly*, 37(3): 271–96.
    1995a. "Partners in Peace? The UN, Regional Organizations, and Peace-Keeping." *Review of International Studies*, 21(4): 411–33.
    1995b. "Sovereignty, Nationalism, and Regional Order in the Arab States System." *International Organization*, 49(3): 479–510.

Barnett, Michael and Etel Solingen. 2007. "Designed to Fail or Failure to Design? The Origins and Legacy of the Arab League." In Acharya, Amitav and Alistair Iain Johnston, eds. *Crafting Cooperation*. Cambridge University Press: 180–220.

Barnett, Michael and Martha Finnemore. 2004. *Rules for the World*. Cornell University Press.

Baxter, Kylie and Shahram Akbarzadeh. 2012. *US Foreign Policy in the Middle East: The Roots of Anti-Americanism*. New York: Routledge Press.

Bayart, Jean-Francois. 2000. "Africa in the World: A History of Extraversion." *African Affairs*, 99(365): 217–67.

Beall, Katherine. 2022. "The Global South and Global Human Rights: International Responsibility for the Right to Development." *Third World Quarterly*, 43(10): 2337–56.

2024a. "Empowering to Constrain: Procedural Checks in International Organizations." *Review of International Organizations*, 19: 443–68.

2024b. "Trading Sovereignty for Self-Determination." *International Studies Quarterly*, 68(1): sqad094.

Bebr, Gerhard. 1955. "Regional Organizations: A United Nations Problem." *American Journal of International Law*, 49(2): 166–84.

Bedjaoui, Mohammed. 1968. "First Report on Succession of States in Respect of Rights and Duties Resulting from Sources Other than Treaties." A/CN.4/204 and Corr.1.

1979. *Towards a New International Economic Order*. UNESCO.

Bekker, Gina. 2007. "The African Court on Human and Peoples' Rights: Safeguarding the Interests of African States." *Journal of African Law*, 51(1): 151–72.

Bellamy, Alex J. and Paul D. Williams. 2011. "The New Politics of Protection? Côte d'Ivoire, Libya and the Responsibility to Protect." *International Affairs*, 87(4), 825–50.

Bengtsson, Rikard and Ole Elgström. 2012. "Conflicting Role Conceptions? The European Union in Global Politics." *Foreign Policy Analysis*, 8(1): 93–108.

Benham, Joseph. 1977. "Why Latin Americans Are Bitter about Carter." *U.S. News and World Report*. 4 April.

Bernardi, Bruno Boti. 2018. "Silence, Hindrances and Omissions: The Inter-American Commission on Human Rights and the Brazilian Military Dictatorship." *International Journal of Human Rights*, 22(9): 1123–43.

Beti, Mongo. 1981. "Human Rights Hypocrisy." *Index on Censorship*, 10(6): 77–79.

Bially Mattern, Janice and Ayşe Zarakol. 2016. "Hierarchies in World Politics." *International Organization*, 70(3): 623–54.

Bicchi, Federica. 2002. "From Security to Economy and Back? Euro-Mediterranean Relations in Perspective." Draft presented at the symposium organized by the Institute for European Studies of Berkeley University, Lisbon, Portugal.

Bielefeldt, Heiner. 1995. "Muslim Voices in the Human Rights Debate." *Human Rights Quarterly*, 17(4): 587–617.

Binaisa, Godfrey. 1977. "Organization of African Unity and Decolonization: Present and Future Trends." *The Annals of the American Academy of Political and Social Science*, 43: 52–69.

Binder, David. 1975. "US Relations with Chile have Reportedly Deteriorated in Recent Weeks." *New York Times Abstracts*, 19 November.

Blackburn, Peter. 1984. "Sekou Toure's Legacy to Guinea: Warming Ties to West, Repression." *Christian Science Monitor*. 2 April.

Blanton, Shannon. 2000. "Promoting Human Rights and Democracy in the Developing World: U.S. Rhetoric versus U.S. Arms Imports." *American Journal of Political Science*, 44(1): 123–31.

Blanton, Shannon, and Robert Blanton. 2007. "What Attracts Foreign Investors? An Examination of Human Rights and Foreign Direct Investment." *Journal of Politics*, 69(1): 143–55.

Blau, Peter. 1963. "Critical Remarks on Weber's Theory of Authority." *American Political Science Review*, 57(2): 305–16.

Bloomfield, Lincoln. 1982. "From Ideology to Program to Policy: Tracking the Carter Human Rights Policy." *Journal of Policy Analysis and Management*, 2(1): 1–12.

Boilard, Marie Christine. 2019. "Debating Development as a Human Right." Unpublished PhD dissertation, University of Jyvaskyla.

"Bokassa's Accomplices." 1979. *The Globe and Mail*. 28 September.

Borstelmann, Thomas. 2013. *The 1970s: A New Global History from Civil Rights to Economic Inequality*. Princeton University Press.

Börzel, Tanja and Thomas Risse, eds. 2016. *The Oxford Handbook of Comparative Regionalism*. Oxford University Press.

Börzel, Tanja and Vera van Hüllen, eds. 2015. *Governance Transfer by Regional Organizations*. London, United Kingdom: Palgrave MacMillan.

Boumans, Etienne and Monica Norbart. 1989. "The European Parliament and Human Rights." *Netherlands Quarterly Human Rights*, 7(1): 36–56.

Boutros-Ghali, Boutros. 1979. "Two International Organizations of the Third World." In P. C. Jessup, ed. *Jus et Societas*. The Hague, The Netherlands: Springer: 21–37.

Brand, Laurie. 1998. *Women, The State, and Political Liberalization: Middle Eastern and North African Experiences*. Columbia University Press.

Brier, Robert. 2015. "Beyond the Quest for a 'Breakthrough': Reflections on the Recent Historiography on Human Rights." In Sarah Panter, ed. *Mobility and Biography*. Berlin, Germany: De Gruyter Oldenbourg: 155–73.
Brown, Wendy. 2004. "'The Most We Can Hope For…': Human Rights and the Politics of Fatalism." *The South Atlantic Quarterly*, 103(2): 451–63.
Brumberg, Daniel. 2003. "Liberalization versus Democracy: Understanding Arab Political Reform." Carnegie Endowment for International Peace, Democracy and Rule of Law Project Working paper, Number 37. Available at: https://carnegieendowment.org/pdf/files/wp37.pdf.
Brysk, Alison. 1993. "From Above and Below: Social Movements, the International System, and Human Rights in Argentina." *Comparative Political Studies*, 26(3): 259–85.
Buchanan, Allen. 2013. *The Heart of Human Rights*. Oxford University Press.
Buergenthal, Thomas. 1971. "The American Convention on Human Rights: Illusions and Hopes." *Buffalo Law Review*, 21(1): 121–36.
Burke, Roland. 2008. "From Individual Rights to National Development: The First UN International *Conference* on Human Rights, Tehran, 1968." *Journal of World History*, 19(3): 275–96.
  2011. *Decolonization and the Evolution of International Human Rights*. University of Pennsylvania Press.
  2015. "Human Rights Day after the 'Breakthrough': Celebrating the Universal Declaration of Human Rights at the United Nations in 1978 and 1988." *Journal of Global History*, 10(1): 147–70.
Burns, William. 1982. "The Reagan Administration and the Philippines." *The World Today*, 38(3): 97–104.
Buszynski, Leszek. 1981. "SEATO: Why It Survived Until 1977 and Why It was Abolished." *Journal of Southeast Asian Studies*, 12(2): 287–96.
Buzan, Barry and Ole Wæver. 2003. *Regions and Powers: The Structure of International Security*. Cambridge University Press.
Búzás, Zoltán. 2013. "The Color of Threat: Race, Threat Perception, and the Demise of the Anglo-Japanese Alliance (1902–1923)." *Security Studies*, 22(4): 573–606.
Cabranes, Jose. 1967. "Human Rights and Non-Intervention in the Inter-American System." *Michigan Law Review*, 65(6): 1147–82.
  1968. "The Protection of Human Rights by the Organization of American States." *American Journal of International Law*, 62(4): 889–908.
Cameron, David, Gustav Ranis, and Annalisa Zinn. 2006. *Globalization and Self-Determination*. New York: Routledge.

CARICOM Reparations Commission. 2021. "Message from the CARICOM Reparations Commission: On the Occasion of the United States Congressional Hearing on the HR40 Bill." 18 February. Available at: https://caricomreparations.org/message-from-the-caricom-reparations-commission/. Accessed on 28 January 2025.

Carleton, David and Michael Stohl. 1985. "The Foreign Policy of Human Rights: Rhetoric and Reality from Jimmy Carter to Ronald Reagan." *Human Rights Quarterly*, 7(2): 205–29.

Carlson, Melissa and Barbara Koremenos. 2021. "Cooperation Failure or Secret Collusion? Absolute Monarchs and Informal Cooperation." *Review of International Organizations*, 16(1): 95–135.

Carothers, Thomas. 2003. "Promoting Democracy and Fighting Terror." *Foreign Affairs*, 82(1): 84–97.

Carpenter, Charli. 2007. "Setting the Advocacy Agenda: Theorizing Issue Emergence and Nonemergence in Transnational Advocacy Networks." *International Studies Quarterly*, 51(1): 99–120.

2014. *"Lost" Causes: Agenda Vetting in Global Issue Networks and the Shaping of Human Security*. Cornell University Press.

Cassese, Antonio. 1995. *Self-Determination of Peoples*. Cambridge University Press.

Chaabane, Sadak. 1982. "La Réforme du pacte de la Ligue des États Arabes." *Revue Générale de Droit International Public Paris*, 86(3): 508–42.

Chase, Anthony and Amr Hamzawy. 2008. *Human Rights in the Arab World: Independent Voices*. Philadelphia: University of Pennsylvania Press.

Chase, Kerry. 2006. "Multilateralism Compromised: The Mysterious Origins of GATT Article XXIV." *World Trade Review*, 5(1): 1–30.

Chayes, Abram and Antonia Handler Chayes. 1995. *The New Sovereignty: Compliance with International Regulatory Agreements*. Harvard University Press.

Chimni, B. S. 2007. "A Just World Under Law: A View From the South." *American University International Law Review*, 22(2): 199–220.

Chomsky, Noam and Edward Herman. 1979. *Political Economy of Human Rights: The Washington Connection and Third World Fascism*. Black Rose Books.

Ciută, Felix. 2008. "Region? Why Region? Security, Hermeneutics, and the Making of the Black Sea Region." *Geopolitics*, 13(1): 120–47.

Clapham, Christopher. 1996. *Africa and the International System: The Politics of State Survival*. Cambridge University Press.

Claude, Inis. 1956. *Swords into Plowshares*. New York: Random House.

1966. "Collective Legitimization as a Political Function of the United Nations." *International Organization*, 20(3): 367–79.

Clymer, Kenton. 2003. "Jimmy Carter, Human Rights, and Cambodia." *Diplomatic History*, 27(2): 245–78.
Coe, Brooke. 2019. *Sovereignty in the South*. Cambridge University Press.
Cohen, Jean. 2012. *Globalization and Sovereignty: Rethinking Legality, Legitimacy, and Constitutionalism*. Cambridge University Press.
Cole, Wade. 2009. "Hard and Soft Commitments to Human Rights Treaties, 1966–2000." *Sociological Forum*, 24(3): 563–88.
"Commission on Killings Ruled Out by Burundi." 1988. *The Globe and Mail*. 29 August.
Cooley, Alexander. 2015. "Authoritarianism Goes Global: Countering Democratic Norms." *Journal of Democracy*, 26(3): 49–63.
Corbett, Michael. 2013. "Oil Shock of 1973–1974." *Federal Reserve History*. Available at: www.federalreservehistory.org/essays/oil-shock-of-1973-74. Accessed on 28 January 2025.
Cornwall, Andrea, and Celestine Nyamu-Musembi. 2004. "Putting the 'Rights-based Approach' to Development into Perspective." *Third World Quarterly*, 25(8): 1415–37.
Corrales, Javier, and Richard E. Feinberg. 1999. "Regimes of Cooperation in the Western Hemisphere: Power, Interests, and Intellectual Traditions." *International Studies Quarterly*, 43(1): 1–36.
Crapol, Edward. 2000. *James G. Blaine: Architect of Empire*. Lanham, Maryland: Rowman & Littlefield Publishers.
Crawford, Gordon. 1996. "Whither Lomé? The Mid-term Review and the Decline of Partnership." *Journal of Modern African Studies*, 34(3): 503–18.
Crittenden, Ann. 1976. "World Bank's Loan to Chile is Assailed." *New York Times*, 24 March.
Dahl, Robert. 1989. *Democracy and Its Critics*. New Haven: Yale University Press.
[Dakar Draft] African Charter on Human and Peoples' Rights. 1979. Preliminary draft prepared by Dakar Meeting of Experts. Printed in Christof Heyns, ed. 1999. *Human Rights Law in Africa 1999*. Human Rights Law in Africa Series. The Hague, The Netherlands: Kluwer Law International: 81–91.
Dakhlallah, Farah. 2012 "The League of Arab States and Regional Security: Towards an Arab Security Community?" *British Journal of Middle Eastern Studies*, 39(3): 393–412.
Dalacoura, Katerina. 2005. "US Democracy Promotion in the Arab Middle East since 11 September 2001: A Critique." *International Affairs*, 81(5): 963–79.
Dash, Leon. 1979. "Dispute Erupts at African Summit over Tanzanian Action in Uganda." *Washington Post*. 18 July.

Debre, Maria. 2021. "Clubs of Autocrats: Regional Organizations and Authoritarian Survival." *Review of International Organizations*, 17: 1–27.
Deci, Edward and Richard Ryan. 2000. "The 'What' and 'Why' of Goal Pursuits: Human Needs and the Self-Determination of Behavior." *Psychological Inquiry*, 11(4): 227–68.
deCharms, Richard. 1968. *Personal Causation*. New York: Academic Press.
"De Cuellar Urges Non-Interference in Latin America." 1983. *Xinhua General Overseas News Service*. 21 December.
Dehm, Julia. 2019. "Righting Inequality: Human Rights Responses to Economic Inequality in the United Nations." *Humanity* 10(3): 443–59.
de la Serre, Françoise. 1980. "The Community's Mediterranean Policy after the Second Enlargement." *Journal of Common Market Studies*, 19(4): 377–88.
de Nevers, Renée. 2007. "Imposing International Norms: Great Powers and Norm Enforcement." *International Studies Review*, 9(1): 53–80.
de Onis, Juan. 1976a. "O.A.S. Appealing to Chile on Rights." *New York Times*, 17 June.
1976b. "OAS Makes Gains on Rights Issues." *New York Times*, 20 June.
1976c. "OAS Chief Irks Chile Prisoners." *New York Times*, 22 June.
de Perini, Pietro. 2020. "The Inconsistent Human Rights Agenda of EU Mediterranean Policy." *European Foreign Affairs Review*, 25(3): 445–66.
de Soto, Álvaro. 2018. "Javier Pérez de Cuéllar, 1982–1991." In Manuel Fröhlich and Abiodun Williams, eds. *The UN Secretary-General and the Security Council: A Dynamic Relationship*. Oxford University Press: 116–37.
de Waal, Alex. 2003. "Human Rights Organizations and the Political Imagination: How the West and Africa have diverged." *Journal of Human Rights*, 2(4), 475–94.
DeYoung, Karen. 1977. "Vance to Latins: Trade, Aid are Linked to Human Rights." *Washington Post*, June 15, 1976.
Diehl, Paul. 2007. "New Roles for Regional Organizations." In Chester Crocker, Fen Osler Hampson, and Pamela Aall, eds. *Leashing the Dogs of War: Conflict Management in a Divided World*. US Institute of Peace Press: 535–52.
Dietrich, John. 2006. "U.S. Human Rights Policy in the Post-Cold War Era." *Political Science Quarterly*, 121(2): 269–94.
Dietrich, Simone and Amanda Murdie. 2017. "Human Rights Shaming through INGOs and Foreign Aid Delivery." *Review of International Organizations*, 12: 95–120.
Dirlik, Arif. 1992. "The Asia-Pacific Region: Reality and Representation in the Invention of the Regional Structure." *Journal of World History* 3(1): 55–79.
Diuguid, Lewis H. 1974. "OAS Ministers Table Study of Brazil Rights Violations." *Washington Post*, 2 June.

Doidge, Mathew. 2004. "Inter-regionalism and Regional Actors: The EU-ASEAN Case." In Wim Stokhof, Paul van der Velde, and Yeo Lay Hwee, eds. *The Eurasian Space: Far More than Two Continents*. Pasir Panjang, Singapore: ISEAS Publications: 39–57.

Donno, Daniela. 2010. "Who is Punished? Regional Intergovernmental Organizations and the Enforcement of Democratic Norms." *International Organization*, 64(4): 593–625.

Dreier, John. 1968. "New Wine and Old Bottles: The Changing Inter-American System." *International Organization*, 22(2): 477–93.

Du Bois, W.E.B. 1961. *The Souls of Black Folk*. New York: Crest Books.

Dunning, Thad. 2004. "Conditioning the Effects of Aid: Cold War Politics, Donor Credibility, and Democracy in Africa." *International Organization*, 58(2): 409–23.

Dussel, Enrique. 1981. *A History of the Church in Latin America*. Grand Rapids: Michigan: William B. Erdmans Publishing.

Duursma, Allard. 2020. "African Solutions to African Challenges: The Role of Legitimacy in Mediating Civil Wars in Africa." *International Organization*, 74(2): 295–330.

Dworkin, Gerald. 1988. *The Theory and Practice of Autonomy*. Cambridge University Press.

Dwyer, Kevin. 1991. *Arab Voices: The Human Rights Debate in the Middle East*. University of California Press.

Eckel, Jan. 2019. *The Ambivalence of Good: Human Rights in International Politics Since the 1940s*. Oxford University Press.

Eckel, Jan and Samuel Moyn. 2013. *The Breakthrough*. University of Pennsylvania Press.

Eckert, Andreas. 2012. "African Nationalists and Human Rights, 1940s–1970s." In Stefan-Ludwig Hoffman, ed. *Human Rights in the Twentieth Century*. Cambridge University Press: 283–300.

"Economic Measures Set." 1975. *Facts on File World News Digest*. 12 April.

"ECOWAS Delegation in Ghana: Aid for Deportees." 1983. *BBC Summary of World Broadcasts*, February 12.

Eide, Asbjørn. 1966. "Peace-Keeping and Enforcement by Regional Organizations: Its Place in the United Nations System." *Journal of Peace Research*, 3(2): 125–44.

Ejdus, Filip. 2017. "Here Is Your Mission, Now Own It!": The Rhetoric and Practice of Local Ownership in EU Interventions." *European Security*, 26(4): 461–84.

"El secretario general de la OEA habla de los derechos humanos en Chile." 1976. *El Pais*. 28 June. Available at: https://elpais.com/diario/1976/06/29/internacional/204847213_850215.html.

Elgström, Ole. 2000. "Lomé and Post-Lomé: Asymmetric Negotiations and the Impact of Norms." *European Foreign Affairs Review*, 5(2): 175–95.

Esedebe, P. Olisanwuche. 1994. *Pan-Africanism: The Idea and Movement, 1776–1991*. Washington, D.C: Howard University Press.
Esposito, John and James Piscatori. 1991. "Democratization and Islam." *Middle East Journal*, 45(3): 427–40.
European Commission. 1978a. *The Courier*. No. 47. January–February. Available at: http://aei.pitt.edu/36721/1/A2000.pdf.
  1978b. *The Courier*. No. 51. September–October. Available at: http://aei.pitt.edu/36956/1/A2004.pdf.
  1979. "The European Commission and ASEAN." *Europe Information*, 16/79. Available at: http://aei.pitt.edu/8240/1/31735055282192_1.pdf.
  1980a. *The Courier*. No. 59, January–February. Available at: http://aei.pitt.edu/37064/1/A2012.pdf.
  1980b. *The Courier*. No. 61, May–June. Available at: http://aei.pitt.edu/37066/1/A2014.pdf.
  1983. *The Courier*. No. 82. November–December. Available at: http://aei.pitt.edu/37194/1/A2034.pdf.
  1991. *The Courier*. No. 128. July–August. Available at: http://aei.pitt.edu/39174/1/Courier.128.pdf. Accessed on 29 January 2024.
  1994. *The Courier*. No. 146. July–August. Available at: http://aei.pitt.edu/39191/1/Courier.146.pdf.
  1995. *The Courier*. No. 153. September–October. Available at: http://aei.pitt.edu/39198/1/Courier.153.pdf.
  1976. "Extracts from Mr Cheysson's Statement at the First Session of the Consultative Assembly." 1 June. Available at: http://aei.pitt.edu/12801/1/12801.pdf. Accessed 29 January 2024.
European Parliament. 1983a. "Draft Report on Human Rights in the World and Community Policy on Human Rights." Political Affairs Committee Working Group on Human Rights. 30 November. Available at: http://aei.pitt.edu/99331/1/30_nov_1983.pdf.
  1983b. "Report Drawn up on behalf of the Committee on Development and Cooperation on the Outcome of the Work of the ACP-EEC Joint Committee and Consultative Assembly." European Parliament Working Documents. Document 1-1143/83. 12 December.
  1993. "Report of the Committee on Foreign Affairs and Security on Human Rights in the World and Community Human Rights Policy for the Years 1991–1992." 23 February. Available at: http://aei.pitt.edu/48468/1/A9397.pdf.
  2009. "The Role of Regional Human Rights Mechanisms." Directorate-General for External Policies of the Union. Available at: www.europarl.europa.eu/RegData/etudes/etudes/join/2010/410206/EXPO-DROI_ET(2010)410206_EN.pdf. Accessed on 28 January 2025.

Evans, Tony. 1996. *US Hegemony and the Project of Universal Human Rights*. New York: Springer.
Fabry, Mikulas. 2010. *Recognizing States*. Oxford University Press.
Fajardo, Margarita. 2022. *The World that Latin America Created*. Harvard University Press.
Farber, Daniel. 2002. "Rights as Signals." *Journal of Legal Studies*, 31(1): 83–98.
Farer, Tom. 1997. "The Rise of the Inter-American Human Rights Regime: No Longer a Unicorn, Not Yet an Ox." *Human Rights Quarterly*, 19(3): 510–46.
Fawcett, Louise. 2004. "Exploring Regional Domains: A Comparative History of Regionalism." *International Affairs*, 80(3): 429–46.
Fawcett, Louise and Andrew Hurrell. 1995. *Regionalism in World Politics: Regional Organization and International Order*. Oxford University Press.
Fawcett, Louise and Mónica Seranno, eds. 2005. *Regionalism and Governance in the Americas: Continental Drift*. New York: Springer.
Fenn, Peggy. 1963. "México, la no intervención y la autodeterminación en el caso de Cuba." *Foro Internacional*, 4(1): 1–19.
Ferrari, Lorenzo. 2015. "The European Community as a Promoter of Human Rights in Africa and Latin America, 1970–1980." *Journal of European Integration History*, 21(2): 217–30.
Fierro, Elena. 2003. *European Union's Approach to Human Rights Conditionality in Practice*. Leiden, The Netherlands: Martinus Nijhoff Publishers.
Final Declaration of the Barcelona Euro-Mediterranean Ministerial Conference. 1995. 27–28 November.
Finnemore, Martha. 1996. *National Interests in International Society*. Cornell University Press.
  2003. *The Purpose of Intervention*. Cornell University Press.
Finnemore, Martha and Michelle Jurkovich. 2014. "Getting a Seat at the Table: The Origins of Universal Participation and Modern Multilateral Conferences." *Global Governance*, 20(3): 361–73.
Finnemore, Martha, and Kathryn Sikkink. 1998. "International Norm Dynamics and Political Change." *International Organization*, 52(4): 887–917.
Fioretos, Orfeo. 2011. "Historical Institutionalism in International Relations." *International Organization*, 65(2): 367–99.
  2020. "Rhetorical Appeals and Strategic Cooptation in the Rise and Fall of the New International Economic Order." *Global Policy*, 11(3): 73–82.
First Asian-African Conference. 1955. Final Communique of the Asian-African Conference, Bandung, Indonesia. April 18–24.

Foreign Relations of the United States, 1945. 1969. Volume IX, The American Republics. David Stauffer and Almon Wright, eds. Washington: Government Printing Office.

Foreign Relations of the United States, 1969–1976. 2015. Volume E-11, Documents on Mexico; Central America; and the Caribbean, 1973–1976. Halbert Jones and Adam Howard, eds. Washington: Government Printing Office.

Foreign Relations of the United States, 1977–1980. 2013. Volume II, Human Rights and Humanitarian Affairs. Kristin Ahlberg and Adam Howard, eds. Washington: Government Printing Office.

Foreign Relations of the United States, 1977–1980. 2014. Volume I, Foundations of Foreign Policy. Kristen Ahlberg and Adam Howard, eds. Washington: Government Printing Office.

Foreign Relations of the United States, 1977–1980. 2016. Volume XV, Central America. Nathaniel Smith and Adam Howard, eds. Washington: Government Printing Office.

Foreign Relations of the United States, 1981–1988. 2017. Volume XLI, Global Issues II. Alexander Poster and Adam Howard, eds. Washington: Government Printing Office.

Foreign Relations of the United States, 1977–1980. 2018a. Volume XVIII, Middle East Region; Arab Peninsula. Kelly McFarland and Adam Howard, eds. Washington: Government Printing Office.

Foreign Relations of the United States, 1977–1980. 2018b. Volume XXIV, South America, Latin America Region. Sara Berndt and Adam Howard, eds. Washington: Government Printing Office.

Foreign Relations of the United States, 1977–1980. 2018c. Volume XVII, Part 2, Sub-Saharan Africa. Louise P. Woodroofe and Adam Howard, eds. Washington: Government Printing Office.

Forsythe, David. 1991. "Human Rights, the United States and the Organizations of American States." *Human Rights Quarterly*, 13(1): 66–98.

Fox, Donald. 1968. "Protection of Human Rights Through the Inter-American System." *The Virginia Quarterly Review*, 44(3): 369–84.

Franck, Thomas. 1992. "The Emerging Right to Democratic Governance." *American Journal of International Law*, 86(1): 46–91.

Franczak, Michael. 2018. "Human Rights and Basic Needs: Jimmy Carter's North–South Dialogue, 1977–1981." *Cold War History*, 18(4): 447–64.

Fredman, Steven. 1979. "US Trade Sanctions Against Uganda: Legality Under International Law." *Law and Policy in International Business*, 11(3): 1149–92.

Friedman, Marilyn. 2003. *Autonomy, Gender, Politics*. Oxford University Press.

Friedman, Max and Tom Long. 2015. "Soft Balancing in the Americas: Latin American Opposition to US Intervention, 1898–1936." *International Security*, 40(1), 120–56.

"Gabon Nears Accord With IMF." 1986. *Financial Times*, 20 November 20.

Garnick, Laura and Carol Twitchett. 1979. "Human Rights and a Successor to the Lomé Convention." *International Relations*, 6(3): 540–57.

Garriga, Ana Carolina. 2016. "Human Rights Regimes, Reputation, and Foreign Direct Investment." *International Studies Quarterly*, 60(1): 160–72.

Gathii, James Thuo. 2020. "Africa and the Radical Origins of the Right to Development." *Third World Approaches to International Law*, 1(1): 28–50.

Gauhar, Altaf and Pérez de Cuellar. 1984. "Javier Pérez de Cuellar." *Third World Quarterly*, 6(1): 13–24.

Gertzel, Cherry. 1980. "Uganda after Amin: The Continuing Search for Leadership and Control." *African Affairs*, 79(317): 461–89.

Getachew, Adom. 2018. "The Limits of Sovereignty as Responsibility." *Constellations*, 26(2): 1–16.

  2019. *Worldmaking after Empire*. Princeton University Press.

Ginsburg, Tom. 2020. "Authoritarian International Law?" *American Journal of International Law*, 114(2): 221–60.

Gittleman, Richard. 1981. "The African Charter on Human and Peoples' Rights: A Legal Analysis." *Virginia Journal of International Law*, 22(4): 667–714.

Glanville, Luke. 2011. "The Antecedents of 'Sovereignty as Responsibility'." *European Journal of International Relations*, 17(2): 233–55.

Goddard, Stacie. 2012. "Brokering Peace: Networks, Legitimacy, and the Northern Ireland Peace Process." *International Studies Quarterly*, 56(3): 501–15.

  2015. "The Rhetoric of Appeasement: Hitler's Legitimation and British Foreign Policy, 1938–39." *Security Studies*, 24(1), 95–130.

Goddard, Stacie and Ron Krebs. 2015. "Rhetoric, Legitimation, and Grand Strategy." *Security Studies*, 24(1): 5–36.

Goddard, Stacie E., and Colleen Larkin. 2023. "'The Most Humane of All Weapons': Discrimination, Airpower, and Precision Doctrine." *European Journal of International Security*, 8(4): 531–49.

Goldman, Robert. 2009. "History and Action: The Inter-American Human Rights System and the Role of the Inter-American Commission on Human Rights." *Human Rights Quarterly*, 31(4): 856–87.

Goldstein, Avery. 2020. "China's Grand Strategy under Xi Jinping: Reassurance, Reform, and Resistance." *International Security*, 45(1): 164–201.

Goodman, Ryan and Derek Jinks. 2013. *Socializing States*. Oxford University Press.

Grealy, David. 2022a. "An Awkward Partner?: Britain's Human Rights Policy and EC Relations, 1977–9." In Lorenzini, Sara, Umberto Tulli, and Ilaria Zamburlini, eds. *The Human Rights Breakthrough of the 1970s: The European Community and International Relations*. London, United Kingdom: Bloomsbury Publishing: 120–38.

2022b. *David Owen, Human Rights, and the Remaking of British Foreign Policy*. London, United Kingdom: Bloomsbury Publishing.

Grigoryan, Arman. 2020. "Selective Wilsonianism: Material Interests and the West's Support for Democracy." *International Security*, 44(4): 158–200.

Gross, Leo. 1965. "The United Nations and the Role of Law." *International Organization*, 19(3): 537–61.

Grovogui, Siba. 1996. *Sovereigns, Quasi-sovereigns, and Africans: Race and Self-determination in International Law*. University of Minnesota Press.

2002. "Regimes of Sovereignty: International Morality and the African Condition." *European Journal of International Relations*, 8(3): 315–38.

2011. "To The Orphaned, Dispossessed, and Illegitimate Children: Human Rights beyond Republican and Liberal Traditions." *Indiana Journal of Global Legal Studies*, 18(1): 41–64.

Gruber, Lloyd. 2000. *Ruling the World*. Princeton University Press.

Gueye, Par Babacar. 1996. "L'Insertion d'une clause relative aux Droits de l'Homme dans La Convention de Lome: L'Attitude des États africains." *Revue internationale de droit africain*, 28: 7–42.

Guterres, Antonio. 2022. "Cooperation between United Nations, Regional Blocs Will Be Critical in Defusing Evolving Threats, Says Secretary-General, Opening Security Council Debate." Available at: https://press.un.org/en/2022/sgsm21145.doc.htm. Accessed on 29 July 2024.

Gutteridge, William. 1983. "The Organization of African Unity, 1963–1983." *Journal of Contemporary African Studies*, 3(1–2): 21–34.

Hafner-Burton, Emilie. 2005. "Trading Human Rights: How Preferential Trade Agreements Influence Government Repression." *International Organization*, 59(3): 593–629.

2010. *Forced to Be Good*. Cornell University Press.

Hafner-Burton, Emilie and Christina Schneider. 2019. "The Dark Side of Cooperation: International Organizations and Member Corruption." *International Studies Quarterly*, 63(4): 1108–21.

Hafner-Burton, Emilie, Edward Mansfield, and Jon Pevehouse. 2015. "Human Rights Institutions, Sovereignty Costs and Democratization." *British Journal of Political Science*, 45(1); 1–27.

Hafner-Burton, Emilie and James Ron. 2013. "The Latin Bias: Regions, the Anglo-American Media, and Human Rights." *International Studies Quarterly*, 57(3): 474–91.

Halderman, John. 1963. "Regional Enforcement Measures and the United Nations." *Georgetown Law Journal*, 52(1): 89–119.

Halliday, Fred. 1995. "Relativism and Universalism in Human Rights: The Case of the Islamic Middle East." *Political Studies*, XLIII(1), 152–67.

Hamid, Shadi. 2011. "The Struggle for Middle East Democracy." *Cairo Review of Global Affairs*, 23: 18–29.

Hanrieder, Tine. 2016. "Regionalization in the World Health Organization." In Thomas Rixen, Lora Anne Viola, and Michael Zürn, eds. *Historical Institutionalism and International Relations: Explaining Institutional Development in World Politics*. Oxford University Press: 96–119.

Hawes, Gary. 1986. "United States Support for the Marcos Administration and the Pressures That Made for Change." *Contemporary Southeast Asia*, 8(1): 18–36.

Hawkins, Darren. 2004. "Explaining Costly International Institutions: Persuasion and Enforceable Human Rights Norms." *International Studies Quarterly*, 48(4): 779–804.

Hawkins, Darren, David Lake, Daniel Nielson, and Michael Tierney. 2006. *Delegation and Agency in International Organizations*. Cambridge University Press.

Hazelzet, Hadewych. 2005. "Suspension of Development Cooperation: An Instrument to Promote Human Rights and Democracy?" European Centre for Development Policy Management, Discussion Paper No. 64B.

Helfer, Laurence. 1999. "Forum Shopping for Human Rights." *University of Pennsylvania Law Review*, 148(2): 285–400.

Hemmer, Christopher and Peter Katzenstein. 2002. "Why Is There No NATO in Asia? Collective Identity, Regionalism, and the Origins of Multilateralism." *International Organization*, 56(3): 575–607.

Henderson, Errol. 2018. "Unintended Consequences of Cosmopolitanism: Malcolm X, Africa, and Revolutionary Theorizing in the Black Power Movement in the US." *African Identities*, 16(2): 161–75.

Henkin, Louis. 1990. *The Age of Rights*. New York: Columbia University Press.
  1995. "Human Rights and State Sovereignty." *Georgia Journal of International and Comparative Law*, 25(1–2): 31–46.

Hettne, Björn. 2000. "The Fate of Citizenship in Post-Westphalia." *Citizenship Studies*, 4(1): 35–46.
  2005. "Regionalism and World Order." In Mary Farrell, Bjorn Hettne, and Luk Van Langenhove, eds. *Global Politics of Regionalism: Theory and Practice*. London, United Kingdom: Pluto Press: 269–86.

Hettne, Björn, András Inotai, and Osvaldo Sunkel, eds. 1999. *Globalism and the New Regionalism*. London, United Kingdom: Macmillan.
Hettne, Björn and Fredrik Söderbaum. 2000. "Theorising the Rise of Regionness." *New Political Economy*, 5(3): 457–72.
　2006. "The UN and Regional Organizations in Global Security: Competing or Complementary Logics?" *Global Governance*, 12(3): 227–32.
Heyns, Christof. 2004. "The African Regional Human Rights System: The African Charter." *Penn State Law Review*, 108(3): 679–702.
Heyns, Christof and Magnus Killander. 2013. "Universality and the Growth of Regional Human Rights Systems." In *The Oxford Handbook of International Human Rights Law*. Oxford University Press.
Hill, Tony. 1985. "Whither Lomé? A Review of the Lomé III Negotiations." *Third World Quarterly*, 7(3): 661–81.
Hills, Carol and Christopher Shaw. 1990. "An Interview with the Honorable Javier Pérez de Cuéllar, Secretary-General of the United Nations." *Fletcher Forum of World Affairs*, 14(1): 87–92.
Hoffmann, Stefan-Ludwig. 2016. "Human Rights and History." *Past & Present*, 232(1): 279–310.
Hovey, Graham. 1977. "U.S. to Prod O.A.S. To Give More Help To Its Rights Unit." *New York Times*. 10 June.
van Hüllen, Vera. 2015. "Just Leave Us Alone: The Arab League and Human Rights." In Tanja Börzel and Vera van Hüllen, eds. *Governance Transfer by Regional Organizations*. London, United Kingdom: Palgrave MacMillan: 125–40.
Humphrey, John. 1983. "The Memoirs of John P. Humphrey, the First Director of the United Nations Division of Human Rights." *Human Rights Quarterly*, 5(4): 387–439.
Hurrell, Andrew. 1995. "Explaining the Resurgence of Regionalism in World Politics." *Review of International Studies*, 21(4): 331–58.
　2005. "Power, Institutions, and the Production of Inequality." In Michael Barnett and Raymond Duvall, eds. *Power in Global Governance*. Cambridge University Press: 33–58.
Hurst, Steven. 1997. "Regionalism or Globalism? The Carter Administration and Vietnam." *Journal of Contemporary History*, 32(1): 81–95.
Hyde, Susan. 2011. *The Pseudo-Democrat's Dilemma*. Cornell University Press.
Ibhawoh, Bonny. 2011. "The Right to Development: The Politics and Polemics of Power and Resistance." *Human Rights Quarterly*, 33(1): 76–104.
　2018. *Human Rights in Africa*. Cambridge University Press.

Ikenberry, John. 1998. "Institutions, Strategic Restraint, and the Persistence of American Postwar Order." *International Security*, 23(3): 43–78.

Ikenberry, John. 2001. *After Victory*. Princeton University Press.

Ikenberry, John, and Charles Kupchan. 1990. "Socialization and Hegemonic Power." *International Organization*, 44(3): 283–315. Indian Ocean Rim Association. 2014. "Charter of the Indian Ocean Rim Association." 9 October.

Inter-American Commission on Human Rights. 1974. "Report on the Status of Human Rights in Chile." OEA/Ser.L/V/II.34.

1980. "Annual Report of the Inter-American Commission on Human Rights." 2 October 1980, OEA/Ser.L/V/II.50.

Inter-American Juridicial Committee. 1946. "Draft Declaration of the International Rights and Duties of Man and Accompanying Report." *American Journal of International Law*, 40(S3): 93–116.

International Commission of Jurists. 1996. "Arab Charter on Human Rights." *International Commission of Jurists Review*, 56: 57–66.

2015. "The Arab Court of Human Rights: A Flawed Statute for an Ineffective Court." Available at: www.icj.org/wp-content/uploads/2015/04/MENA-Arab-Court-of-Human-Rights-Publications-Report-2015-ENG.pdf. Accessed on 28 January 2025.

International Federation for Human Rights. 2012. "Shanghai Cooperation Organisation: A Vehicle for Human Rights Violations." Available at: www.fidh.org/IMG/pdf/sco_report.pdf. Accessed on 28 January 2025.

International Panel of Eminent Personalities. 2000. "Rwanda: The Preventable Genocide." African Union.

Isham, Jonathan, Daniel Kaufmann, and Lant Pritchett. 1997. "Civil Liberties, Democracy, and the Performance of Government Projects." *World Bank Economic Review*: 11–36.

Jackson, Robert. 1990. *Quasi-States: Sovereignty, International Relations and the Third World*. Cambridge University Press.

Jackson, Robert and Carl Rosberg. 1982. "Why Africa's Weak States Persist: The Empirical and the Juridical in Statehood." *World Politics*, 35(1): 1–24.

Jacoby, Tamar. 1986. "The Reagan Turnaround on Human Rights." *Foreign Affairs*, 64(5): 1066–86.

Jagmohan, Desmond. 2020. "Between Race and Nation: Marcus Garvey and the Politics of Self-Determination." *Political Theory*, 48(3): 271–302.

Jaguaribe, Helio. 1979. "Autonomía periférica y hegemonía céntrica." *Estudios Internacionales* 12(46): 91–130.

Jakobson, Linda. 2016. "Reflections from China on Xi Jinping's 'Asia for Asians'." *Asian Politics & Policy*, 8(1): 219–23.

Jallow, Hassan. 2007. *The Law of the African (Banjul) Treaty on Human and Peoples' Rights*. Victoria, Canada: Trafford Publishing.
Jamal, Amaney. 2012. *Of Empires and Citizens*. Princeton University Press.
James, Laura. 2005. "Nasser and His Enemies: Foreign Policy Decision-Making in Egypt on the Eve of the Six-Day War." *Middle East Review of International Affairs*, 9(2): 23–44.
Jensen, Nathan. 2003. "Democratic Governance and Multinational Corporations." *International Organization*, 57(3): 587–616.
Jensen, Stephen. 2016. *The Making of International Human Rights: The 1960s, Decolonization, and the Reconstruction of Global Values*. Cambridge University Press.
Jones, Toby Craig. 2012. "America, Oil, and War in the Middle East." *Journal of American History*, 99(1): 208–18.
Kamminga, Menno. 1989. "Human Rights and the Lomé Conventions." *Netherlands Quarterly of Human Rights*, 7(1): 28–35.
Kang, David. 2005. "Hierarchy in Asian International Relations: 1300–1900." *Asian Security*, 1(1): 53–79.
Kannyo, Edward. 1981. "Human Rights in Africa." *Bulletin of the Atomic Scientists*, 37(10): 14–19.
Karsh, Efraim and Inari Karsh. 1997. "Myth in the Desert, or Not the Great Arab Revolt." *Middle Eastern Studies*, 33(2): 267–312.
Kat, Quintijn. 2021. "Subordinate-State Agency and US Hegemony: Colombian Consent versus Bolivian Dissent." *International Studies Review*, 23(1): 140–63.
Katzenstein, Peter. 2005. *A World of Regions*. Cornell University Press.
Kaufman, Victor. 1998. "The Bureau of Human Rights during the Carter Administration." *The Historian*, 61(1): 51–66.
Keck, Margaret and Kathryn Sikkink. 1998. *Activists beyond Borders*. Cornell University Press.
  1999. "Transnational Advocacy Networks in International and Regional Politics." *International Social Science Journal*, 51(159): 89–101.
Kelly, Patrick William. 2013a. "'Magic Words' The Advent of Transnational Human Rights Activism in Latin America's Southern Cone in the Long 1970s." In Jan Eckel and Samuel Moyn, eds. *The Breakthrough*. University of Pennsylvania Press: 88–106.
  2013b. "The 1973 Chilean Coup and the Origins of Transnational Human Rights Activism." *Journal of Global History*, 8(1): 165–86.
  2018. *Sovereign Emergencies*. Cambridge University Press.
Kelly, Robert. 2007. "Security Theory in the 'New Regionalism'." *International Studies Review*, 9(2): 197–229.
Kemps, Adri. 1984. "Human Rights Policy of the European Community." *SIM Newsletter No. 5*, 14–21.

Keohane, Robert. 1984. *After Hegemony*. Princeton University Press.
Kerr, Malcolm. 1965. *The Arab Cold War, 1958–1964: A Study of Ideology in Politics*. Oxford University Press.
Keys, Barbara. 2010. "Congress, Kissinger, and the Origins of Human Rights Diplomacy." *Diplomatic History*, 34(5): 823–51.
Khadduri, Majid. 1946a. "The Arab League as a Regional Arrangement." *American Journal of International Law*, 40(4): 756–77.
  1946b. "Towards an Arab Union: The League of Arab States." *American Political Science Review*, 40(1): 90–100.
Khalidi, Rashid. 2009. *Sowing Crisis: The Cold War and American Dominance in the Middle East*. Boston, Massachusetts: Beacon Press.
"Kidnapping Mars IDB Meeting." 1977. *Facts on File World News Digest*. 11 June.
Kim, Soo Yeon. 2010. *Power and the Governance of Global Trade: From the GATT to the WTO*. Cornell University Press.
King, Preston. 1978. "The Arab League and the Organization of African Unity." *Politics*, 13(1): 104–11.
King, T. 1997. "Human Rights in the Development Policy of the European Community: Towards a European World Order?" *Netherlands Yearbook of International Law*, 28: 51–100.
Kingsbury, Benedict. 2000. "Reconstructing Self-Determination: A Relational Approach." In P. Aikio and M. Scheinin, eds. *Operationalizing the Right of Indigenous Peoples to Self-Determination*. Turku/Åbo, Finland: Institute for Human Rights: 19–37.
Kioko, Ben. 2003. "The Right of Intervention under the African Union's Constitutive Act: From Non-interference to Non-intervention." *International Review of the Red Cross*, 85(852): 807–26.
Kirby, James. 2021. "African Leadership in Human Rights: The Gambia and The Commonwealth Human Rights Commission, 1977–83." *Journal of Contemporary History*, 56(1): 191–215.
Kirkpatrick, Jeanne. 1979. "Dictatorships and Double Standards." *Commentary*, 68(5): 34–45.
  1986. "The Myth of Moral Equivalence." *Imprimis*, 15(1).
Klare, Michael. 1969. "The Architecture of Imperial America." *Science and Society*, 33(3): 257–84.
Klotz, Audie. 1995. *Norms in International Relations*. Cornell University Press.
Kodjo, Edem. 1990. "The African Charter on Human and Peoples' Rights." *Human Rights Law Journal*, 11(3–4): 271.
Korpi, Walter. 1985. "Power Resources Approach vs. Action and Conflict: On Causal and Intentional Explanations in the Study of Power." *Sociological Theory*, 3(2), 31–45.

Krasner, Stephen. 1981. "Transforming International Regimes: What the Third World Wants and Why." *International Studies Quarterly*, 25(1): 119–48.

1985. *Structural Conflict*. University of California Press.

1999. *Sovereignty*. Princeton University Press.

Kufuor, Kofi. 2010. *The African Human Rights System: Origin and Evolution*. New York: Springer.

Labonski, Peter and Kunal Parker. 1991. "Human Rights as Rhetoric: The Persian Gulf War and United States Policy towards Iraq." *Harvard Human Rights Journal*, 4: 152–62.

Lake, David. 2009. *Hierarchy in International Relations*. Cornell University Press.

2024. *Indirect Rule: The Making of US International Hierarchy*. Cornell University Press.

Landman, Todd. 2005. "The Political Science of Human Rights." *British Journal of Political Science*, 35(3): 549–72

Langley, Lester. 2001. *The Banana Wars: United States Intervention in the Caribbean, 1898–1934*. Lanham, Maryland: Rowman & Littlefield Publishers.

Lauren, Paul Gordon. 1983. "First Principles of Racial Equality: History and the Politics and Diplomacy of Human Rights Provisions in the United Nations Charter." *Human Rights Quarterly*, 5(1): 1–26.

League of Arab States. 1945. *Charter of the League of Arab States*. 22 March.

1994. *The Arab Charter on Human Rights*. 15 September.

2004. *The Arab Charter on Human Rights*. 22 May.

2014. *The Statute of the Arab Court on Human Rights*. 7 September.

Lebovic, James. 1988. "National Interests and US Foreign Aid: The Carter and Reagan Years." *Journal of Peace Research*, 25(2): 115–35.

Lebovic, James and Erik Voeten. 2009. "The Cost of Shame: International Organizations and Foreign Aid in the Punishing of Human Rights Violators." *Journal of Peace Research*, 46(1): 79–97.

Lerner, Natan. 1980. "Self-Determination: The Latin American Perspective." In Alexander Yonah and Robert Friedlander, eds. *Self-Determination: National, Regional, and Global Dimensions*. New York: Routledge: 63–78.

Letelier, Fabiola. 1986. "I think I have struggled in people's real interests. So I am content, even if I don't live to see the final victory." *NACLA Report on the Americas*, 20(5): 51–55.

Levitsky, Steven and Lucan Way. 2006. "Linkage versus Leverage: Rethinking the International Dimension of Regime Change." *Comparative Politics*, 38(4): 379–400.

Libman, Alexander and Anastassia Obydenkova. 2018. "Understanding Authoritarian Regionalism." *Journal of Democracy*, 29(4): 151–65.
Lightfoot, Sheryl. 2021. "Decolonizing Self-Determination: Haudenosaunee Passports and Negotiated Sovereignty." *European Journal of International Relations*, 27(4): 971–94.
Limon, Marc and Hilary Power. 2014. "History of the United Nations Special Procedures Mechanism: Origins, Evolution and Reform." *Universal Rights Group*. Available at: www.universal-rights.org/urg-policy-reports/history-of-the-united-nations-special-procedures-mechanism-origins-evolution-and-reform/. Accessed on 28 January 2025.
Long, Tom. 2017. "It's Not the Size, It's the Relationship: From 'Small States' to Asymmetry." *International Politics*, 54: 144–60.
Long, Tom and Max Friedman. 2020. "The Promise of Precommitment in Democracy and Human Rights: The Hopeful, Forgotten Failure of the Larreta Doctrine." *Perspectives on Politics*, 18(4): 1088–103.
Lorenzini, Sara, Umberto Tulli, and Ilaria Zamburlini, eds. 2022. *The Human Rights Breakthrough of the 1970s: The European Community and International Relations*. London, United Kingdom: Bloomsbury Publishing.
Lowman, Thomas. 2022. "Amin Reframed: The UK, Uganda, and the Human Rights 'Breakthrough' of the 1970s." *Cambridge Review of International Affairs*, online only: 1–21.
Lutz, Ellen and Kathryn Sikkink. 2000. "International Human Rights Law and Practice in Latin America." *International Organization*, 54(3): 633–59.
  2001. "The Justice Cascade: The Evolution and Impact of Foreign Human Rights Trials in Latin America." *Chicago Journal of International Law*, 2(1): 1–34.
MacDonald, Robert. 1965. *The Arab League: A Study in the Dynamics of Regional Organization*. Princeton University Press.
MacDonald, Scott. 2019. "The Shifting Tides in Caribbean International Relations: Jamaica, China and the United States." *The Global Americas*. 19 December.
Mace, Gordon. 1988. "Regional Integration in Latin America: A Long and Winding Road." *International Journal*, 43(3): 404–27.
MacKay, Joseph. 2019. "Legitimation Strategies in International Hierarchies." *International Studies Quarterly*, 63(3): 717–25.
Mackenzie, Catriona and Natalie Stoljar, eds. 2000. *Relational Autonomy*. Oxford University Press.
Macklem, Patrick. 2015. *The Sovereignty of Human Rights*. Oxford University Press.
Mahmood, Saba. 2011. *Politics of Piety*. Princeton University Press.

Mahoney, James and Kathleen Thelen, eds. 2015. *Advances in Comparative-Historical Analysis*. Cambridge University Press.
Maksoud, Clovis. 1995. "Diminished Sovereignty: United Nations-Arab League Relations at 50." *Middle East Journal*, 49(4): 582–94.
Mansfield, Edward and Helen Milner, eds. 1997. *The Political Economy of Regionalism*. New York: Columbia University Press.
Marantis, Demetrios James. 1994. "Human Rights, Democracy, and Development: The European Community Model." *Harvard Human Rights Journal*, 7: 1–32.
Marino, Katherine. 2019. *Feminism for the Americas*. University of North Carolina Press.
Markell, Patchen. 2008. "The Insufficiency of Non-Domination." *Political Theory*, 36(1): 9–36.
Mathews, K. 1977. "The Organization of African Unity." *India Quarterly*, 33(3): 308–24.
[Mbaye] Draft African Charter on Human and Peoples' Rights. 1979. Draft prepared for Meeting of Experts in Dakar, Senegal. Printed in Christof Heyns, ed. 2002. *Human Rights Law in Africa 1999*. Human Rights Law in Africa Series. The Hague, The Netherlands: Kluwer Law International: 65–80.
M'Baye, Keba. 1992. *Les droits de l'homme en Afrique*. International Commission of Jurists.
McNamara, Kathleen. 2002. "Rational Fictions: Central Bank Independence and the Social Logic of Delegation." *West European Politics*, 25(1): 47–76.
Medina Quiroga, Cecilia. 1988. *The Battle of Human Rights*. Martinus Nijhoff Publishers.
Meyer, John and Brian Rowan. 1977. "Institutionalized Organizations: Formal Structure as Myth and Ceremony." *American Journal of Sociology*, 83(2): 340–63.
Meyer, John, John Boli, George Thomas, and Francisco Ramirez. 1997. "World Society and the Nation-State." *American Journal of Sociology*, 103(1): 144–81.
Al-Midani, Mohammed Amin. 2002. "La ligue des états arabes et les droits de l'homme." *Scienza e Politica*, 26: 101–14.
Al-Midani, Mohammed Amin, Mathilde Cabanettes, and Susan Akram. 2006. "Arab Charter on Human Rights 2004." *Boston University International Law Journal*, 24(2): 147–64.
Milewicz, Karolina and Robert Goodin. 2018. "Deliberative Capacity Building through International Organizations: The Case of the Universal Periodic Review of Human Rights." *British Journal of Political Science*, 48(2): 513–33.

Milner, Helen. 1991. "The Assumption of Anarchy in International Relations Theory: A Critique." *Review of International Studies*, 17(1): 67–85.
Mitzen, Jennifer. 2006. "Ontological Security in World Politics: State Identity and the Security Dilemma." *European Journal of International Relations*, 12(3): 341–70.
Moe, Terry. 2005. "Power and Political Institutions." *Perspectives on Politics*, 3(2): 215–33.
Mohandesi, Salar. 2017. "From Anti-imperialism to Human Rights: The Vietnam War and Radical Internationalism in the 1960s and 1970s." Unpublished PhD Dissertation, University of Pennsylvania.
Moore, Colin. 2012. *American Imperialism and the State, 1893–1921*. Cambridge University Press.
Moore, Margaret. 2014. "Which People and What Land? Territorial Right-Holders and Attachment to Territory." *International Theory*, 6(1): 121–40.
Moravcsik, Andrew. 1995. "Explaining International Human Rights Regimes: Liberal Theory and Western Europe." *European Journal of International Relations*, 1(2): 157–89.
  1997. "Taking Preferences Seriously: A Liberal Theory of International Politics." *International Organization*, 51(4): 513–53.
  2000. "The Origins of Human Rights Regimes: Democratic Delegation in Postwar Europe." *International Organization*, 54(2): 217–52.
Morgan, Michael Cotey. 2011. "The Seventies and the Rebirth of Human Rights." In Ferguson, Niall, Erez Manela, and Daniel J. Sargent, eds. *The Shock of the Global: The 1970s in Perspective*. Cambridge, Massachusetts: Belknap Press: 237–50.
Morsink, Johannes. 1999. *The Universal Declaration of Human Rights: Origins, Drafting and Intent*. University of Pennsylvania Press.
Moses, A. Dirk, Marco Duranti, and Roland Burke, eds. 2020. *Decolonization, Self-Determination, and the Rise of Global Human Rights Politics*. Cambridge University Press.
Mower Jr., A. Glenn. 1969. "The UN and Regional Organizations: The Pattern of Relationships in Political Affairs." *Social Science*, 44(4): 208–14.
Moyn, Samuel. 2010. *The Last Utopia*. Cambridge: Harvard University Press.
Mukherjee, Rohan. 2022. *Ascending Order: Rising Powers and the Politics of Status in International Institutions*. Cambridge University Press.
Muppidi, Himadeep. 1999. "Post-Coloniality and the Production of International Security: The Persistent Puzzle of U.S.-India Relations." In Jutta Weldes, Mark Laffey, Hugh Gusterson, and Raymond Duvall, eds. *Cultures of Insecurity*. University of Minnesota Press: 119–46.

Murray, Rachel. 2004. *Human Rights in Africa: From the OAU to the African Union*. Cambridge University Press.
Mutua, Makau. 2000. "The African Human Rights System: A Critical Evaluation." Prepared for United Nations Development Programme, Human Development Report 2000. Available at: https://digitalcommons.law.buffalo.edu/other_scholarship/16/.
―――. 2004. "African Human Rights Organizations: Questions of Context and Legitimacy." In Paul Tiyambe Zeleza and Philip J. McConnaughay, eds. *Human Rights, the Rule of Law, and Development in Africa*. University of Pennsylvania Press: 191–97.
Muyangwa, Monde and Margaret Vogt. 2000. "An Assessment of the OAU Mechanism for Conflict Prevention, Management and Resolution, 1993–2000." International Peace Academy. Available at: www.ipinst.org/wp-content/uploads/publications/oau_conflict_1993_2000.pdf. Accessed on 28 January 2025.
Narayan, Yasmeen. 2019. "Intersectionality, Nationalisms, Biocoloniality." *Ethnic and Racial Studies*, 42(8): 1225–44.
Nasser, Gamal Abdel. 1954. "The Egyptian Revolution." *Foreign Affairs*, 33(2): 199–211.
Neier, Aryeh. 1996. "The New Double Standard." *Foreign Policy*, 105: 91–102.
Neumayer, Eric. 2003a. "Do Human Rights Matter in Bilateral Aid Allocation? A Quantitative Analysis of 21 Donor Countries." *Social Science Quarterly*, 84(3): 650–66.
―――. 2003b. "Is Respect for Human Rights Rewarded? An Analysis of Total Bilateral and Multilateral Aid Flows." *Human Rights Quarterly*, 25(2): 510–27.
Newsom, David. 1981. "Miracle or Mirage: Reflections on US Diplomacy and the Arabs." *Middle East Journal*, 35(3): 299–313.
Nielsen, Richard. 2013. "Rewarding Human Rights? Selective Aid Sanctions against Repressive States." *International Studies Quarterly*, 52(9): 1–13.
"Nigerian Minister's Criticism of Western and Ghanaian Media." 1983. *BBC Summary of World Broadcasts*. 16 February.
"Nigeria's Ratification of African Charter on Human Rights." 1983. *BBC Summary of World Broadcasts*, 21 March.
Nkrumah, Kwame. 1963. *Africa Must Unite*. Heinemann Publishers.
―――. 1965. *Neo-Colonialism, the Last Stage of Imperialism*. International Publishers, Inc.
"Nnamdi Azikiwe, 'The Future of Pan-Africanism.'" 2009. *Blackpast*. Available at: www.blackpast.org/global-african-history/speeches-global-african-history/1962-nnamdi-azikiwe-future-pan-africanism/. Accessed on 28 January 2025.

Nonneman, Gerd. 2006. "EU-GCC Relations: Dynamics, Patterns and Perspectives." *The International Spectator,* 41(3): 59–74.

Norris, Robert. 1980. "Observations In Loco: Practice and Procedure of the Inter-American Commission on Human Rights." *Texas International Law Journal,* 15(1): 46–95.

Nye, Joseph. 1990. "Soft Power." *Foreign Affairs,* 80: 153–71.

Nyerere, Julius. 1980. "No to IMF Meddling: President Nyerere's New Year 1980 Message to the Diplomats Credited to Tanzania." *Development Dialogue,* 2: 7–9.

OAU Assembly of Heads of State and Government. 1973. "African Declaration on Co-operation, Development and Economic Independence." Resolution adopted at the 10th Meeting of the Heads of State and Government of the Organization of African Unity. CM/ST.12 (XXI).

———. 1990. "Declaration of the Assembly of Heads of State and Government of the Organization of African Unity on the Political and Socio-Economic Situation in Africa and the Fundamental Changes Taking Place in the World." Resolution adopted at the 26th Meeting of the Heads of State and Government of the Organization of African Unity. AHG/Decl.1 (XXVI)

———. 1993. "Declaration of the OAU Assembly Heads of State and Government on the Situation in Angola." Resolution adopted at the 29th Ordinary Session of the Assembly of Heads of State and Government of the Organization of African Unity. AHG/DECL.2 (XXIX).

OAU Council of Ministers. 1980. "Human and Peoples' Rights." Resolution adopted at the 35th Ordinary Session. CM/Res.792 (XXXV).

———. 1991. "Resolution on the Armed Conflict in Liberia." Resolution adopted at the 53rd Ordinary Session of the Council of Ministers of the Organization of African Unity. CM/Res.1317 (LIII).

———. 1992. "Resolution on the Situation in Somalia." Resolution adopted at the 56th Ordinary Session of the Council of Ministers of the Organization of African Unity. CM/Res.1388 (LVI).

———. 1994a. "Resolution on Burundi." Resolution adopted at the Fifty-Ninth Ordinary Session of the Council of Ministers of the Organization of African Unity. CM/Res.1487 (LIX).

———. 1994b. "Resolution on Liberia." Resolution adopted at the Fifty-Ninth Ordinary Session of the Council of Ministers of the Organization of African Unity. CM/Res.1488 (LIX).

OAU Secretariat. 1979. "What Kind of Africa by the Year 2000?" Final Report of the Monrovia Symposium on the Future Development Prospects of Africa towards the Year 2000, Monrovia, Liberia, 12–16 February.

Oberdorfer, Don. 1977. "The U.S. Response to Uganda." *Washington Post*, 4 March.

Obregón, Liliana. 2009. "The Universal Declaration of Human Rights and Latin America." *Maryland Journal of International Law*, 24(1): 94–8.

Obydenkova, Anastassia and Alexander Libman. 2019. *Authoritarian Regionalism in the World of International Organizations: Global Perspective and the Eurasian Enigma*. Oxford University Press.

Odinkalu, Anselm Chidi and Camilla Christensen. 1998. "The African Commission on Human and Peoples' Rights: The Development of Its Non-State Communication Procedures." *Human Rights Quarterly*, 20(2): 235–80.

Organization of African Unity. 1963. *Charter of the Organization of African Unity*. 13 September.

    1981. *The African Charter on Human and Peoples' Rights* ("Banjul Charter"). 27 June.

Organization of American States. n.d. "IACHR on-site Visits." Available at: www.oas.org/en/iachr/activities/countries-all.asp. Accessed on 7 August 2020.

    1948. *Charter of the Organization of American States* ("Pact of Bogota"). 30 April.

    1959. Final Act. Fifth Meeting of Consultation of the Ministers of Foreign Affairs. 12–18 August.

    1969. *American Convention on Human Rights* ("Pact of San Jose"). Costa Rica, 22 November.

    1979. *Statute of the Inter-American Commission on Human Rights*, O.A.S. Off. Rec. OEA/Ser.P/IX.0.2/80, Vol. 1 at 88, 1 October.

Ottaway, Marina and Thomas Carothers. 2004. "Think Again: Middle East and Democracy." *Foreign Policy*, 145(22–24): 26-28.

Ouguergouz, Fatsah. 2003. *The African Charter of Human and People's Rights: A Comprehensive Agenda for Human Dignity and Sustainable Democracy In Africa*. Martinus Nijhoff Publishers.

Owen, Roger. 1981. "The Arab Economies in the 1970s." *Middle East Report*, 11(8–9). Available at: www.merip.org/mer/mer100-101/arab-economies-1970s. Accessed on 28 January 2025.

Oyewumi, Aderemi. 1991. "The Lomé Convention: From Partnership to Paternalism." *The Round Table*, 80(318): 129–37.

Özsu, Umut. 2015. "'In the Interests of Mankind as a Whole': Mohammed Bedjaoui's New International Economic Order." *Humanity*, 6(1): 129–43.

Pace, Michelle. 2009. "Paradoxes and Contradictions in EU Democracy Promotion in the Mediterranean: The Limits of EU Normative Power." *Democratization*, 16(1): 39–58.

Padelford, Norman. 1954. "Regional Organization and the United Nations." *International Organization*, 8(2): 203–16.
"Papa Bok is a Millstone to France." 1979. *Globe and Mail*, 28 September.
Peretz, Don. 1965. "Nonalignment in the Arab World." *The Annals of the American Academy of Political and Social Science*, 362(1): 36–43.
Pevehouse, Jon. 2002. "Democracy from the Outside-In? International Organizations and Democratization." *International Organization*, 56(3): 515–49.
  2005. *Democracy from Above*. Cambridge University Press.
  2016. "Regional Human Rights and Democracy Governance." In Tanja Börzel, and Thomas Risse, eds. *The Oxford Handbook of Comparative Regionalism*. Oxford University Press: 486–509.
Pflüger, Friedbert. 1989. "Human Rights Unbound: Carter's Human Rights Policy Reassessed." *Presidential Studies Quarterly*, 19(4): 705–16.
Phung, Tracy ThuTrang, Ian Coxhead, and Chang Lian. 2014. "Lucky Countries?" In Ian Coxhead, ed. *Routledge Handbook of Southeast Asian Economics*. Routledge.
Pierson, Paul. 2004. *Politics in Time*. Princeton University Press.
  2015. "Power and Path Dependence." In James Mahoney and Kathleen Thelen, eds. *Advances in Comparative-Historical Analysis*. Cambridge University Press: 123–46.
Pitts, Jennifer. 2018. *Boundaries of the International: Law and Empire*. Harvard University Press.
Poast, Paul, and Johannes Urpelainen. 2013. "Fit and Feasible: Why Democratizing States Form, Not Join, International Organizations." *International Studies Quarterly*, 57(4): 831–41.
Podeh, Elie. 1993. "The Struggle over Arab Hegemony after the Suez Crisis." *Middle Eastern Studies*, 29(1): 91–110.
  1996. "The Drift towards Neutrality: Egyptian Foreign Policy during the Early Nasserist Era, 1952–1955." *Middle Eastern Studies*, 32(1): 159–78.
Poe, Steven. 1991. "Human Rights and the Allocation of US Military Assistance." *Journal of Peace Research*, 28(2): 205–16.
Pogany, Istvan. 1986. "Arab Attitudes towards International Human Rights Law." *Connecticut Journal of International Law*, 2(2): 367–74.
Pomonti, Jean-Claude. 1982. "Mitterrand's Embarrassing 'Friend' in Africa; Guinea's Leader Seeks a Wider Role." *Guardian Weekly*, 25 July.
Porath, Yehoshua. 1986. *In Search of Arab Unity: 1930–1945*. Frank Cass Publishers.
Pouliot, Vincent. 2017. "Against Authority: The Heavy Weight of International Hierarchy." In Ayşe Zarakol, ed. *Hierarchies in World Politics*. Cambridge University Press: 113–33.

Powers, Kathleen E. and Dan Altman. 2023. "The Psychology of Coercion Failure: How Reactance Explains Resistance to Threats." *American Journal of Political Science*, 67(1): 221–38.

Prashad, Vijay. 2007. *The Darker Nations*. Leftword Books.

Presidential Directive NSC-30: Human Rights. 1978. Presidential Directives. Jimmy Carter Presidential Library. 17 February. Available at: www .jimmycarterlibrary.gov/assets/documents/directives/pd30.pdf.

Pritchett, Lant, and Daniel Kaufmann. 1998. "Civil Liberties, Democracy, and the Performance of Government Projects." *Finance and Development*, 35: 26–29.

Quintana, Francisco-José. 2024. "The (Latin) American Dream? Human Rights and the Construction of Inter-American Regional Organisation (1945–1948)." *Journal of the History of International Law*, 25(4): 560–91.

Quiroga-Villamarín, Daniel. 2019. "'An Atmosphere of Genuine Solidarity and Brotherhood': Hernán Santa-Cruz and a Forgotten Latin American Contribution to Social Rights." *Journal of the History of International Law*, 21(1): 71–103.

Rabe, Stephen. 1996. "The Caribbean Triangle: Betancourt, Castro, and Trujillo and U.S. Foreign Policy, 1958–1963." *Diplomatic History*, 20(1): 55–78.

Ramphul, Krishna. 1983. "The Role of International and Regional Organizations in the Peaceful Settlement of Internal Disputes (with Special Emphasis on the Organization of African Unity)." *Georgia Journal of International and Comparative Law*, 13: 371–84.

Randal, Jonathan C. 1982. "Mitterrand Visits Africa to Offer Reassurance of Close French Ties." *The Washington Post* May 21.

Reed, Michael. 1987. "Gabon: A Neo-Colonial Enclave of Enduring French Interest." *Journal of Modern African Studies*, 25(2): 283–320.

"Return to Gabon of Member of 'Government-in-Exile.'" 1985. *BBC Summary of World Broadcasts*. 8 October.

Ridpath, John Clark. 1893. *The Life and Work of James G. Blaine*. Philadelphia, Pennsylvania: World Publishing Co.

"Rights Issue Dominates OAS Parley." 1977. *Facts on File World News Digest*, July 2.

Rishmawi, Mervat. 2005. "The Revised Arab Charter on Human Rights: A Step Forward?" *Human Rights Law Review*, 5(2): 361–76.

2008. "Human Rights Commission of the Arab States." *Max Planck Encyclopedias of Public International Law*. Oxford University Press.

Risse, Thomas. 2016. "The Diffusion of Regionalism." In Tanja Börzel and Thomas Risse, eds. *The Oxford Handbook of Comparative Regionalism*. Oxford University Press: 87–108.

Risse-Kappen, Thomas, Stephen Ropp, and Kathryn Sikkink, eds. 2013. *The Persistent Power of Human Rights: From Commitment to Compliance*. Cambridge University Press.
1999. *The Power of Human Rights*. Cambridge University Press.
Rixen, Thomas, Lora Anne Viola, and Michael Zürn, eds. 2016. *Historical Institutionalism and International Relations: Explaining Institutional Development in World Politics*. Oxford University Press.
Roberts, Sean. 2017. "The Eurasian Economic Union: The Geopolitics of Authoritarian Cooperation." *Eurasian Geography and Economics*, 58(4): 418–41.
Rodney, Walter. 1972. *How Europe Underdeveloped Africa*. Bogle-L'Ouverture Publications.
Rondos, Alex. 1983. "Mitterrand's Two-Year Record." *Africa Report*, 28(3): May–June, 8–11.
Rowen, Hobart. 1977. "Agenda: Recovery, Aiding the Poor; United States, Allies Facing Touch Agenda for Summit; The London Summit." *Washington Post*, 24 April.
Rubin, Barry. 1991. "Pan-Arab Nationalism: The Ideological Dream as Compelling Force." *Journal of Contemporary History*, 26(3/4): 535–51.
Rubner, Nathaniel. 2011. "The Origins of the 1981 African Charter on Human and Peoples' Rights." Unpublished PhD Dissertation, Cambridge University.
Russell, Roberto, and Juan Gabriel Tokatlian. 2003. "From Antagonistic Autonomy to Relational Autonomy: A Theoretical Reflection from the Southern Cone." *Latin American Politics and Society*, 45(1): 1–24.
Ryan, Richard and Edward Deci. 2006. "Self-Regulation and the Problem of Human Autonomy: Does Psychology Need Choice, Self-Determination, and Will?" *Journal of Personality*, 74(6): 1557–86.
Sahraoui, Hassiba Hadj. 2004. "'Modernising' the Arab Charter on Human Rights." In Ian Seiderman, ed. *Yearbook of the International Commission of Jurists*. Intersentia: 339–98.
Saksena, K. P. 1982. "Human Rights in Asia: Assessing the Prospects for a Regional Approach." *International Studies*, 21(1): 1–17.
Salman, Munir. 1986. *The Arab League: A Critical Assessment of the Political Efficacy of a Regional Organization*. Unpublished PhD dissertation. Northern Arizona University.
Salomon, Margot. 2013. "From NIEO to Now and the Unfinishable Story of Economic Justice." *International & Comparative Law Quarterly*, 62(1): 31–54.
Sanders, Thomas. 1970. "The Church in Latin America." *Foreign Affairs*, 48(2): 285–99.

Sandholz, Wayne. 2016. "United States Military Assistance and Human Rights." *Human Rights Quarterly*, 38(4): 1070–101.
Sandifer, Durward. 1965. "Human Rights in the Inter-American System." *Howard Law Journal*, 11(2): 508–28.
Santa-Cruz, Arturo. 2013. *International Election Monitoring, Sovereignty, and the Western Hemisphere: The Emergence of an International Norm*. New York: Routledge Press.
Santa Cruz, Hernán. 1995. "The Creation of the United Nations and ECLAC." *CEPAL Review*, 57: 17–34.
Al-Sayyid, Mustapha K. 1997. "Theoretical Issues in the Arab Human Rights Movement." *Arab Studies Quarterly*, 19(1): 23–30.
Schmitter, Philippe and Terry Lynn Karl. 1991. "What Democracy Is... and Is Not." *Journal of Democracy,* 2(3): 75–88.
Schmitz, David and Vanessa Walker. 2004. "Jimmy Carter and the Foreign Policy of Human Rights: The Development of a Post-Cold War Foreign Policy." *Diplomatic History*, 28(1): 113–43.
Schreiber, Anna. 1970. *The Inter-American Commission on Human Rights*. A.W. Sitjhoff.
Scoble, Harry and Lisa Wiseberg. 1981. "Problems of Comparative Research on Human Rights." In Ved Nanda, James Scarritt, and George Shephard, Jr., eds. *Global Human Rights: Public Policies, Comparative Measures, and NGO Strategies*. Westview Press: 147–71.
Scott, David. 2012. "Norms of Self-Determination: Thinking Sovereignty Through."*Middle East Law and Governance*, 4(2–3): 195–224.
Scott, James. 1985. *Weapons of the Weak*. New Haven, Connecticut: Yale University Press.
  1990. *Domination and the Arts of Resistance: Hidden Transcripts*. New Haven, Connecticut: Yale University Press.
Senghor, Léopold. 1963. "Négritude et civilisation de l'universel." *Présence africaine*, 46: 8–13.
Shanghai Cooperation Organisation. 2005. *Declaration by the Heads of the Member States of the Shanghai Cooperation Organization* ("Ashtana Declaration"). 5 July.
Shrinkhal, Rashwet. 2021. "'Indigenous Sovereignty' and Right to Self-determination in International Law: A Critical Appraisal." *AlterNative: An International Journal of Indigenous Peoples*, 17(1): 71–82.
Sikkink, Kathryn. 1993. "Human Rights, Principled Issue-Networks, and Sovereignty in Latin America." *International Organization*, 47(3): 411–41.
  2004. *Mixed Signals*. Cornell University Press.
  2014. "Latin American Countries as Norm Protagonists of the Idea of International Human Rights." *Global Governance*, 20(3): 389–404.

Simmons, Beth. 2009. *Mobilizing for Human Rights*. Cambridge University Press.
Simon, Joshua. 2017. *The Ideology of Creole Revolution*. Cambridge University Press.
Simpson, Bradley. 2009. "Denying the 'First Right': The United States, Indonesia, and the Ranking of Human Rights by the Carter Administration, 1976–1980." *International History Review*, 31(4), 798–826.
  2019. "Indonesia-US Relations, 1949–1999." In *Oxford Research Encyclopedia of American History*.
Slaughter, Joseph. 2018. "Hijacking Human Rights: Neoliberalism, the New Historiography, and the End of the Third World." *Human Rights Quarterly*, 40(4): 735–75.
Slim, Hugo. 2002. "Making Moral Low Ground: Rights as the Struggle for Justice and the Abolition of Development." *Praxis*, 17: 1–5.
Smith, Matthew. 2005. "An Island Among Islands: Haiti's Strange Relationship with the Caribbean Community." *Social and Economic Studies*, 54(3): 176–95.
Smits, Rene. 1980. "The Second Lomé Convention: An Assessment with Special Reference to Human Rights." *Legal Issues of European Integration*, 7(2): 47–74.
Sneh, Itai Nartzizenfield. 2008. *The Future Almost Arrived: How Jimmy Carter Failed to Change US Foreign Policy*. New York: Peter Lang.
Söderbaum, Fredrick. 2016. "Old, New, and Comparative Regionalism." In Tanja Börzel and Thomas Risse, eds. *The Oxford Handbook of Comparative Regionalism*. Oxford University Press: 16–37.
Söderbaum, Fredrik and Timothy Shaw. 2003. "Theories of New Regionalism." *Theories of New Regionalism*. New York: Palgrave Macmillan: 1–21.
Spanu, Maja. 2020. "The Hierarchical Society: The Politics of Self-Determination and the Constitution of New States after 1919." *European Journal of International Relations*, 26(2): 372–96.
Stilz, Anna. 2015. "Decolonization and Self-Determination." *Philosophy and Policy*, 32(1), 1–24.
Stone, Randall. 2008. "The Scope of IMF Conditionality." *International Organization*, 62(4): 589–620.
Stormorken, Bjørn. 1984. "Menneskerettigheter – vilkår for samarbeid med EF?" *Mennesker og Rettigheter*, 2(2): 16–19.
Sunkel, Osvaldo. 1969. "National Development Policy and External Dependence in Latin America." *The Journal of Development Studies*, 6(1): 23–48.
Tallberg, Jonas, Magnus Lundgren, Thomas Sommerer, Theresa Squatrito. 2020. "Why International Organizations Commit to Liberal Norms." *International Studies Quarterly*, 64(3): 626–40.

Tallberg, Jonas and Michael Zurn. 2019. "The Legitimacy and Legitimation of International Organizations: Introduction and Framework." *Review of International Organizations*, 14: 581–606.

"The Arusha Initiative." 1980. *Development Dialogue*, 2: 11–23.

"The British Cabinet's 'New Approach' to Chile." 1979. *BBC Summary of World Broadcasts*. 18 August.

Thomas, Jr., A. J. 1959. "Non-Intervention and Public Order in the Americas." *Proceedings of the American Society of International Law*, 53: 72–80.

Thomas, Ann Van Wynen and A. J. Thomas, Jr. 1974. "Human Rights and the Organization of American States." *Santa Clara Lawyer*, 12(2): 319–76.

Thomas-Greenfield, Linda. 2023. Address of the U.S. Representative to the United Nations. 28 March.

Thornton, Christy. 2018. "A Mexican International Economic Order? Tracing the Hidden Roots of the Charter of Economic Rights and Duties of States." *Humanity*, 9(3): 389–421.

Thompson, Alexander. 2006. "Coercion through IOs: The Security Council and the Logic of Information Transmission." *International Organization*, 60(1): 1–34.

Tickner, Arlene. 2014. "Autonomy and Latin American international relations thinking." In *Routledge Handbook of Latin America in the World*. New York: Routledge Press: 74–84.

Tieku, Thomas. 2013. "Exercising African Agency in Burundi through Multilateral Channels." *Conflict, Security & Development*, 13(5): 513–35.

Tolley Jr., Howard. 1983. "Decision-Making at the United Nations Commission on Human Rights, 1979–1982." *Human Rights Quarterly*, 5(1): 27–57.

   1984. "The Concealed Crack in the Citadel: The United Nations Commission on Human Rights' Response to Confidential Communications." *Human Rights Quarterly*, 6(4): 420–62.

   1989. "Popular Sovereignty and International Law: ICJ Strategies for Human Rights Standard Setting." *Human Rights Quarterly*, 11(4): 561–85.

Tomayo, Juan. 1981. "Mexico and France Friday recognized El Salvador's Leftist Alliance." *United Press International*. 29 August.

Tourinho, Marcos. 2015. "For Liberalism Without Hegemony: Brazil and the Rule of Non-intervention." In Oliver Stuenkel and Matthew M. Taylor, eds. *Brazil on the Global Stage: Power, Ideas, and the Liberal International Order*. Palgrave Macmillan: 79–94.

Tsoukalis, Loukas. 1977. "The EEC and the Mediterranean: Is 'Global' Policy a Misnomer?" *International Affairs*, 53(3): 422–38.

Tulli, Umberto. 2021. "Wielding the Human Rights Weapon against the American Empire: The Second Russell Tribunal and Human Rights in Transatlantic Relations." *Journal of Transatlantic Studies*, 19(2): 215–37.

Umozurike, Oji. 1979. "The Domestic Jurisdiction Clause in the OAU Charter." *African Affairs*, 78(311): 197–209.

——— 1983. "The African Charter on Human and Peoples' Rights." *American Journal of International Law*, 77(4): 902–12.

Umozurike, U. O. 1970. "Nationalization of Foreign-Owned Property and Economic Self-Determination." *East African Law Journal*, 6(2): 79–99.

UN Commission on Human Rights. 1968a. "Report of the Ad Hoc Study Group Established under Resolution 6(XXIII) of the Commission on Human Rights." 26 January. E/CN.4/966.

——— 1968b. "Report of the Ad Hoc Study Group Established under Resolution 6(XXIII) of the Commission on Human Rights: Communication Received from the Secretariat-General of the League of Arab States." 19 February. E/CN.4/966/Add.1.

UN General Assembly. 1960. "Declaration on the Granting of Independence of Colonial Countries and Peoples." 15th Session. A/RES/1514(XV).

——— 1962. "Permanent Sovereignty over Natural Resources." A/RES/1803 (XVII).

——— 1965a. "Declaration on the Inadmissibility of Intervention in the Domestic Affairs of States and the Protection of their Independence and Sovereignty." 20th Session. A/RES/20/2131.

——— 1965b. Official Records of the General Assembly, 20th Session, 1408th Meeting, 21 December. A/PV.1408.

——— 1966. Official Records of the First Committee, 21st Session, 1475th Meeting, 7 December.

——— 1967. Official Records of the General Assembly. 22nd Session, 1570th Meeting, 27 September. A/PV.1570.

——— 1968. Official Records of the General Assembly. 23rd Session. 1702nd Meeting. A/PV.1702.

——— 1970. "Declaration on Principles of International Law concerning Friendly Relations and Co-operation among States in Accordance with the Charter of the United Nations." A/RES/2625(XXV).

——— 1974a. "Charter of Economic Rights and Duties of States." A/RES/3281 (XXIX).

——— 1974b. Summary Records of the 2015th to 2110th Meetings, 3rd Committee, 29th Session. A/C.3/SR.2051-2110.

——— 1975a. "Alternative Approaches and Ways and Means within the United Nations System for Improving the Effective Enjoyment of Human Rights and Fundamental Freedoms." Draft resolution. A/C.3/L.2189.

1975b. Summary Record of the 2151st Meeting, 3rd Committee, 30th Session. A/C.3/SR.2151.
1975c. Official Records of the Third Committee, 30th Session, 2152nd Meeting, 6 November. A/C.3/SR.2152.
1975d. Summary Record of the 2153rd Meeting, 3rd Committee, 30th Session. A/C.3/SR.2153.
1975e. Official Records of the 3rd Committee, 30th Session, 2168th Meeting, 24 November. A/C.3/SR.2168.
1976a. Summary Record of the 46th Meeting, 3rd Committee, 31st Session. A/C.3/31/SR.46
1976b. Summary Record of the 54th Meeting, 3rd Committee, 31st Session A/C.3/31/SR.54.
1976c. Summary Record of the 55th Meeting, 3rd Committee, 31st Session A/C.3/31/SR.55.
1976d. Summary Record of the 56th Meeting, 3rd Committee, 31st Session A/C.3/31/SR.56.
1976e. Summary Record of the 57th Meeting, 3rd Committee, 31st Session. A/C.3/31/SR.57.
1976f. Summary Record of the 58th Meeting, 3rd Committee, 31st Session. A/C.3/31/SR.58.
1977a. "Alternative Approaches and Ways and Means within the United Nations System for Improving the Effective Enjoyment of Human Rights and Fundamental Freedoms." Draft resolution. A/C.3/32/L.25.
1977b. "Alternative Approaches and Ways and Means within the United Nations System for Improving the Effective Enjoyment of Human Rights and Fundamental Freedoms." Draft resolution. A/C.3/32/L.32.
1977c. "Alternative Approaches and Ways and Means within the United Nations System for Improving the Effective Enjoyment of Human Rights and Fundamental Freedoms." Draft resolution. A/C.3/32/L.28.
1977d. Official Record of the 7th Plenary Meeting, 32nd Session. A/32/PV.7.
1977e. Official Records of the 8th Plenary Meeting, 32nd Session. A/32/PV.8.
1977f. "Protection of Human Rights in Uganda." Draft Resolution. A/C.3/32/L.49.
1977g. "Regional Arrangements for the Promotion and Protection of Human Rights." Draft resolution. A/C.3/32/L.63.
1977h. Summary Record of the 53rd Meeting, 3rd Committee, 32nd Session. A/C.3/32/SR.53.
1977i. Summary Record of the 60th Meeting, 3rd Committee, 32nd Session. A/C.3/32/SR.60.

1977j. Summary Record of the 72nd Meeting, 3rd Committee, 32nd Session. A/C.3/32/SR.72.

1977k. Summary Record of the 75th Meeting, 3rd Committee, 32nd Session. A/C.3/32/SR.75.

1977l. Summary Record of the 43rd Meeting, 3rd Committee, 32nd Session. A/C.3/32/SR.43.

1978a. Official Records. 33rd session, 90th plenary meeting, Wednesday, 20 December 1978. A/33/PV.90.

1978b. Summary Record of the 54th Meeting, 3rd Committee, 33rd Session. A/C.3/33/SR.54.

1979a. Official Records of the 34th Session, 18th Plenary Meeting. 3 October. A/34/PV.18.

1979b. Summary Record of the 25th Meeting, 3rd Committee, 34th Session. A/C.3/34/SR.25.

1979c. Summary Record of the 28th Meeting of the 3rd Committee, 34th Session, A/C.3/34/SR.28.

1979d. Summary Record of the 29th Meeting of the 3rd Committee, 34th Session, A/C.3/34/SR.29.

1980a. Official Record of the 4th Plenary Meeting, 35th Session. A/35/PV.4).

1980b. Official Record of the 25th Plenary Meeting, 35th Session. A/35/PV.25.

1981. Official Record of the 17th Plenary Meeting, 36th Session. A/36/PV.17.

2001. Promotion of a Democratic and Equitable International Order. A/RES/56/151

2023. Official Record of the 50th Plenary Meeting, 78th Session. A/78/PV.50.

United Nations. 1966. *International Covenant on Civil and Political Rights*. 16 December.

Universal Declaration on the Rights of Peoples. 1976. Adopted in Algiers, Algeria. 4 July.

UN Office on Drugs and Crime. n.d. "Regional Counter-terrorism Approaches: The Asian Region." Available at: www.unodc.org/e4j/en/terrorism/module-5/key-issues/asian-region.html. Accessed on 28 January 2025.

UN Secretariat. 1992. "An Agenda for Peace: Preventive Diplomacy, Peacemaking and Peace-keeping." Report of the Secretary-General pursuant to the statement adopted by the Summit Meeting of the Security Council. 31 January. [ST/]DPI/1247.

Uribe, Armando. 1975. *The Black Book of American Intervention in Chile*. Boston, Massachusetts: Beacon Press.

"U.S. Cuts Back Ties." 1979. *Facts on File World News Digest*. 6 April.
US House of Representatives. 1977. Human Rights and United States Foreign Policy: A Review of the Administration's Record: Hearing before the Subcommittee on International Organizations, 95th Congress, 1st Session, 25 October.
Van Boven, Theo. 1977. "The United Nations and Human Rights: A Critical Appraisal." *Bulletin of Peace Proposals*, 8(3): 198–208.
Vasak, Karel. 1982. "Introduction." In Karel Vasak and Philip Alston, eds. *The International Dimension of Human Rights*. Westport, Connecticut: UNESCO and Greenwood Press: 3–10.
Veeser, Cyrus. 2002. *A World Safe for Capitalism: Dollar Diplomacy and America's Rise to Global Power*. Columbia University Press.
Viljoen, Frans. 2007. *International Human Rights Law in Africa*. International Human Rights Law in Africa. Oxford University Press.
"Vive la France?" 1979. *Washington Post*, 25 September.
Voeten, Erik. 2017. "Competition and Complementarity between Global and Regional Human Rights Institutions." *Global Policy*, 8(1): 119–23.
Vogelgesang, Sandra. 1978. "What Price Principle?: U.S. Policy on Human Rights." *Foreign Affairs*, 56(4): 819–41.
Waever, Ole. 1993. "Culture and Identity in the Baltic Sea Region." In Pertti Joenniemi, ed. *Cooperation in the Baltic Sea Region*. Washington, DC: Taylor and Francis: 23–48.
Waltz, Susan. 2004. "Universal Human Rights: The Contribution of Muslim States." *Human Rights Quarterly*, 26(4): 799–844.
Walzer, Michael. 1983. *Spheres of Justice*. New York: Basic Books.
Wang, Jian, and Shuming Wang. 2008. "The Middle Eastern Democratization in the Context of Anti-Americanism." *Journal of Middle Eastern and Islamic Studies (in Asia)*, 2(1): 59–68.
Wang, Pei-Chen. 2012. "Normative Power Europe and Asia-Europe Relations." Southeast Asian Studies at the University of Freiberg, Occasional Paper No. 10. Available at: www.southeastasianstudies.uni-freiburg.de/documents/occasional-paper/op10.pdf. Accessed on 28 January 2025.
Weinraub, Bernard. 1982. "Reagan's Human Rights Chief: No 'Liberal Mole.'" *New York Times*, 19 October.
Weinstein, Warren. 1976. "Africa's Approach to Human Rights at the United Nations." *Issue: A Journal of Opinion*, 6(4): 14–21.
  1980. "Human Rights in Africa: A Long-Awaited Voice." *Current History*, 78(455): 97–101.
Weissbrodt, David. 1977. "Human Rights Legislation and US Foreign Policy." *Georgia Journal of International and Comparative Law*, 7: 231–87.

Welch, Claude. 1981. "The O.A.U. and Human Rights: Towards a New Definition." *Journal of Modern African Studies*, 19(3): 401–20.
Wilcox, Francis. 1965. "Regionalism and the United Nations." *International Organization*, 19(3): 788–811.
Wilder, Gary. 2015. *Freedom Time*. Duke University Press.
Williams, Paul. 2007. "From Non-Intervention to Non-Indifference: The Origins and Development of the African Union's Security Culture." *African Affairs*, 106(423): 253–79.
Wright, Quincy. 1968. "Legal Aspects of the Middle East Situation." *Law and Contemporary Problems*, 33(1): 5–31.
Xanthaki, Alexandra. 2007. *Indigenous Rights and United Nations Standards*. Cambridge University Press.
Yalem, Ronald. 1962. "Regionalism and World Order." *International Affairs*, 38(4): 460–71.
Young-Anawaty, Amy. 1980. "Human Rights and the ACP-EEC Lomé II Convention: Business as Usual at the EEC." *NYU Journal of International Law and Politics*, 13(63): 63–98.
Youngs, Richard. 2002. "The European Union and Democracy Promotion in the Mediterranean: A New or Disingenuous Strategy?" *Democratization*, 9(1): 40–62.
Zarakol, Ayşe, ed. 2017. *Hierarchies in World Politics*. Cambridge University Press.
Zerrougui, Leila. 2008. "The Arab Charter on Human Rights." Lecture given at the High-Level Panel on the 60th Anniversary of the Universal Declaration of Human Rights, University of Essex, 4–6 July.
Životić, Aleksandar, and Jovan Čavoški. 2016. "On the Road to Belgrade: Yugoslavia, Third World Neutrals, and the Evolution of Global Non-Alignment, 1954–1961." *Journal of Cold War Studies*, 18(4): 79–97.
Zoller, Adrien-Claude. 1989. "Moving in Fits and Starts: The 45th Session of the Human Rights Commission Gets a Mixed Reception," *Netherlands Quarterly of Human Rights*, 7(2): 199–215.
  1990. "46th Session of the United Nations Commission on Human Rights." *Netherlands Quarterly of Human Rights*, 8(2): 140–75.

Index

Adedeji, Adebayo, 42
affirmation, 11, 39–41
Africa, 16
African, Caribbean, and Pacific states, 38, 74, 86, 124, 128–29, 138–39, 143
African Charter on Human and Peoples' Rights, 3, 23, 119, 136, 182
African Commission on Human and Peoples' Rights, 3, 126, 135, 144
African Court on Human and Peoples' Rights, 144, 178
African Declaration on Co-operation, Development, and Economic Independence, 47, 127
African Union, 24, 52, 144
agency, 26, 28, 171, 174, 180
Alexandria Protocols, 150
Algeria, 162
All-African Peoples' Conference, 122
Allende, Salvador, 67–68, 78, 88, 98
alliances, 46, 83
American Convention on Human Rights, 3, 91, 94, 96, 111
American Declaration on the Rights and Duties of Man, 93–94
Amin, Idi, 13, 16, 73, 80, 118, 123
Amnesty International, 62, 67–68, 74, 76, 80, 97, 119, 124, 130, 160
Andrés Pérez, Carlos, 108
Angola, 80
anti-communism, 83–84
apartheid, 66–67, 121
Arab Charter on Human Rights, 4, 166
Arab Charter on Human Rights (1994), 164
Arab Cold War, 155
Arab Committee on Human Rights, 4

Arab Conference on Human Rights, 146, 153
Arab Court on Human Rights, 4, 167
Arab League Expert Human Rights Committee, 167
Arab nationalism, 149
Arab Permanent Committee on Human Rights, 153, 164, 166
arbitration, 44, 92
Argentina, 78–79
Association of Southeast Asian Nations (ASEAN), 2, 24, 84
  Brussels Committee, 84
  Human Rights Declaration, 5
  Intergovernmental Commission on Human Rights, 4
  way, 2, 25
asymmetric interdependence, 38, 60, 157, *See* interdependence
Atlantic Charter, 120
AU Peace and Security Council, 51
autarky, 38–39, 42
authoritarian governments, 6, 58, 102, 147, 168, 172
authoritarian regional organizations, 178
authority, 6, 9, 34–35, 52, 59–60
autonomy, 37, 48, 107
Azikiwe, Nnamdi, 122

Baghdad Pact, 151, 155
Bahrain, 167
Banana Wars, 92
Bandung Conference, 46
Barcelona Process, 163
Baroody, Jamil, 147
Belgrade Conference, 62
Biafran civil conflict, 122
Bokassa, Jean-Bédel, 74, 130
Bongo, Omar, 136

Index

boomerang pattern, 59
Botswana, 119
Brazil, 78, 97
bureaucrats, 14, 53–54, 59
Burundi, 122, 136

Calvo Doctrine, 42
Cambodia, 85
Caribbean, 28, 95
Caribbean Community, 177
Carter, Jimmy, 6, 12, 15, 70–71, 77–78, 82, 85, 105, 108, 115, 124, 126, 140, 156
Central African Economic and Monetary Community, 144
Central African Empire, 74, 80–81, 119, 122, 125, 130
Central Asia, 179
Charter of Economic Rights and Duties of States, 43
Charter of the League of Arab States, 150, 152
Chile, 15, 18, 66–69, 71, 73, 78–79, 88–89, 97–102
China, 9, 175, 179
civil society, 6, 12, 17, 19, 40, 49, 53, 59, 68, 76
Cold War, 16, 57, 70, 72, 97, 155
  end of, 20
  post-Cold War, 26, 54, 176–77
collective legitimation, 9, 177
Colombia, 94, 103, 107–9
colonialism, 37, 66, 120, 181
Common Market for Eastern and Southern Africa, 144
Commonwealth of Nations, 118
conditionality, 6, 12, 43–44, 63, 108, 125, 142–43
contestation, 29, 48, 60–61, 174, 176, 179
Cooperation Agreement between Member Countries of ASEAN and the European Community, 85
Costa Rica, 69, 86, 103–4
critical juncture, 23
Cuba, 92, 95
cultural imperialism, 10

Declaration on the Granting of Independence to Colonial Countries and Peoples, 36, 66

Declaration on the Inadmissibility of Intervention in the Domestic Affairs of States and the Protection of their Independence and Sovereignty, 43, 106
Declaration on Principles of International Law Concerning Friendly Relations and Cooperation among States, 43
decolonization, 2, 36–37, 45, 59, 70, 120–21, 151, 170–71
delegation, 11, 27, 54, 56, 174–75
democracy, 11, 18, 21, 39
democratic leaders, 6, 17, 94, 172
democratization, 4, 18–21, 111, 142, 183
dependence, 12, 41, 59, 175
dependency theory, 107
development assistance, 19, 71, 75, 105
disappearances, 68
Doe, Samuel, 136
domination, 14, 21, 37, 39, 61, 85, 149, 175, 183
Dominican Republic, 92, 95–96
Du Bois, WEB, 120

East Timor, 84
Economic Community of Central African States, 144
Economic Community of West African States, 139, 144
economic dependence, 6, 37, 42, 79, 107, 126
economic development, 38, 42, 75, 183
economic enforcement, 63, 71, 85, 110, 140, 158, 172
economic independence, 42, 47, 107, 127
Egypt, 151, 155, 159
Eisenhower Doctrine, 155
El Salvador, 78, 80, 114
Equatorial Guinea, 81, 122, 125
Ethiopia, 133
Euro-Arab Dialogue, 83, 157
European Economic Community, 12, 38, 73–75, 82, 84, 124, 156
European Parliament, 7, 75, 163
everyday resistance, 60

Ford, Gerald, 71, 115
foreign direct investment, 19

forum shopping, 22
France, 74, 130, 149
Franco-African Summit, 119
Fraser, Donald, 71
French federation, 46, 127

Gabon, 136
Gambia, The, 118–19, 131, 134
global capitalism, 18, 21, 40, 68
global governance, 8, 27, 174, 177–78
Global South, 1, 21, 25, 40, 57, 69–70, 86, 171, 174, 182–84
Global War on Terror, 158, 165
great powers, 8, 26, 48
Guatemala, 114
Guinea, 136
Gulf Cooperation Council, 179

Haig, Alexander, 72
Haiti, 92
hegemon, 45
hegemony, 176
hierarchy, 9, 17, 26–29, 61, 182
historical institutionalism, 23–24
Honduras, 112
human rights, 29, 48, 65, 180
  breakthrough of, 18, 23, 30, 152, 168
  enforcement, 7, 13, 20, 57, 63, 88, 108, 116, 172
  protection, 63, 69
humanitarian intervention, 161

imperialism, 6, 14, 18, 57, 68, 107, 152
imposition, 9–10, 41, 50, 175, 180
  of human rights enforcement, 6, 9, 56, 61, 105, 168, 172
individual petitions, 95, 119, 130, 167
Indonesia, 84
inequality, 31, 37, 39, 59, 65, 181
institutional design, 23, 55, 57, 135
integration, 42, 183, *See* unequal integration
Inter-American Commission on Human Rights, 3, 90–91, 94–96, 102–3, 110–11, 113
Inter-American Conference on War and Peace, 93
Inter-American Court on Human Rights, 3, 111

Inter-American Development Bank, 78, 101
Inter-American Juridicial Committee, 93
interdependence, 11–12, 38, 42, 59, 157, *See* asymmetric interdependence
International Commission of Jurists, 7, 131
International Commission of the Red Cross, 97
international cooperation, 10–11, 174
international courts, 44
International Covenant on Civil and Political Rights, 67
International Criminal Court, 178
international financial institutions, 38, 45, 48, 73, 80
international institutions, 12, 39, 46, 49
international interference, 1, 11, 55–56
  economic, 6, 43
  legitimate, 6–7, 34, 67, 85, 88, 100
international law, 6, 37, 39
International Monetary Fund, 43, 45–46, 136
international norms, 29, 176, 180
  diffusion, 18–21, 181
  localization, 22–23, 55, 182
  norm entrepreneur, 59
  socialization, 181
international order, 8, 25–27, 174–76, 183
international organizations, 39, 45–46, 108, 178
International Union of American Republics, 92
investment regime, 37–38
Iran, 82, 157
Iraq, 161, 166
Islam, 147
Islamic Declaration on Human Rights and Duties, 160
Israel, 82, 151, 155–56

Jamaica, 174

Khmer Rouge, 85
Kirkpatrick, Jeanne, 72
Kissinger, Henry, 71, 105
Kodjo, Edem, 6, 120, 127, 131, 134
Korea, 84

Lake, Anthony, 77–78, 82–83, 156
Lake Chad Basin Commission, 177
Larreta Doctrine, 94
Law of Lagos, 122
League of Arab States, 24, 150
League of Nations, 149
legitimacy, 7, 34, 60, 85, 115, 173, 177, *See* collective legitimation
legitimation, 9
Lesotho, 119
liberal international order, 25–27, 49, 175
liberation movements, 121, 151
Liberia, 81, 120, 127, 131, 136, 142
local ownership, 54
Lomé Convention, 38, 73–74, 81, 86, 124–25, 128–29, 133, 138, 141–42
López Michelsen, Alfonso, 108

Mandela, Nelson, 142
marginalization, 142, 180–81
Mauritius, 123, 131
M'Baye, Keba, 120, 131, 133
Mediterranean Group, 83, 157
Middle East, 17
military intervention, 92, 165
Mitterrand, Francois, 74
Monroe Doctrine, 66
Mozambique, 80
multilateralism, 45, 115
multipolarity, 176

Namibia, 143
Nasser, Gamal, 151–52
National Security Council, 79, 84, 115
nationalization, 37, 151
Nehru, Jawaharlal, 41, 46
neocolonialism, 6, 36, 57, 86, 121, 126
Netherlands, The, 12, 73, 124
New International Economic Order, 21, 43, 47–48, 86
new regions, 178
NGOs, 14, 54, 68, 167
Nicaragua, 78–79, 92, 113
Nigeria, 69, 119, 122, 131, 136, 138
Nkrumah, Kwame, 36, 125
Nobel Peace Prize, 62
non-alignment, 41, 62, 68, 152
non-interference, 11, 66, 85, 131
    norm of, 13, 87–88, 91, 97, 103, 119, 122, 141, 144, 152, 172
    rules of, 2, 43
    to non-indifference, 145
Nordic countries, 12, 73
North–South relations, 7, 49, 86–87, 183
Nyerere, Julius, 44–45, 132

OAS Charter, 94, 106
OAS General Assembly, 98–99, 102–4, 110
OAU Assembly of Heads of State and Government, 123, 131–32, 135
OAU Charter, 122
OAU Liberation Committee, 121
oil, 16, 82–83, 154–55, 157
oil boycott, 82, 155
Optional Protocol to the ICCPR, 67, 112, 137
Orfila, Alejandro, 102
Organization of African Unity (OAU), 24
Organization of American States (OAS), 15, 24, 94, 99, 101
Organization of Islamic Cooperation, 160
Organization of Petroleum Exporting Countries, 82
organized hypocrisy, 29
Owen, David, 77

Palestine, 146, 151
Pan-African Congresses, 120
pan-Africanism, 25, 120, 126
Panama, 92
pan-Americanism, 25
pan-Arabism, 25, 149
pan-regionalism, 24
Paraguay, 110, 112
participation, 11, 26, 39, 44–45, 127, 176, 180, 182
partnership, 38, 128, 139
Pérez de Cuéllar, Javier, 116
Permanent Arab Committee on Human Rights, 146
permanent sovereignty over natural resources, 37, 42
Philippines, The, 83–84
Pinochet, Augusto, 13, 15, 18, 89, 97

post-Cold War, 142, 144, 161
post-sovereign, 24
property rights, 37, 41–42

racial discrimination, 66, 121
raw commodities, 37, 80
Reagan, Ronald, 71
regime survival, 15, 17, 58, 90, 102, 158, 168, 173
regional authority, 6–7, 9, 13, 48, 52, 88, 97, 172, 178
regional autonomy, 22–23, 27
regional enforcement, 6
regional federation, 11, 38
regional institutions, 7, 21, 90, 174
regional integration, 42
regional norms, 22–23, 25, 55, 108, 173
regional solutions to regional problems, 9, 26, 48, 114, 141, 176–77
regionalism, 20, 175–76, 182
regionalization, 12, 87, 116, 176
regionness, 27, 178
resistance, 48–49, 60, 174–75, 179, *See* everyday resistance
right to development, 23, 86, 121, 182
Rodney, Walter, 12, 42, 126–27
Russell Tribunals, 107
Russia, 179
Rwandan genocide, 145

sanctions, 6, 12, 124
Santa Cruz, Hernán, 66
Saudi Arabia, 151, 155–56, 160
security assistance, 71
self-determination, 3, 6, 9–12, 35–40, 50, 60, 66, 106, 125–27, 144, 170–71, 183
Senegal, 69, 118–20, 129
Senghor, Léopold, 46, 120, 127, 131
Shanghai Cooperation Organisation, 179
Six-Day War, 151–52
soft power, 60
solidarity groups, 73, 79
Somalia, 142
South Africa, 67
Southeast Asia, 17, 83–85
Southern African Development Community, 144

South-North Conference on the International Monetary System and the New International Economic Order, 44
sovereign equality, 36–37, 92
sovereignty, 2, 11, 19, 21, 36, 42, 65, 67, 69, 85, 121, 149
Soviet Union, 70
spheres of influence, 79, 152
state-building, 38
Stroessner, Alfredo, 112
Sudan, 142
Suez Canal, 151
Sykes–Picot Agreement, 149

Tanzania, 80, 132
terrorism, 72, 82, 156, 162, 166, 168
Third World Approaches to International Law, 40
Tolbert, William, 120, 126–27, 131
Touré, Sekou, 136
trade, 6, 19, 48, 71, 78–79, 83–84, 105
transnational advocacy networks, 17–21, 54, 59, 68, 88, 124, 159
Trujillo, Rafael, 95

Uganda, 13, 16, 73, 80, 118, 123–24, 129, 131
Uganda Guidelines, 74, 81, 125
Umozurike, UO, 36, 126
UN *ad hoc* working group on Chile, 98–100, 103
UN Charter, 26, 48, 53, 65, 70, 177
  Chapter VIII of, 53
UN Commission on Human Rights, 66, 69, 97, 109, 116, 153
UN Economic Commission for Africa, 42
UN Economic and Social Council, 69, 119
UN General Assembly, 100–1, 103, 170
UN High Commissioner for Human Rights, 20, 69, 119, 160
UN human rights covenants, 43, 66–67, 106
UN Secretary General, 9, 116
UN Security Council, 9, 46, 51–52, 144, 177
unequal integration, 37–38, *See* integration

Index 229

uneven enforcement, 7, 16
unintended consequences, 23
United Kingdom, 12, 73, 77, 124, 149
United Nations, 21, 27, 70, 89, 100
United States, 12, 16, 71, 155
Universal Declaration of Human Rights, 65–67, 147
Universal Declaration on the Rights of Peoples, 40
universality, 8, 53, 89, 113, 176
Uruguay, 71, 78, 110
US Congress, 67, 71, 101
US Department of State, 16, 71–72, 79, 84

Vance, Cyrus, 70, 78, 105, 156
Venezuela, 95, 108, 114
Vietnam, 85

Vietnam War, 83
voice, 14, 26, 49, 88, 131, 171, 174, 177

West African Economic and Monetary Union, 144
Western Europe, 16, 73, 82, 155
women's rights, 40, 107
World Bank, 46
World Conference on Human Rights, 152
World Health Organization, 48
World Islamic Congress, 150

Yankee imperialism, 86, 92, 115
Yom Kippur War, 82, 152, 155

Zambia, 80

For EU product safety concerns, contact us at Calle de José Abascal, 56–1°, 28003 Madrid, Spain or eugpsr@cambridge.org.

www.ingramcontent.com/pod-product-compliance
Ingram Content Group UK Ltd.
Pitfield, Milton Keynes, MK11 3LW, UK
UKHW020332080126
466737UK00019B/242